# FIRST COMMUNION

*"When I was a child, I spoke as a child.*
*I understood as a child.*
*I thought as a child."*
(1 Cor 13:11)

**"Mother Loyola's name** is becoming one that in itself is an endorsement of every book over which it appears…A careful use of Mother Loyola's work will be productive of the best results."  —Rosary Magazine, November 1901

Having taught in the convent school most of her life, Mother Loyola was encouraged by Father John Morris, S.J. to write a book for children preparing for First Communion. It was issued anonymously in 1896 as part of the Jesuit Quarterly Series, but it quickly became so popular that she was persuaded to publish it and all her subsequent books in her own name. Because of its happy combination of thorough catechesis and readability, it remained in common use even after *Quam Singulari* was promulgated by Pope Pius X in 1910, lowering the age for reception of First Communion from twelve to seven.

### Contemporary praise for *First Communion*:

☞ "This book is intended to prepare children for First Communion by giving them an insight into our Lord's life and mission on earth. Its aim is to fill the heart of the child with a true and earnest love for our Lord in the Blessed Sacrament, a strong love which the struggles of later life will not weaken, a love which cannot be inspired by the dry, dogmatic facts of the catechism…Although written for children, it is not childish, and persons of any age will find it interesting and profitable reading, and especially suited as a preparation for Holy Communion"  —*The Rosary Magazine*

☞ "Each chapter is really a little sermon, devised with great skill, abounding in anecdote, and written with simplicity never degenerating into triviality."  —*The Boston Pilot*

☞ "We cannot speak too highly of its merits. It is meant to be a picture-book in words designed specially for the little ones, to whom pictures appeal so readily. But it is more than this. The *dulce* and the *utile* are happily blended throughout."  —*The Catholic Times*

To learn more about Mother Mary Loyola, visit our website at
www.staugustineacademypress.com.

# First Communion

By

Mother Mary Loyola

of the Bar Convent, York

Edited by

Reverend Herbert Thurston, S.J.

2015
St. Augustine Academy Press
Homer Glen, Illinois

This book is newly typeset based on the 1913 edition published by Burns & Oates. All editing strictly limited to the correction of errors in the original text, the addition of selected footnotes, and minor clarifications in punctuation or phrasing. Any remaining oddities of spelling or phrasing are as found in the original.

Nihil Obstat:
> CHARLES BLOUNT, S.J.,
> *Censor Deputatus.*

Imprimatur:
> ✠HERBERTUS CARD. VAUGHAN,
> *Archiepisc. Westmonasteriensis*

Imprimatur:
> ✠GULIELMUS,
> *Episc. Loidensis.*

This book was originally published in 1896 by Burns & Oates. This edition ©2011 by St. Augustine Academy Press. All editing by Lisa Bergman

Second printing with updated illustrations September 2015

ISBN: 978-1-936639-13-7
Library of Congress Control Number: 2011939866

Unless otherwise noted, all illustrations in this book, including the cover, are either the original illustrations as found in the book, or are public domain images.

To the Sacred Heart of Him

Who Loves Little Children

and Embraced them

and Blessed them

and Said

"Suffer the Little Children

to Come Unto Me"

# Contents

| | | |
|---|---|---|
| Preface | | xi |
| To the Children | | xvii |

**Part the First: Our Lord's Preparation for Coming to Us in Holy Communion**

| | | |
|---|---|---|
| I | Eternity, and What the Saints Thought of It | 1 |
| II | Eternity, and What I Must Think of It | 11 |
| III | The Promise in Paradise | 21 |
| IV | "Behold He Cometh, Leaping upon the Mountains, Skipping over the Hills." | 31 |
| V | The Sacrifice of Melchisedech, and the Prophecy of Malachias | 39 |
| VI | The Manna in the Desert and the Food of Elias | 49 |
| VII | "Learn of Me" | 59 |
| VIII | Bethlehem | 70 |
| IX | Egypt | 83 |
| X | Nazareth | 96 |
| XI | Jerusalem | 107 |
| XII | Nazareth Again: The Hidden Life | 123 |
| XIII | The School of Christ | 134 |
| XIV | "Who Went About Doing Good" | 151 |
| XV | Feeding of the Five Thousand | 162 |
| XVI | The Promise of the Eucharist | 172 |
| XVII | "Will you also go away? Lord, to whom shall we go?" | 184 |
| XVIII | The Last Supper | 195 |
| XIX | Calvary | 209 |

## Part the Second: Our Preparation for Meeting Our Lord in Holy Communion

| XX | Our Enemies Abroad | 227 |
| XXI | Our Enemy at Home | 240 |
| XXII | More About the Enemy at Home | 248 |
| XXIII | How We Must Meet Our Enemies | 256 |
| XXIV | The Pet Passion | 265 |
| XXV | The Wedding Garment | 272 |
| XXVI | The Lost Sheep | 298 |
| XXVII | Who Comes? | 304 |
| XXVIII | To Whom Does He Come? | 314 |
| XXIX | Why Does He Come? | 322 |
| XXX | Come Lord Jesus! | 338 |

## Part the Third: "Thanks be to God for His Unspeakable Gift!"

| XXXI | Our First Communion | 355 |
| XXXII | "Stay with us, Lord!" | 366 |
| XXXIII | "Lord, Give us always this Bread." | 379 |
| XXXIV | "He that Eateth this Bread Shall Live Forever." | 396 |
| INDEX | | 413 |

# Preface

THIS book of Preparation for First Communion, which it is my privilege to introduce to the reader, was originally undertaken at the suggestion of the late Father John Morris, S.J., who—as long as he lived—took the warmest interest in its progress. Unhappily, only a few chapters had been completed at the time of his lamented death, and in the sense of that great loss, the work for a while was laid aside. It would have been a matter for much regret if the author had made this decision a final one. The book now completed has suffered, we cannot doubt, from the lack of Father Morris's always helpful criticisms, but the originality of its conception and the knowledge of child nature displayed in it can hardly fail to justify its publication.

In the address "To the Children" which will be found further on, it is stated that the book is intended to aid the little ones to *prepare themselves* for First Communion. Perhaps it may be well to add a word of explanation here, to anticipate possible misconceptions. It is not in any way the idea of the author that a child should be presented with a copy of this work and then cut adrift without further help, in the expectation that when the proper time comes the needful process of preparation will have worked itself out automatically. None the less, it is believed that many children are quite capable, under the supervision of parents or teachers, of reading for themselves instructions couched in simple child's language such as this book offers them, and furthermore the author has assumed that it may be helpful to some who have to prepare others for First Communion, and who, while conscious of the importance, are not a little embarrassed by the difficulty of their task. To cram children's minds with certain facts of dogmatic knowledge about the Blessed Eucharist is comparatively easy; to prepare their hearts so that they may approach this Divine Mystery full not only of faith, but of love—this is a duty sometimes relegated by teachers to a secondary place, simply from a sense of helplessness and ignorance of how to set about it. While the method developed in this volume does not pretend to be better than many others which might be devised, it will be found, I believe, to possess many advantages of its own. And here I cannot do better than quote a few sentences from a Prospectus previously issued, in which the idea of the book is described in the author's own words:

"To make the Life of our Blessed Saviour enter largely into preparation for First Communion seems the most natural way of drawing the hearts of the young to Him. It would be sad to think of children coming to the altar-rails knowing little or nothing of His Life beyond such facts as the doctrine of the Holy Eucharist supposes. Yet there is danger of this. There is so much to be done in the simple teaching of the Christian doctrine during a child's school life, that the time devoted to it barely suffices. But in the preparation for First Communion time might surely be found, and ought to be found. Their hearts are fresh and tender, and full of an eager longing, that will never again in their lives be quite the same. If we could tell them a little more about Him then—His character, His ways of dealing with us—and so bring them to the altar able to say, in their own fashion and degree: 'I *know* Whom I have believed,' would there not be solid work for the future done in their souls? Knowing Him better, they would come to love Him more. Faith, Hope, and Charity would have a firmer foundation; they would make the acts more easily and more fervently, for there would be a living picture of Him in their hearts."

It should be noted, therefore, that the book is not intended to do more than supplement the work of the catechist. It is not meant to be a Manual of Instruction. It is meant to be a *picture-book* in words, designed specially for the little ones, to whom pictures appeal so readily. This may perhaps be some excuse for its size, which might otherwise be considered unpardonable. To prepare children for their First Communion by a retreat suited to their capacity is not always possible. It is hoped that they may find here the same sort of help; the contemplation of the Life of our Blessed Saviour being made, as it often is in a retreat, the backbone of all the moral instruction. Obviously the usefulness of these meditations is by no means limited to those who are looking forward to receive our Blessed Lord for the first time; and the work, apart from its original purpose, may well be recommended to Catholics as an attempt to provide for quite young people a sort of Primer or attractive introduction to that science of all sciences, the science of self-conquest.

As long as Catholics are agreed that nothing is more precious in after-life than the practice of spiritual reading, it must be held desirable that even from early years children should be enticed to form such a habit *for themselves*. To encourage them in other sensible pursuits, such as a taste for science, or poetry, or history, many books are provided in which writers, often of the highest eminence, have been at pains to make knowledge attractive to the young. To secure a successful book of piety the same means must be resorted to. If the minds of our little folk are to be led on to appreciate the beauties of Christian Faith and Christian Holiness, these must be brought down to the level of their intelligence, just as we endeavour to simplify for their comprehension the marvels of astronomy or geology. In the Prospectus already referred to, the author asks very pertinently:

"Is the instruction given to children such as to bear a proportion to the fruit looked for, and as a matter of fact, is the fruit apparent, at least in the majority of cases? Supposing there to be fault anywhere, where are we to look for it? Scarcely in the children. Their minds and hearts respond readily enough to instruction that really appeals to them. But it *must* appeal to them; we must make it easy and interesting, putting the doctrine as simply as possible, 'with illustrations to make it clear, and stories to make it attractive and impressive. When a point occurs of special importance to a child, several stories must be told to hammer it in well. A story well told and vivid in its details will often be invaluable to a child, and will call up a picture to its little mind which will have lasting effects for good. No one with any knowledge of children will dispute this."

To avoid a multiplicity of Prefaces in a book intended for the young, it has been thought well to dispense with any further Introduction than the Author's Address to the children and to forego elaborate references to authorities or acknowledgment of obligations. With the exception of one story taken from the *Annals of the Propagation of the Faith*, hardly any printed book has been cited textually in the course of the volume. Facts and interpretations have occasionally been borrowed from ordinary sources of information accessible to all, such as the works of Father Coleridge, the Abbé Fouard, and Père Didon among Catholics, and those of Dr. Edersheim among Protestants, but the use made of these writers has not been such as to call for detailed mention. With regard, however, to the share of Father Morris in inspiring these pages, it is only fitting that I should put on record the deep sense of indebtedness to which the author has given expression in the following words:

"To say how much I am indebted to Father Morris would be impossible. He used to say of himself that he could never be grateful enough for having been brought under the influence of Père Petit, S.J., and made familiar with his treatment of scenes in our Lord's Life. With far greater reason I may say the same of Father Morris's influence and help. If this book, undertaken at his instance and revised by him up to the time of his death, should prove in any degree interesting and helpful to children, this will be entirely due to him. Perhaps I ought to add a word more. Those who have followed his retreats may possibly say that in chapter XV, 'The Feeding of the Five Thousand,' I have made an unfair use of his beautiful meditation, 'Twenty-four hours with our Lord.' I feel that this blame is not altogether undeserved, and in self-defence I will only plead the difficulty of going over the same ground without using his thoughts and at times even his very words."

To economize space, a portion of chapter XXXI, containing an arrangement of devotions for the children at the Mass of their First Communion, has been regretfully excluded, but the prayers have been printed separately in a little booklet which may be obtained from the publishers at a trifling cost. [EDITOR'S NOTE: these prayers were much more suited to the older First Communicant of that time; we recommend instead those found in Mother Mary Loyola's *The Little Children's Prayer Book*.]

It may be added that the *You* which is uniformly used instead of *Thou* when Almighty God is addressed in the prayers at the end of the chapters has been adhered to in deference to the author's feeling that a child will talk most naturally and unconstrainedly to its Heavenly Father in the language in which it habitually addresses its father and mother on earth.

HERBERT THURSTON, S.J.<br>
Feast of the Patronage of St. Joseph,<br>
April 26th, 1896.

# To The Children

This, dear children, is a book put into your hands in the hope that it may help you to prepare yourselves for First Communion. Yes, *prepare yourselves;* for this great work, the greatest of your lives, must be done by yourselves. No one can do it for you. Others may help you, but the real work of preparing your hearts for Jesus must be your own doing.

A tiny child, all in rags, found its way one morning into a poor school just as work was starting. It was taken to the master, who said, kindly, "And where do you come from, poor little thing? Did your father or your mother send you here?"

"Please, I haven't got no father nor mother."

"Your sister, then, or whoever looks after you. Who has brought you up?"

"Please, I've brought myself up."

None of us, thank God, are like that poor little friendless child. But the bringing up part of its story is true of us all. We all *bring ourselves up.* For God has given to all of us a free-will, and on the way in which we use that free-will depends the way in which we grow up. If we use it well, we shall grow up good. If we use it well now, we shall be well prepared for our First Communion and pleasing to our Lord when He comes. So we are all going to be thoroughly in earnest; we are going to put our whole heart into our preparation and refuse our Lord nothing He asks of us.

Yes, we must be really in earnest. If up to now we have been careless about serving God and saving our souls, we must not be so any longer. We must think seriously about what we are going to do. We must look upon our First Communion as an event in our lives for which we cannot prepare too carefully and too heartily. God is coming to visit us. Can any pains in getting ready for Him be too great?

Here there will be some thinking deep down in their hearts, "I wish I could feel as I ought about my First Communion, but I can't, so this is not said for me, and it is no use for me to try." Yes, it *is* said for you, and what you have to get well into your mind from the very beginning is that *feelings* do not matter in the least. The notion that to love God you must *feel* a very hot love for Him is not true, and you must get rid of it at once or it will harm you very much and prevent your preparation being what it ought to be. Among the children preparing for First Communion all the world over, there are some who *feel* a great desire to have our Lord with them, and are ready to do anything and everything to prepare themselves for Him. And there are others who do not *feel* this strong desire, but wish they had it. These last are inclined to be sad and discouraged. Others are looking forward to their First Communion with an eager joy they do not feel, and so they think there must be something wrong in their hearts, that they do not really love our Lord, and cannot get to love and long for Him as others do. These thoughts trouble and cast them down, when there is nothing to be troubled about at all.

*Feeling* is not in our power, but *fervour* is. Fervour means a goodwill, and this we can always have. We can always *desire* to love God with all our heart. We can always do *what we can*, and this is all He asks.

You will say now: "What must I do to show my good-will, for I really do want to do all that God wants of me?" Do this—

take the different lessons as they come each day in this book as if our Blessed Saviour Himself were teaching you. Fix your attention on them as you do on a lesson you are going to study carefully. The lessons will be mostly from the Life of our Lord. By studying them you may come to know Him with something of the knowledge and love of those who lived with Him during His earthly Life. One reason why some children do not look forward with any great longing to their First Communion, is that they know so little of our Lord. He is almost a Stranger to them. How can we long to be with those we do not know! Now our time of preparation is to be a time for coming to know Him better and so to love Him more. No one can know Jesus without loving Him. So let us study His Blessed Life lovingly during these few weeks, spending them as it were in His Company. See our Lord in the scene before you. Listen to His words. Notice what He does. And then hear what He has to say to you about all this. Sometimes He will reproach you gently that you are so unlike Himself. Sometimes He will draw you to love Him as you have never loved Him before, and to show Him your love by trying to be like Him. Sometimes He will move you to sorrow for your sins, to a more prompt obedience, to acts of kindness to others for His sake. Listen to Him speaking in your heart, and take away with you some resolution for the day.

When you come to the prayer, do more than this. See if your heart has not something to say to our Lord about what you have been reading. Use your own words; they are better than those of the book, and He likes them better. As we go on, we shall come to prayers made by quite little children, who said what they had to say to Him just as it came. He does not care for grand words, but, great God as He is, He does love the prayer that comes straight from the heart of a little child. Tell Him that you want to prepare fervently for His Coming—that you will try to do all He asks of you—to correct your faults and to make your soul pleasing to Him. Tell Him when you have been naughty. If you are in trouble, if you find it hard to be good, ask His advice and His help. He will not keep you waiting. His answer will come quickly and sometimes in a way that will surprise you. Try.

Another thing you must do, if you want this book to be of any use to you. You must read the meditation for the day *only*, and read it, not at railway speed, but slowly and thoughtfully. If it is too long and you begin to get tired, stop at once and go straight to the prayer. The meditation on the Wedding Garment, which is about confession, is far too long for one reading.

The meditation for the day *only*. You will not like this, especially if you have found out that there are stories coming. Never mind the liking. We are not going to begin our preparation by thinking of our likes and dislikes, but of what will help us most.

We see, then, how we ought to use our book. Shall we see now how we are *not* to use it?

A kind old uncle had a little niece aged five who had lived in his house since she was a baby of a year old. The two loved one another dearly and were never so happy as when they were together. One day he took the trouble to hide a pill for her in a beautiful apple. Having cut it in half, and stuck the pill inside, he joined the halves together so cleverly that there was no sign of a join anywhere. Why did he not take the precaution to notice whether anyone was watching him! "Here, Dot," he said, "is a nice rosy apple for you." Dot took the apple, split it open, picked out the pill and presented him with it, "Yes, uncle, and there is the pip *for you.*"

Now we are not to use our book as Dot used the apple. It was given to her not because it was nice in itself, but to make the pill go down easily. Something good for us will often be hidden in a story; we must not think of the story *only*, but of what it is meant to bring home to us. Do you understand?

Of course you will want to know if the stories are true. Yes, they are true, and, moreover, the greater number relate what happened not so long ago. So you may be quite happy on that score. Here and there you will find mention of a little boy named Urban. His thoughts during his preparation may interest and help you.

One word more. If there are others preparing with you, pray for them. Say an Our Father and a Hail Mary for them every day. Our Lord has promised to hear the prayer of two or three gathered together in His Name, and by praying for one another we shall be wonderfully helped and get far more grace than if we thought only of ourselves.

# Part the First:

# Our Lord's Preparation for Coming to Us in Holy Communion

# I
# Eternity, and What the Saints Thought of It

That is a beautiful story, among the many beautiful stories of the conversion of the Saxon Heptarchy, which tells how Edwin, King of Northumbria, hesitating still whether to receive or reject the doctrines brought by Paulinus from Rome, called together his priests and nobles, and bade each man speak his mind freely.

Then Coifi, chief priest of the idols, rose and said, "When, O King, in mid-winter, you and your nobles are seated at supper, here in the great hall, a blazing fire on the hearth, a sparrow, chased by the wind and snow, flies in by one door and escapes by another. Our eyes follow her for a moment during her flight, and then she passes again into the wintry night and is seen no more. Such is the life of man. We see it for a little while, but what went before and is to come after, we know not. If these new teachers can tell us anything certain of these matters, we ought to hear them."

What Coifi desired to learn, the Catholic child knows from the first page of its Catechism. We know that we came from God and that we are returning to God. We know that He thought of us from all eternity; that there never was a time when He was not thinking of us and loving us; that He wants us to be happy; wants to see our bright faces among those of His Saints who are to stand before Him for ever. And so He made us instead of many others, who perhaps would have loved and served Him better than we have done. He has sent us into this world for a little while *on our trial,* that He may see whether we will love and serve Him, and so deserve the happiness He has in store for us.

It is very important that we should understand *what we are—where we are—*and *where we are going.* So we will go very thoughtfully through this meditation, and try to let it sink into our hearts.

When our baby days are past, and we are old enough to think at all seriously about ourselves and all we see around us, we find that we are here in God's great world, surrounded by many creatures of His—some without reason, as the plants and animals—and some like ourselves with souls that have three powers: memory, understanding, and will.

Now, what were all these different kinds of creatures made for? If the plants and animals had sense, they would answer: "*We* are made for the service of those favoured creatures, whom God has made to His own image and likeness, and to whom He has given souls that will never die. We are made to serve for their food and clothing, to labour for them, and then to die. When we have done this, we have done all we were made for. For us there is no life to come, and so we may well try to get all the enjoyment we can out of this life. We bask in the sunshine, we eat, and drink, and sleep, and find our pleasure in these things, for God has not made us for anything higher. How happy are those other creatures of His, who are made to live for ever, and be for ever happy with Him! What can it matter to them if their short life here is hard or sad, when their real life is to come, when they can look forward to joys and delights which eye has not seen, nor ear heard, nor heart conceived? Surely none of them will live as we do—just to eat and drink, and sleep, and sport about. But they will live wisely in this world, remembering they are not going to live here always, and all their care will be to get ready for that other world which is never to pass away."

So these lower creatures would speak, so they would envy us, if they knew the difference between ourselves and them. Oh, yes, how happy we are—to be made, not for any creature, however noble, but for the God Who made them all! Do we understand and feel our happiness? Do we thank Him for it?

The attendants of a little prince were watching him one day, as he stood at a window of the palace, gazing intently into the street below. Suddenly he burst into tears, and the whole place was filled with such piteous cries and sobs, that for some time there was no getting to know what was the matter. And what was the matter? Down there in the gutter, a number of little ragged boys were enjoying themselves, making a mud tower—and His Royal Highness was upset because he could not be of the party. Poor little prince! You think him very silly, yet how many there are like him! How many children of the King of kings there are, who care for nothing but the dirt of this world—money and comforts, good eating and drinking, and enjoyments for the body, forgetting the delights of their Father's Palace, and their dignity as princes and princesses in the Kingdom of Heaven!

Whether we forget it or not, are ready for it or not, Eternity is coming. What do we do when something is coming which we cannot escape, and for which we are expected to be prepared—say—an examination? We try to find out first, what it will be about, and next, when it will be. If we are told that we may be dropped upon at any time, there is nothing for it but to be ready at any moment. So we act in the things of this life. Why are we less wise—*why are we so stupid*, when our examination is to decide, not a little matter of this life, but our happiness or misery in the everlasting life to come?

Our summons may come at any time. It may be soon. Not one of us can be sure when we lie down to rest at night, that we shall not wake up in the other world. Our Lord says He will come like a thief in the night, when we least expect him. If He were to come to-night, should I be ready? Am I doing what He sent me into this world to do, and doing it diligently?

An English Bishop once found himself in a railway carriage with a lady, who had plenty to say to her fellow-travellers. She was a clever lady, whose conversation showed that her mind was well stored with information on many subjects. She spoke of plants and animals; of the laws by which this world is governed; of the heavenly bodies, their nature and movements, and of many other things. The Bishop listened quietly from his corner, waiting for an opportunity of putting in his word. It came at last. "Madam," he said, "I have followed with much interest all you have been saying. You have spoken, and spoken well, of the end for which so many things in this grand creation have been made. Can you tell us now for what *you* were made?" She was thunderstruck at so extraordinary a question. What was *she* made for? For some moments she remained silent and thoughtful, her countenance betraying her discomfort. Then she said, in gentler tones than the company had heard hitherto, "I confess, sir, that this thought has never occurred to me before." There was no time for anything further. The train stopped for an instant to set the Bishop down at his destination, and then went whistling on its way. He watched it till it was out of sight. One of God's creatures was there, who had never thought till now why she had been sent into this world, who had busied herself about everything but the one thing necessary, who had found everything in this wonderful world interesting *except* her own immortal soul. What would become of her? Would the words that had startled her for a moment be forgotten directly, or would they sink into her heart and make her think at last, although so late, of Eternity and of her salvation?

"What a stupid woman," some of you are saying. "Why, any one could have answered the Bishop's question, it was quite easy." Wait a bit. Suppose, instead of asking how this poor lady could be so stupid, we ask *ourselves*: Which is more stupid—never to have thought of eternity before, or, having heard about it ever since we can remember, believing firmly that it is coming, and coming fast, and that everything depends on our being ready for it—to be taking no pains, or very little pains, to get ready? Is this what I have been doing? What have I done up to now, what am I doing now, which shows that I understand perfectly that I was made for Eternity and am making my life a preparation for it?

Oh, that wonderful thought of Eternity—never, never, never to come to an end! If we remembered it, could we help getting ready for it? The Saints remembered it, and got ready. The chief thought of all the Saints is—to save my soul—to do nothing that will harm it—to do everything that will help it. "What is this for Eternity?" was a question St. Aloysius often asked himself, and he fast became a Saint. "What shall I think of this when I come to die?" St. Ignatius used to say: "How will it look at the Judgment?"

It was the thought of Eternity that made the Saints so afraid of sin, the only thing that could deprive them of God and eternal happiness. The martyrs feared it so much that they bore cruel torments and a dreadful death rather than commit sin. Multitudes of men, women, and children have feared it so much as to be resolved never to commit a wilful sin for the love or fear of anything whatsoever.

In the early ages of the Church, there were numbers of men and women so determined to save their souls and secure a happy Eternity, that, fearing the concerns of this life might take up all their thoughts and make them forget the life to come, they left their home and country, and went to live far away from the cares and the comforts of the world. The deserts of Egypt and Palestine were filled with these holy solitaries, living for one thing only, the one thing necessary—to serve God and get ready for Eternity.

The Church knows that the greater number of her children are not called to leave the world in order to serve God faithfully and save their souls. But she warns all without exception against setting their hearts upon the things of this world, and bids them pray so to pass through the good things of time as not to lose those of Eternity.

And now I want you to go back in thought nearly four hundred years, and to come with me far away from these leaden skies of ours to a bright land in the south, to beautiful Spain, and the sky of fair Castile.

We will take our stand on this old bridge and watch the passers-by. There will be two coming up presently whom you must notice. Turn this way—so, with your face towards Avila. Now we can hardly miss them. No, not those gay cavaliers on their prancing Arabians, nor these stately Castilian ladies, nor the bare-headed friars, nor that noble-looking boy yonder, who is attracting your attention, though we might well be waiting to have a look at him. His name is Francis Borgia. He will be Duke of Gandia by-and-bye, and later on, third General of the Society of Jesus. His father, one of the grandees of Spain, and a great man at Court, is with him over here in Castile, on business probably—King Ferdinand, the boy's grandfather, being Regent of the Kingdom.

You are tired of waiting for the two I have told you to expect? Have a little patience, they are worth waiting for, one does not meet such children every day. Ah! here they come at last, hand in hand. That boy of ten is Rodrigo de Cepeda. We should never have heard of him but for the little eager creature at his side, his sister evidently, who is urging him on. She cannot be more than six, but there are signs already of the generosity and greatness of soul that will make her later one of God's grandest Saints. Look at her well. It is she who will be known later as Teresa of Jesus. Her writings will enlighten the most learned, and her burning love of God be felt throughout the length and breadth of the Church to the end of time.

How earnestly the two are talking. What can it be all about? If we were nearer we should catch the word that falls so often from their lips, "Eternity, Eternity." Their conversation is, as usual, about the Saints, the happiness of dying for God, the happiness of living for ever with Him. What strange deep thoughts, you say, for minds so young. Deep, yes—but not strange. For those who are fond of reading the Lives of the Saints come to have the thoughts of the Saints, and this little brother and sister delight in these Lives—those of the martyrs especially. At an age when other children are satisfied with toys and trifles, their hearts are set on joys that will last for ever. Their favourite talk is about the happiness of Heaven, and they have learnt already to despise all that passes with time. What seems to have made most impression on them is the thought of Eternity. They are amazed to find that both the pain and the glory of the next life are to last for ever, and they repeat again and again, "For ever, for ever, for ever!" Envying the Saints their everlasting happiness, they often say to one another, "What, they will see God for ever!" The martyrs seem to them to have bought Heaven very cheap by their torments, and of late the thought has been growing upon them that it would be a grand thing for themselves if *they* could buy it at the same price. And why not? The country of the Moors is not far off. They are cruel people, and hate the Christians, and put to death all they can find. "If we were to go to them," said Teresa, "they would cut off our heads, and we should be in Heaven directly, and see God for ever."

At last she has persuaded Rodrigo to go in search of martyrdom, and after watching for an opportunity, they have found one this morning. No one at home has seen them set out, and here they come across the bridge, praying with great fervour that God will give them grace to lay down their lives for Christ. Rodrigo's step is not so brisk as his little sister's, and at times he has his misgivings, which it takes all her energy and powers of persuasion to allay. They have crossed the bridge, and are hastening along the road to Salamanca, when—alas for their hopes of martyrdom!—an uncle meets them. They have been missed at home, and search is being made for them in every direction. Another moment and they are captured, and without more ado, taken back to their mother. When questioned by her, Rodrigo does not show himself a very valiant comrade in adversity, laying all the blame of the escapade on "the little one," who, he says, "wished to see God, and to die soon that she might do so."

I could tell you many other stories of the little Teresa. How she and Rodrigo, finding they could not be martyrs, tried next to be hermits, and to build themselves hermitages amongst the trees in the orchard, where they wanted to live as the solitaries of the desert, whose lives had interested them almost as much as those of the martyrs. How Teresa, becoming more and more inflamed with the love of God, spent many hours alone in prayer, and, looking up to the blue Castilian sky above her, as she walked in her father's garden, would say over and over again, "O Eternity, Eternity, Eternity!" And how, when she grew older, the devil, suspecting perhaps that she would save many souls beside her own, began to lay his snares for her. But we have no time for all this. If you want to see what became of her later, you must get her Life and read for yourselves.

What is that you are saying? You just want to know if she went on being good, or if the devil did catch her in his snares? Well, yes, he did, and the Saint tells us so herself. She is so given to exaggerate her faults, that it is not easy to know what we ought to think of her at this period of her life. If we are to trust her own account, silly books and frivolous occupations so engrossed her thoughts, that for a time she became a thoroughly worldly girl. She certainly fell away sadly from her first fervour, and her faults, if not grave, were real infidelities in one who had been so highly favoured by God. Her feet were on the dangerous slope that leads to grave sin, when again the thought of the Eternity to which she was hastening brought her back to the right way.

Great and glorious Saint! Safe now for ever, and high in the Kingdom of God, how she must bless Him for that thought of Eternity, which for her guidance and protection through life, he impressed so deeply on her heart as a little child!

My God, impress it on *my* heart too. I do want to save my soul. I know that if I save it once, it is saved for ever, and if I lose it once, I cannot have another chance. Make me understand this as St. Ignatius, and St. Aloysius, and St. Teresa understood it, as they all understand it in Eternity. And help me to remember it when temptation comes, that I may turn away from sin—every sin—with the same horror with which the Saints turned away from it, because sin alone can make me lose my place in Heaven. O my God, *make me afraid of sin*. Keep me safe from all sin that would separate me from You. Let me be so helped by the prayers of all those who have saved their souls, that I may love and serve You faithfully in this world as they did, and like them, come to be happy with You for ever in the next.

# II
# Eternity, and What I Must Think of It

"What, more about Eternity!" some of you will say; "we shall never get on with our preparation if we begin so far off. And what has Eternity to do with First Communion?" It has a great deal to do with it; it has everything to do with it. Those who get the great thought of Eternity well into their minds will make an excellent preparation, like a man who having a high building to raise, lays a solid foundation. Those who pass lightly over this thought will not do very much. Indeed it will be well for them if their house is not built upon the sand, and they are not swept away by the first storm. So let us be patient and stay a little longer where the Saints stayed all their lives.

Our next thought must be this. The one thing necessary for the Saints is the one thing necessary *for me*. My soul is as much to me as theirs was to them. How comes it then that there is such a difference between them and me, between so many children, who at this moment are leading good and even holy lives, and me? It comes from this, that they think a great deal about what is to come and I think about it so little. *I* think all will come right of course; I shall get to heaven of course. *They* think they can never be too careful or too safe. Is my way as wise as theirs? Is it well for me to make so sure? Must I not think more about saving my soul? Surely, if the determination to secure their salvation could make two little children start off in search of martyrdom, and has made thousands upon thousands give up every other concern in this life, it ought to make me more careful than I am, more in earnest than I am.

I have to save my soul. No one can do it for me. I shall either save it or not save it. I must either be intensely happy or utterly miserable throughout Eternity. What a difference between the two!

To save my soul, I have to know, love, and serve God. Am I trying to know Him? It is very easy to learn about Him, for He has told everything in this world to teach me. The stars over my head; the flowers beneath my feet: the birds that delight me with their song—all the beautiful things He has made, speak to me of Him, show me how great and glorious He must be Who has made them all. When I hear a piece of music that pleases me, or see a beautiful picture, I say at once, "Who is the composer?" or "I should like to see the man who painted that." Why do not the wonderful things God has made—made on purpose to raise my heart to Him—why do they not make me think of Him?

Mother Church teaches me more about Him still. All that I need and can know about God in this world, she teaches me by her priests, by her words in my Catechism, by the Lives of her Saints, and other holy books. Much of all this I am *bound* to know, and I *must* know in order to save my soul. *Do I try to know it?* Am I attentive at Catechism, and do I strive to understand what I hear?

To save my soul, I must not only know God, but love and serve Him. The more we know of God, the more we shall love and the better we shall serve Him. We must learn to love God, the Catechism tells us, by begging Him to teach us to love Him.

We must often think how good He is, often speak to Him in our hearts, and always try to please Him. Any one who does this, really loves God, even though he may not have in his heart any strong *feeling* of love. Love is shown by deeds more than by words or feelings. And thus it is that to love God truly and to serve Him are the same thing.

Those whom we love we are anxious to please and afraid to displease, *because* we love them. Who is it I love best in this world? Would I willingly offend that one? When I do sadden the heart that I love, am I not sad and sorry? Have I a greater pleasure than to please those I love, to save them pain or trouble, to do them some little service? Am I not careful above all to do their bidding? Now we love and serve God just in the same way, and if our love and service to Him is not shown like this, it is no love and service at all.

Let me ask myself then: Do I often think how good God is, often speak to Him in my heart, and try in all I do to please Him? Do I fear to displease Him? Am I afraid of sin? Do I serve Him by keeping His Commandments, as a good servant does the bidding of his master?

If in this way I am trying to know, love, and serve God, I am saving my soul, I am doing what I was sent into this world to do, what our Lord calls "the one thing necessary." If I am neglecting this, all the rest will profit me nothing. I may work from morning till night—be rich, clever, successful—I may have plenty of the pleasures and amusements of this life—but if I do not serve God, if I lose my soul, I shall have lost everything and be eternally miserable.

Supposing the story to be true, that Queen Elizabeth on coming to the throne of England, said, "Give me forty years of glory, and I care not what follows," how would those words have come back to her when her forty years of earthly glory came to a close, and her soul was going to its account! In any case, what did all the splendour of her proud, prosperous reign profit her then? On the other hand, what did all their torments matter to the martyrs she so cruelly put to death, once they were over? They lasted some of them many years, for the prisons of England at that period—to say nothing of the tortures there inflicted—were worse than death. But what are fifty or a hundred years compared to Eternity? For more than three hundred years these blessed martyrs have been enjoying all the delights of Heaven, and their happiness will last as long as God shall be God. If He were to require of *us* all He required of them, it would be very little—it would be nothing compared to the reward. But He does not ask this. He only bids us avoid sin, keep His Commandments, and bear patiently the troubles He sends us for our good. Oh, how glad we shall be when we come to die if we have done this, if we have served Him faithfully!

And not only shall we be glad *then*, but all our life through we shall be happy with a peaceful happiness that no trouble can take from us. We may be poor, suffering, friendless; we may have to work hard for the necessaries of this life, and enjoy few of its pleasures, yet, if we are doing that for which God created us, if we are trying to save our souls, we shall be happier far, even here, than those who think only of enjoying themselves. One of the things that will fill the lost with rage and envy at the Last Day, will be to see, that those who have saved their souls have suffered less in gaining eternal happiness, than *they* have done in procuring for themselves never-ending misery.

How foolish I am then, if I am not using my life as God meant me to use it. It is not a very grand or important life in the eyes of men. But it may be a life very dear to God and very pleasing in His sight, if like the Saints I am in earnest about my salvation. Am I? Is it not just the want of earnestness that makes me so unlike the Saints? I wish I could come to be like them. I know as they did that my soul is worth more than all the world beside. But, somehow, it is so difficult to care much for things we cannot see, to feel interested in them, to think much about them. I believe they are all true, but as to thinking any more about them, I cannot do it.

No, not unless you can *get* interested in them. If we look at a picture, in the twilight, we see it as in a haze; it puzzles instead of pleasing us, and we are not interested. But bring it out into the light and there examine it again, and how different it looks, how quickly interest is awakened, and admiration and delight. The difference between us and the Saints is this: *we* look at Divine things in the dusk, superficially, carelessly, and they do not move us—the wonder would be if they did—the Saints examine them closely by the light of faith, till their hearts are kindled with the love and desire of them, and their resolve is taken to secure them at any price. If we could understand like them the worth of our souls, we should have their determination, their courage, and their perseverance in working out our salvation.

What must we do for this? Bring them out into the light and there examine them. God is the Light of light. In His light all things are seen as they are. If we want to know what a thing is worth, there is no better way than to ask: "What does God think about it?" It is clear that what *He* thinks must be right, that the value He puts on a thing must be its true value.

Now what does God think of my soul? He values it so much that He has been always occupied about it. As long as He has been God, He determined to create it and do for it all that He has done. From all eternity He has been looking at it with love, and making plans for its happiness. From all eternity He appointed the Angel who was to be its guardian, the graces He would give it, the time when it should be sent into the world. This was to be, not that dark, dreadful time before our Lord came, but the time since his coming, since the foundation of His Church and the institution of His Sacraments, that so my soul might have its share in all these priceless blessings. It was to work out its salvation, not in a Pagan country, but in a Christian land and in a Christian home. Holy Church was to make it His child and an heir of Heaven by Baptism, and prepare it by her teaching and her sacraments for its place in His Kingdom. The Precious Blood is to be always at hand that its sins may be washed away. Every morning the graces stored up in Holy Mass are to be unlocked for it, that it may come and help itself freely. More favoured than the child of any earthly king, it is to be admitted at any hour of the day or night into the Royal Presence to ask for all it needs or desires. Any one harming it will incur the anger of God; all who love and help it will be rewarded by Him. Angels and saints are to be its brothers and sisters; the Blessed Mother of God is to take it into her motherly keeping; and God Himself it is to call by the tender name of Father.

What could this Father do for me that He has not done? What has He spared that my soul may be eternally happy? Nothing—not even His only Son. For its sake this well-beloved Son came down from Heaven, lived a life of sorrow, and died a death of shame. For its sake He rose again and ascended into Heaven, that He might prepare its place there. And—as if all this were not enough—He is coming down from Heaven again to bring it a Gift, greater than all He has yet given—His own very Self—*to be its Food.*

This is the value God puts upon my soul. This is how He treats it. All this He does not think too much to secure its salvation. And what value do *I* set upon it? How have I treated it up to now? Was it safe to trust *to me* what He has loved so long and so intensely?

O my God, my God, I fall on my knees before You, and hide my face in my hands. No, it was not safe to trust this precious soul to *me*. Had it been worth nothing at all, worth less than my worthless body, I could scarcely have treated it worse. Heaven and earth are set to serve it. The God of Heaven and earth is become its Food—and I treat it as a thing of no account. I take little care to keep it from sin. I have not the fear I ought to have even of mortal sin, which would expose it to the frightful danger of losing You for ever. I am doing so little, so very little, to make it fit for Your company in Heaven. Oh, no, I do not deserve to have this precious soul in my keeping. I am not fit to be trusted with it any longer. And so, my God, I give it into Your Hands to keep it for me. When I was very little I used to take to my mother any treasure I was afraid of losing, and lay it in her lap saying, "Save that for me." And now, my Heavenly Father, I come to You with the greatest treasure I have, my immortal soul, and I give it into Your keeping. Save it for me. Do not trust it to me, I shall only lose it. Have pity on it because it is my only one. Have pity on it still more because it is Your own, and the work of Your Hands. It is more Yours than mine. It was Yours before it was mine. I give it back to You. Take it, O Lord, and receive it. Teach me to love it and care for it as You do—to hate all that would harm it, to lay hold on all that will help it—to try to make it worthy of Your love. That so, when You shall call for it again, it may be found pleasing in Your sight and worthy of its place in Your Kingdom.

Some years ago an English gentleman was disinherited by his father for becoming a Catholic. His home, however, was not, as is the case with so many converts, closed against him. He was free to go there whenever he pleased, and was kindly received. Our story is about one of these visits, when he was accompanied by his little boy.

It was one of those stately homes, of which we have so many in the land, beautiful at every season of the year, but never more beautiful than when the surrounding foliage was putting on its autumnal tints, and greens of every hue, passing here and there into yellow or scarlet, framed it in on every side. The child gazed at it with a sort of wondering awe and his eye wandered over terrace, park, and garden—he thought no place in the world could be half so nice as the house which was once his father's home.

There was no little curiosity among the visitors invited for the shooting party, when the last two arrivals were announced. All knew how the son's inheritance had been lost to him, and many things were said—some of them not very kind things—by those who did not understand that to a Catholic, the Faith is more than all the world beside. "What a strange fancy to throw away a place like this!" said one. "If he did not want it himself, he might have thought of the child," remarked another. "I wish I cared for my religion as he must care for his," said a third, quietly. And so they talked, wondering, blaming, or admiring, when they met the boy and his father strolling hand in hand through the grounds.

One evening the guests had betaken themselves to a fine old room, whose western windows opened out upon the lawn. Conversation was brisk. The morning's sport had put them all in high spirits. Many had adventures to tell and retell, and at times the merriment of the younger ones broke out in a somewhat noisy fashion. Then the discreet finger of one of the elders would point to the corner, where, apart from the rest, the old man and his son sat silent and thoughtful. They were watching the little fellow who stood so motionless at the window, looking out upon the scene beyond. It was a scene whose beauty might well have arrested even a child's eye. The sun was going to set. His beams were still golden, and turned to gold the rippling waters of the lake and the foliage of the trees that studded the lawn. Oaks and elms and quivering aspens reflected his parting rays, all except the two solemn cedars, that looked more solemn than usual against the brilliant sky. Suddenly every one in the room was startled by a shrill cry from the window. "O father, do come and look, it is so beautiful out there." There was no need for the father to look. He knew it all so well. It was the home of his childhood, and might have been his home yet. Every inch of ground he knew. Every tree, every curve round the water's edge was familiar to him, and reminded him of the olden days when he played about there, and people used to say it would one day be his own. Oh, no, there was no need for him to go and look. Calling the boy to him, he took the little hands into his own, and said: "Yes, it *is* beautiful—tell me now, would you rather have that or Heaven?" The child returned to his post and looked out once more upon the outstretched lands and the glittering lake. Long and earnestly he looked. Then, coming again to his father's side, and putting his hand into his, he said: "I would rather have Heaven." "Thank God, my boy; it was the choice your father made before you," was the quiet answer.

For some minutes the room was very still—still with a solemn silence. Many a heart was stirred to its depths, and there were tears in many eyes. For all felt that a lesson of heavenly wisdom had been taught that night by the choice of a little child.

My God, let *me* learn that lesson. Let me see, as that little boy saw, that I cannot give up Heaven in exchange for anything in this world. Show me that nothing matters *very much* except to save my soul. It does not matter whether my life is long or short, bright and happy, or full of trial; whether I am rich or poor; liked by everybody, or not cared much about. All this does not matter much—it will all be over soon. What *does* matter is, that I never do anything which would risk the salvation of my soul, and that when temptation comes, I am ready to lose everything rather than lose Your love and Your grace. Help me to do this, as You have helped so many in this country to give up home and friends and all they loved, as You helped our dear English Martyrs to give up life itself.

>Faith of our Fathers, holy Faith,
>We will be true to thee till death.

# III
# THE PROMISE IN PARADISE

What a sad, sad story it is, that Fall of our first parents! To think that God, Who was infinitely happy in Himself from all eternity, should have made them to share His happiness; should have been so generous to them, body and soul; given them in that beautiful garden all that could make them happy even in this life, and promised to take them to Heaven without dying, there to fill up the places of the fallen angels; and in return for all this love and liberality have required of them one thing only, one act of self-restraint, and such a little one, that so they might show their submission to Him and earn the reward He had in store for them! To think that when He had loved them *like that*, they should have disappointed Him, broken His easy laws, and spoilt His perfect plan—how sad it all is! So sad that we wonder He did not sweep them from off the face of the earth, and make in their place a new and better race. But He did not do this. He loved them still, and pitied them, and promised to put all right again for them and their children, by sending His only Son into the world to open again the gates of Heaven which their sin had shut.

We cannot understand this love of God. Our Lord Himself, when He came on earth; could only say of it, "God *so* loved the world *as to send His Son.*"

Who ever heard of the son of a king wishing to die in

order to atone for the crime of a servant he loved! Or of a king consenting to give the life of his only son for a favourite! But that the son should offer his life, and the father be willing he should die, not for a friend or favourite, but for an enemy—can we imagine love like this? Yet this was God's love for us. And even this was not enough to satisfy His love. It seems as if He could never do enough for us.

The least act of our Lord after His Incarnation would have atoned for all our sins, had he so willed. A word, a tear would have redeemed a thousand worlds. Why then did He do and suffer so much? His Human Nature shrank, as ours does, from the things that hurt it. Hunger and thirst, unkindness and pain He felt even more than we do. Why, then, did He choose what was so hard, when He might have had a bright, unsorrowing life?

And if He was determined to die for us, why must it be the most cruel and shameful death He could find? No one can tell us why. The Church herself cannot tell us. She is as much amazed as we are that God should have loved us so, and can only cry out in her admiration and gratitude: "O happy fault that deserved to have such a Redeemer!"

What have I done up to now to show my grateful love to Jesus, my Redeemer? What am I going to do? "If," says St. Bernard, "I owe my whole self to Him for being made, what shall I give Him for being so wonderfully restored, when I had been ruined by sin? For it cost Him much more to redeem me than to make me at first." To create us cost Him only a word; to redeem us cost Him a life of sorrow and a death of shame. Have we ever thought what it cost our Lord to save us as He did?

When we want to know the worth of a thing, we ask what it cost. "What did you give for it?" we say, and we come to know something of the love of Jesus for us when we see what he gave up for our sakes. Unless we can bring this home to ourselves in some way, we cannot be grateful to Him and love Him as we ought. We must try then to bring it home.

Some children are very fond of fairy-tales. They like to get away from the hum-drum life at home or at school, and wander about in fairy-land. They love to hear of places impossibly beautiful, of fields of golden grass, palaces of precious stones, princes and princesses of dazzling loveliness. These things interest them somehow, though they know they are not real. How much more interested would they be if fairy-land were a reality! Well, there is a place, a real place, where everything is so rich and beautiful that all we read or can imagine of fairy-land is ugliness compared with it. That place is Heaven, the palace where God reigns in His majesty, surrounded by the princes of His Court. Look up through the open heavens, and see Him there as the Saints have seen Him on the throne of His glory. He is "King of kings, and Lord of lords, and on His Head are many diadems. Around the throne there is a rainbow like an emerald, and before the throne a sea of glass like crystal." See the magnificence of His Court. "Thousands of thousands minister to Him, and ten thousand times a hundred thousand stand before Him." Angels are there in such multitudes that God alone can number them. And glorious even among the Angels, is the great multitude that no man can number, of all nations, and tribes, and peoples, and tongues, clothed with white robes and palms in their hands. There are the Saints standing with their harps on the crystal sea; and the four living creatures that rest not day and night, saying: "Holy, Holy, Holy, Lord God Almighty;" and the four-and-twenty ancients clothed in white with golden crowns on their heads, who fall down on their faces and adore Him, and cast their crowns before the throne.

Turn now from His throne in Heaven, and look at Him as He appeared on earth and was seen by men. See in Bethlehem the throne He chose for love of us, and the courtiers there—the stable and the manger, the ox and the ass, the darkness and the cold.

St. Bernard says that, rising from His throne, he laid aside the purple robes of His royalty, and stepping down to the earth, clothed Himself with the sackcloth of our mortality. Shall we not love Him for it? "The Lord is great and exceedingly to be feared. The Lord is little and exceedingly to be loved."

We sometimes hear that certain poor people are deserving of special pity, because they have known better days. This is because those who have once been well off feel the hardships of poverty more than others who have never known anything else. And so we pity them more. But if it is a king who is in distress, how our hearts are moved. No one can help pitying Charles I, at least when he fell into the hands of his enemies; and that royal child in a French prison, whose sufferings touch us still more than those of our Stuart King.

When you read some day the history of the French Revolution, you will come upon one of the saddest stories that has ever been told, the story of a little prince born and brought up in the splendour of a palace, and dying after a short life of ten years within the walls of a dungeon, in want of all things. You will read how, after the execution of the King, his father, the young Louis XVII was taken from his mother and given into the keeping of a ruffian, who tormented the fragile, sensitive child in every way that cruelty could invent. Blows, kicks, fierce threats, coarse and scanty food—this was the little prisoner's treatment during eighteen months till death put an end to his sufferings.

We pity the poor little captive King more than we should pity an ordinary child who had suffered the same cruelty and neglect. We think how he must have contrasted the Palace of Versailles, where he had been so delicately reared, with the gloomy prison, or rather den, in which the last eighteen months of his life were spent. How he, who had been accustomed to the fondest love of father and mother—and as the heir of France, to the homage of the most ceremonious of Courts, must have felt the cruelty and contempt of those into whose hands he had fallen. We keep saying to ourselves, this poor little sufferer was no ordinary child, but a King. It is because we remember always who he was and what he had once been, that our hearts are so stirred by his wrongs.

The same thought should be in our minds always when we think of our Lord's pains—His bodily pain and the pain of His Sacred Heart. If we feel our hearts touched by the sorrows of the little captive King, because he was rejected by his people and delivered over by them to a lingering death; because it was such an innocent victim that was mocked and struck and wounded in his tenderest affections, who heard his mother insulted, and saw his father hated and despised; because he suffered in silence the punishment of a guilt that was not his—if all this fills our hearts to overflowing, how is it we are not touched by the bitter sorrows of another Captive King, a Divine King, Who suffered more by far, all His Life through, than the child in the Temple prison? We feel for a King in distress; what ought we to feel for a God in distress, and in distress for love of us!

Was He not a little Captive King that first Christmas night, held captive in the manger and in His swathing-bands by His love for us? Was He not a Captive all through His earthly Life? Is He not a Captive still in His sacramental Life? He does not mind it; He is quite willing, for love and sacrifice go together, and He *does* love us. All He asks of us is that we love Him in return. He has come a long way to seek our love, all the way from Heaven. He has done much—oh, how much to win it! Are we going to disappoint Him? He told one of His Saints that He had done all He could to show us how much He loves us; but if she could think of anything more, He would do it. Is there anything more? Yes, there is this one thing, He can give us the grace we need to return Him love for love.

A little boy, named Urban, was preparing like you for his First Communion. One day a thought struck him as it had never done before—the thought of our Lord's love *for him*. Our Lord loves all men and died for all—he knew that of course. But he had never thought, or at least it had never come home to him, how much our Lord had loved *him* and done for *him*. It had come home now. And then came another thought—how little love our Lord had had from him in return. His was a loving little heart, and he could not bear to think he had been ungrateful to One Who had loved him so dearly. What could he do to show he was not ungrateful? The words of the Catechism came to his mind: "How must we learn to love God? We must often think how good God is, often speak to Him in our hearts, and always seek to please Him." Oh, that was not hard. It would be nice to think of Him, to speak to Him, to try to please Him. He could do that. And he did do it, and what is more, persevered in doing it, till at last he came to love our Blessed Lord with a very real and a very tender love. Would you care to know how he used to speak to our Lord in his heart? "I tell him," he said, "that as He has loved me so much and done so much for me, He might as well do a little more and make me love Him back."

This is what we all want, to love Him back. We should love Him back if we tried to bring His love more home to our hearts; and to remember, not only Who He was that came to save us, but the willingness with which He came and suffered. Shall we try to bring home to ourselves, by another story, this willingness of His?

Some years ago a Catholic gentleman whose life is spent in the service of the poor, heard of the miserable places in which many of them are forced to seek shelter at night. The description was so terrible that he felt something must be done to help them. But what could he do? He turned the subject over in his mind again and again, and at last a thought struck him. He would go amongst them and find out from his own experience what they have to bear. Out of such a knowledge of their misery would come the best means of remedying it. So he made his plans.

One evening after dusk, a gentleman entered a little cottage on the high-road to M——. Half an hour later, a tramp in tattered clothes came out. Can you guess who it was? He joined other tramps on the road and made his way with them to the casual ward, where he was to spend the night. What a night it was and what a day succeeded it! It makes us shudder to think of all the suffering that was crowded into those forty hours. The dirt, the wretched bedding and food, the hard work for hands unused to it, this was bad enough. But the companions he had to mix with, this was worse by far. In the home he had left all were good and gentle, lovable and kind. Here he was in the midst of the bad, and of the very worst among the bad. The manners and the language, the coarse rough usage from which there was no escape—how hard it all was to bear! Some of us who are dainty or particular as to food and clothing and the way we are treated, can guess perhaps something of the pain.

"And what did he gain by it?" you will say. This—that he knows now by his own experience how hard and dangerous life is for so many; that he is better able to bring their misery before the notice of the charitable and the generous, and thus may hope to win for our homeless poor some measure of comfort and relief.

And this was what the Son of God gained by coming amongst us, this was what He came on earth to seek. As God,

He knew our miseries, but He could not, as God, know them by experience, which is learning things at our own cost, by feeling them ourselves. He wanted to have this experience. He wanted to know—as we know—hunger and thirst, and unkindness, and sorrow, and fear, that He might be like us in all things, and be able to give us in all our troubles the sympathy of His Sacred Human Heart.

Oh, what a Redeemer it was that was promised to us in Paradise! If Adam and Eve had known Him as we know Him, they would have loved Him and longed for Him even more than they did. As it was, they handed down to their children the Promise of His Coming as the most precious thing they had to leave them. And surely during their nine hundred years of penance in the cold gloomy world outside the gates of Eden, their first thought as the sun rose each morning would be, "Oh, will He come to-day?"

They did not know—but God knew—all, that in His loving designs, the Promise meant. It meant a Redeemer not only for the whole world in general, but for each of us one by one. And it meant not a coming after four thousand years and then a going away, but a coming that should have no going away at all. Our Lord would indeed ascend to His throne at the right hand of His Father after paying the price of our redemption. But His Blessed Presence He would never take away from us. In the Sacrament of the Altar He would be with us all days, even to the end of the world; coming to each one of us as soon as we are ready to receive Him—the Friend, the Companion of each one all through our life, till He brings us safely to His eternal Kingdom through the gates of Heaven which He has opened for us.

What would the love of poor Adam and Eve have been, could they have dreamed of this! What shall our love be when we know it all so well!

A great servant of God used to say, when he heard people thanking God for this or that: "It is not so much for things like these we should thank Him, as for having become Man to save us." The Church is never weary of thanking Him for it. She teaches us to bend our knee in honour of our Lord's Incarnation twice during Mass; first at the words in the Creed, *Et Homo factus est*—"And He was made Man;" and again at the *Verbum caro factum est*—"The Word was made Flesh," in the last Gospel.

All creatures in Heaven, on earth, and under the earth, teach us the reverence and grateful love we owe to Jesus, God made Man for us. The very devils whom He cast out of the bodies of the poor possessed, when He was on earth, teach us. They know He came to snatch their prey from them, and they hate and fear Him. They know He preferred us to them; came for us, not for them; chose us, and passed them by. And they envy us our happiness in having God Himself for our Redeemer. It was envy and rage that forced from them that miserable cry which we hear in the Gospels; "What have *we* to do with Thee, Jesus, Son of God?"

It is gratitude to our Lord made Man for us, that the Church teaches us by the *Angelus*. The Angelus bell once brought a Protestant to the true Faith. Staying with a friend in the country, he asked what that bell meant, that rang so regularly several times a day from the little chapel near. He was told it was the voice of the Catholic Church, summoning all her children to adore three times a day the Word made Flesh. These words were like a flash of light to him. Could the Church which so honoured this unspeakable mystery, be any other than the one true Church of which he was in search? He began to inquire and to read and pray. God gave him the light of faith, and he became a Catholic.

O Jesus, Son of God, very God of very God, I believe that in Your love for us, You came down from Heaven and were made Man. I thank You with all my heart for this wonderful love, for all it cost You to come *to me*. O my Redeemer and my Saviour, to think that my First Communion was part of the Promise made so long ago! To think that You thought of it in Paradise, and planned everything for it, and longed for the time to come! Shall not I long for it too and prepare for it heartily? You have loved me so dearly. Teach me, my God, to love You back. Teach me how to speak to You in my heart, to please You in all I do. I will try to show You I am thankful to You whenever I say the *Angelus*. Help me to say it so, that You may always be able to take it as an act of thanksgiving.

# IV
## "Behold He Cometh, Leaping upon the Mountains, Skipping over the Hills."

Looking back upon the long four thousand years and more before our Lord came, we see how the hand of God directed all that happened in that olden time, and gradually prepared the world for the greatest event in its history, the coming of its Redeemer.

Little by little He unfolded His Divine plan. First the race, then the tribe, and at last the family was pointed out from which the Messiah should come. The promise made to Adam and Eve was renewed again and again, and each time with greater clearness. In the first promise the Redeemer is spoken of in general terms, as one of Adam's race. Then it is said that He shall be of the posterity of Sem. Out of these Abraham is chosen. Of the children of Abraham, Isaac. Of Isaac's children, Jacob. Among the twelve sons of Jacob, Juda. And out of the families of the tribe of Juda, the family of David.

Turn to the first chapter of St. Matthew's Gospel, and you will find the long list of our Lord's ancestors. "Abraham begot Isaac, and Isaac begot Jacob, and Jacob begot Judas and his brethren." And so the line runs on till we come to "David the King." Then on again and on, till at last, it ends with another

Jacob: "And Jacob begot Joseph, the husband of Mary, of whom was born Jesus, Who is called Christ."

Perhaps you think this list of hard names very dry and uninteresting. The Church does not think so, for she bids her priests read it as the Gospel of the Mass on some of her greatest feasts. And St. Bernard did not think so. He has a beautiful thought about this list of names: "It is delightful," he says, "to contemplate the manner of Christ's coming, for His ways are beautiful ways. 'Behold He cometh, leaping upon the mountains, skipping over the hills.' The mountains and hills we may consider to be the Patriarchs and the Prophets, and we may see His leaping and skipping in the book of His genealogy, "Abraham begot Isaac, and Isaac begot Jacob."

Think of this leaping upon the mountains next time you hear the names at Mass.

If on opening your book to-day you caught sight of Abraham, David, or Nabuchodonosor, you may well have said: "Surely we are not going to have a Scripture History lesson? These men have nothing to do with preparation for First Communion, and we know all about them if they had." That you know all about them is good news, and just what is wanted. But as to their having nothing to do with our preparation, are you so sure of that?

It is possible that you have gone through your Scripture History more with the view of getting up the facts than of getting out of them the good that lies hidden there. You know, at least in part, the story of God's chosen people, and of His dealings with them. And yet perhaps you have not noticed, or at least not noticed sufficiently, what that wonderful history of the Jews teaches us. There, better than anywhere else except in the holy Gospels, we come to know God, because we see there a picture of Him drawn by His own Hand. And because we learn to know Him, we learn to love Him. This is what we want, this

## Isaac

"Take thy only-begotten son, Isaac, whom thou lovest,...and offer him for an holocaust upon one of the mountains, which I will show thee." (Genesis 22:2)

is *all* that we want—*to learn to love God*. If our Lord finds love in our hearts when He comes to us in Holy Communion, He will be quite satisfied. Scripture History teaches us this love by showing us how lovable God is, and how worthy of all our love. It shows us that He is not only infinitely good in Himself, but infinitely good to us. From beginning to end, it is nothing but the wonderful story of God working out His designs for our redemption, through the history of the people He had chosen. Now nothing so strongly draws us to love as to see that we are loved. If then, by bringing home to us that God loves us dearly, we are led to love Him in return, who shall say that Scripture History has nothing to do with our work of preparation? Mind, we are not speaking of studying it in a dry way, as if we had to get it up for an examination, but of looking back upon the dear familiar story quietly and reverently in order to see God in it throughout—God guiding, guarding, cherishing through two thousand years the chosen nation, for the sake of His Son Whom it was to bring to the world for the redemption of all nations.

How can we help loving God when we see Him loving like that? It is true that the love He showed His chosen people in that Old Law, which has been called the law of fear, is as nothing compared with the love He shows the children of the Church, His chosen people under the New Law, the law of love. And yet what faithful, untiring love it was. Love in His miraculous help so freely given; love in His promises and threats and warnings; love in His very chastisements. Love most of all in that fidelity to His first promise in Paradise, for the sake of which all other blessings were given. It was to keep that promise and give us a Redeemer that He was so patient with a wayward and ungrateful race, that He worked so many miracles for it, and guided the events, not of its history alone, but of all other histories that were going on at the same time. But do not be afraid, we are not going to have a Scripture

History lesson. All we are going to do is to take a rapid glance at Jewish history, and the histories of the four great Empires of ancient times, that we may see the Providence of God working in them and through them. It mast be a very rapid glance, for we have not time for more.

You know that out of all the nations of the earth, God chose one to be His own in a peculiar way. With this Jewish nation, of which Abraham was the father and founder, He took up His abode. He gave it a special knowledge of Himself, a chosen priesthood, and a glorious ritual, with privileges and means of holiness such as no other nation possessed. You know that Jacob, Abraham's grandson, went down into Egypt, and that for four hundred years his descendants lived there, and were cruelly oppressed. That after their deliverance by Moses, and their entrance into the Promised Land, they were governed by Judges for four hundred years, and then by Kings. Saul reigned, and David, the man according to God's own heart, and Solomon, who built the first Temple. Then in Roboam's reign came the great schism. Ten out of the Twelve Tribes revolted, and formed the Kingdom of Israel. Two tribes remained faithful to Roboam, and formed the Kingdom of Juda. The Kings of Israel were all wicked, and their kingdom, after lasting two hundred and fifty years, was destroyed by Salmanasar, King of the Assyrians of Niniveh, who led the Ten Tribes into a captivity from which they never returned. Of the Kings of Juda, some were wicked and some were good. This kingdom lasted four hundred years, and was then destroyed by Nabuchodonosor, King of Babylon, who took the Two Tribes captive to Babylon. For seventy years their captivity lasted, and then they returned, and built the second Temple.

Now all this time—that is, from the time of Abraham—the great Assyrian Empire was running its course. It was used by

God again and again to punish His people when they sinned. But its hour came at last, and it fell. The Prophet Daniel, then a captive in Babylon, foretold its fall. You remember how he saw in vision four great beasts which trod down and devoured one another. These represented the four great Empires which were to rise and fall, one after the other, during two thousand years before the coming of Christ. With each of them the chosen nation had to do. Under the Assyrians, the Jews became a captive people. Under the Persians, who conquered the Assyrians, they were allowed to return to their native land and rebuild their Temple. Under the Macedonian, or Greek Empire, which lasted only twelve years, they lived in peace, subject to Alexander the Great. And when Alexander's Empire fell to pieces, and the various nations which had composed it came under the rule of the all-conquering Romans, the Jews, who for a brief space had recovered their independence, and were ruled by their own kings, were conquered too, and the Roman Empire filled the then-known world.

Like its predecessors, this Empire had a place of its own in God's plan, and a special work to do. That work was not only to prepare the world for the coming of the Messiah, which it did in various ways, but to make the preaching of the Gospel easier for the Apostles and their successors by bringing all nations under one rule.

It was an edict of the Roman Emperor ordering the whole world to be enrolled, that took our Lady and St. Joseph to Bethlehem, and when at last the King of kings came into the world, He came as a Roman subject. He was very near now. Whilst we have been following the fortunes of His people through the pagan world around them, He has been "leaping upon the mountains, skipping over the hills," and now He is almost in sight. The pagan world itself was watching for Him. Among the Gentiles there had been from the beginning a glimmering of the light which the Jews had in its fulness. This is plain from the words of Job, the Idumean: "I know that my Redeemer liveth;" from the prophecy of Balaam, "A star shall rise out of Jacob and even from the utterances of the heathen oracles, one of which is said to have declared that the greatest foe to the Roman power was a Child to be born among the Hebrews. In China there is said to have been a strong belief that a great Saint was about to appear in the West. And we know that as soon as the Eastern Kings saw the unknown star in the heavens, they set out in search of Him Who was "born King of the Jews," to lay their costly offerings at His Feet.

We must not then suppose that because the Jews were the chosen people, in whom the promises were to be fulfilled, God did not care for the rest of the poor world outside, and was not the God of all peoples. To the Gentiles also He gave some knowledge of His truth, and as the time drew near, He so disposed things that they too were eager with expectation. It was by a wonderful ordering of His Providence that several hundred years before Christ, the Jews were dispersed all over the earth, so that, as ancient historians tell us, there was scarcely a place of any importance where they were not to be found. They were on all the shores of the Mediterranean, and of Asia Minor; at the mouths of all the great rivers: the Nile, Danube, Tigris, and Euphrates. They were in Greece and Italy, and had gone eastward as far as China. They carried with them the writings of the Prophets, which in a hundred different forms foretold not only the time when the Messiah was to come, and the land in which He would appear, but the city in which He was to be born, His family, His character, actions, and sufferings, and the chief events of His Life. And thus, towards the close of the four thousand years, there was a universal expectation that a great Prophet and Deliverer was about to appear in the West. Among the Jews themselves, this expectation was naturally stronger still. When the Romans, setting aside the royal Jewish line, raised a stranger to the throne of the Machabees, and made Judea a Roman Province, all true Israelites and children of Abraham consoled themselves for the loss of their liberty by remembering that He must now be close at hand, Who was to deliver them, not from any earthly bondage, but from the slavery of the devil, and so make them truly free. For so Jacob had prophesied: "The sceptre shall not be taken away from Juda till He come that is to be sent, and He shall be the expectation of nations." The four thousand years of waiting had run their course. The whole world was in peace for the coming of the Prince of Peace. God's time for the redemption of the world had come, and the Redeemer came.

In her *Magnificat* our Lady poured forth her full heart in adoration, thanksgiving, and love. What was it that made her silent lips break forth into that glorious song of praise? It was the remembrance of God's goodness to the human race from the beginning; of His goodness to her people in particular; of His mercy from generation to generation; of His fidelity to His promises to Abraham and his seed. Let us look back on the history of her people as she did, and the spirit of the *Magnificat* will be ours too. With her we shall love and thank Him when we see how He has been working in the world since that promise to Adam and Eve in Paradise; using all kinds of instruments; now by His friends, now by His enemies, carrying out His designs, and all that by Redemption He might save us, and all that by Holy Communion He might come into our hearts.

"Behold He cometh, leaping upon the mountains, skipping over the hills." I stand, dear Lord to watch Your coming. Thousands of years of travelling over those mountains and hills, the Patriarchs and Prophets of the Old Law—and all that

You might find Your way at last into the tabernacle, and so into my heart. O Jesus, Jesus, to think of Your coming all that way for a little child like me! To think that You thought of me all the way as You came, and longed for the time when You would reach my heart, and rest. The Church is filled with wonder that You did not mind coming to Your Holy Mother, who was full of grace. And to think that You should come to *me*—You so great and I so small, You so holy, and I so weak and full of faults. To think that the Desired of all nations should desire to come *to me*. Blessed be Your Sacred Heart that made You think it worth Your while to come so far for such a welcome as I can give You. It has been a long long journey, and now You are drawing near. I stand and watch Your coming, and stretch out my arms to embrace You, and to welcome You to my heart. If only it could be such a welcome as You deserve. If only my desires could equal Yours, and I could long to be with You as much as You long to be with me. You say to me, "With desire I have desired to come to you." And I too say, "With desire I desire to be with You, my God." Would that my heart could thirst after You as David's did; that I could be like Daniel, "the man of desires." Since You are journeying so far to reach me, stay with me, Lord, when You come, *and rest*. Make my heart a place where You *can* rest. Come, Lord Jesus, come!

# V

# THE SACRIFICE OF MELCHISEDECH, AND THE PROPHECY OF MALACHIAS

Among the ways by which Almighty God prepared the world for its promised Redeemer, one, and a very important one, was by *types* and *prophecies*. Let us try to understand what these were and why they were needed.

History tells us that about two hundred years after the Deluge, the descendants of Sem, Cham, and Japhet left their old home round the Tigris and Euphrates and were dispersed over the earth. The descendants of Japhet went north and west and peopled Europe; those of Cham went south into Africa; and Sem's journeyed east and peopled Southern Asia. They carried away with them into their distant homes a knowledge of the true God and of the duty of worshipping Him by sacrifice, the six precepts of Noah, which were in substance what God afterwards gave to Moses on Mount Sinai as the Ten Commandments; and the belief in the birth of a Redeemer from the family of Sem. But they did not preserve incorrupt this simple religion, or keep the precepts God had given them. They not only became as wicked as the people who lived before the Deluge, but they fell into a terrible sin which, as far as we know, was not committed by these who lived before the Deluge. The sin was idolatry, and the way they fell into idolatry seems to have been this.

God is a pure Spirit Who cannot be seen. Men began to wish for some object of worship which they could see, and fancying from the beauty of the sun, the moon, and the stars, that they might be gods, they came to worship them as such. Next they took the image set up in honour of some great man and worshipped that. Growing worse and worse, they came to worship images of the animals they were accustomed to offer in sacrifice, and even shapeless blocks of stone, which had once served as altars for sacrifice.

All this while they were growing more and more wicked in other ways, so that it was a sad world of sin and misery on which Almighty God looked down not long after the Deluge, and whilst the memory of that terrible punishment ought to have been still fresh in the minds of men. But in the midst of all this wickedness the coming Redeemer was not forgotten. Who He was to be, and what He was to do, men did not know, but He was to be a mighty Conqueror and subdue all nations, and somehow set right all that had gone wrong, and bring peace and joy to the world.

Now Almighty God knew all this. And He knew that although in this confused kind of way a Redeemer was expected, He would take men by surprise when He came. His coming would be so unlike anything they were looking out for, that unless they were prepared in some way to recognize Him as the Redeemer, they would not know Him at His coming. So He prepared them by making use of *types* and *prophecies*.

*Types* foreshadow, and *prophecies* foretell something that is to come. When you are out walking on an autumn afternoon, with the sun shining faint and low behind you, you notice that your shadow is thrown a long way before, so that your companions on in front see it and know you are coming. You are foreshadowed. Our shadows are like and yet unlike us.

They are poor empty likenesses at best, still you know that by throwing a strong light upon a wall, we can get such a general outline of ourselves as our friends recognize at once.

So is it with the types of our Lord. Adam, and Abel, Isaac, Melchisedech, Moses, Jonas, the Paschal Lamb, the Brazen Serpent, the Manna—all these foreshadowed in one way or another His character, His office, or His actions.

Poor and very imperfect likenesses they were, but they were likenesses, and when our Lord came, He spoke of them as figures of Himself.

We will pass over all these types to come to one that has more to do with our work of preparation—a type of the Holy Eucharist as a Sacrifice.

And first of all, we must be clear as to the object and duty of sacrifice. From the beginning of the world God made known to men that He is to be worshipped by an act of supreme worship, which, because it is supreme, can be offered to Him alone. This act is *sacrifice*. It consists in the destruction or complete change of something which we can see or perceive by our senses, in order to show by this act that we acknowledge God to be the Giver of life and the Lord of all things. Cain and Abel offered sacrifice. The Patriarchs offered sacrifice. When God chose for Himself a special nation, He Himself appointed the sacrifices that were to be offered, first in the Tabernacle of the wilderness, and afterwards in the Temple of Solomon. These sacrifices were to foreshadow the Great Sacrifice to come, by which the Redeemer was to offer Himself once a bleeding Victim on the Cross for our salvation, and to the end of time in an unbloody manner on the altars of the Catholic Church, in order to apply to our souls the fruit of His Sacrifice on Calvary. Think of having to go back four thousand years in the world's history to find a type of the Mass we heard this morning!

You remember how Abraham and Lot went out of Mesopotamia into that lovely strip of land which forms the eastern boundary of the Mediterranean Sea, a land which was then called Canaan, and which we know later as the Land of Promise, Palestine, the Holy Land; how they separated, and Lot went to live in Sodom, one of the five wicked Cities of the Plain; and how four Kings swept down on Sodom and carried off Lot, who was afterwards rescued by Abraham. It was on Abraham's return home after the rescue, that Melchisedech, the King of Salem, came out to meet him, bringing bread and wine, for, says Holy Scripture, he was the Priest of the Most High God. Melchisedech is called a type of our Lord both by David and by St. Paul.

St. Paul points out that he was King of Salem, that is king of justice, and king of peace, and David seems to remind us of his sacrifice of bread and wine when he says: "Thou art a priest for ever after the order of Melchisedech." Notice the words, "for ever." They show that His Sacrifice under the appearances of bread and wine was to be offered not once only, but to the end of the world.

And now we will turn from type to prophecy. Our Blessed Saviour's unending Sacrifice on our altars was not only foreshadowed by type, it was also foretold by prophecy.

Why? Because, as we have seen, our Lord meant to come in a way so different from the way men expected, that they had to be taught beforehand when and what to look for.

If we have to go to the station to meet a stranger whom we have never seen, we not only find out the time of his arrival, but we get to know what he is like, his height, age, general appearance, so that on the crowded platform we may be able to recognize him.

And thus it was that hundreds of years before the coming of His Son, God made known to the Prophets the chief

## Melchisedech

"Melchisedech, the king of Salem, bringing forth bread and wine, for he was the priest of the Most High God, blessed him." (Genesis 14:18,19)

circumstances of His Life, that the chosen nation having learned so much about Him beforehand, might welcome Him when He came. The time of His coming was known, and His family; and that He should be born in Bethlehem, go into Egypt, and have His home in Nazareth; that He should be gentle and compassionate, work miracles of mercy, and in spite of all this be despised, hated, and rejected by His own people; that He should be betrayed and sold by one of His disciples, and abandoned by the rest; that His Hands and Feet should be pierced; that His garments should be parted, that gall and vinegar should be given to Him, and that He should die and rise again. When all these prophecies are put together, do they not sound more like a history of Him after His coming than a foretelling of Him many hundred years before He came?

This foreknowledge of their coming Redeemer was a treasure confided to the Jews, and kept safely in the Holy Scriptures, not for the Jews only, but for the poor pagan nations also, whom the Redeemer was coming to save. And as in Holy Scripture we find His bloody Sacrifice clearly foretold, so also is the unbloody Sacrifice of the Holy Mass.

Malachias, one of the last of the Prophets, says: "I have no pleasure in you, saith the Lord of Hosts, and I will not receive a gift of your hand. For from the rising of the sun even to the going down, My Name is great among the Gentiles; and in every place there is sacrifice, and there is offered to My Name a clean oblation; for My Name is great among the Gentiles, saith the Lord of Hosts." The sacrifices of which Almighty God here speaks were those He ordained in the Jewish Law to be offered first in the Tabernacle in the wilderness, and afterwards in Solomon's glorious Temple. These sacrifices were of four kinds, and they answered to the four duties which we have as God's sinful and needy creatures. First, we have to praise and glorify Him; secondly, to thank Him for all His goodness to us; thirdly, to ask His forgiveness for our many sins; and fourthly, to beg of Him all we need for soul and body. In the Old law, there were separate sacrifices for these four ends, and for a thousand years these sacrifices were offered. Morning and evening a little lamb was led to the altar to be slain, and at the times of the yearly feasts, especially at the feast of the Passover, these innocent victims were slain by thousands. All these sacrifices were pleasing to God only because they were figures or *types* of the great Sacrifice to come. It was only because of this Sacrifice that they had any value in His sight, and when He came they were to stop.

But sacrifice was not to stop. God was to be worshipped to the end of time in the way He had appointed from the beginning, and so, on the night before the offering of His bloody Sacrifice, which was to be offered only once, our Blessed Saviour instituted the unbloody Sacrifice which was to continue to the end of the world. In this unbloody Sacrifice He no longer dies or suffers, but by the separate consecration of the bread and the wine, the Sacrifice of Calvary is renewed in a mystical—that is—a hidden and mysterious way, and He is laid upon the altar as St. John saw Him in Heaven—"the Lamb standing, *as it were* slain." He took the bread. He took the wine. He changed the bread and the wine into His Body and Blood. He said to His beloved disciples who looked on in wondering silence: "Do this in commemoration of Me."

And so He made them priests of the New Law, priests to act in His Name, doing what He had done, He Himself being at each Mass they and their disciples should ever offer, the invisible Priest and Offerer—"a Priest for ever according to the order of Melchisedech." How plain it is that the Mass is the Sacrifice foretold by David and by Malachias. It is offered amongst *the Gentiles*, that is, all the nations of the world. It is a real *sacrifice*. It is offered in *every place*, amongst all nations.

It is a *clean* oblation, the offering of the Immaculate Lamb of God, and it is as our Lord commanded, a *memorial* of Him and of His Passion and Death. The bloody Sacrifice offered once on Calvary redeemed us. The unbloody Sacrifice offered daily applies the merits of that redemption to our souls.

Shall we see how the prophecy of Malachias is being fulfilled now day by day, and hour after hour, in different parts of the earth?

Open the map of the world, or better still, take your globe and find England and China. Now turn the globe slowly from west to east and watch. When it is midnight with us, the Masses, which often succeed each other in the same place for several hours, are beginning to be offered up in Western China.

At 1 o'clock, in India on the Eastern Coast.

At 2 o'clock, in India on the Western Coast.

At 3 o'clock, in the islands of the Indian Ocean.

At 4 o'clock, in Mesopotamia, where Abraham lived; in Palestine where the first Mass was said, and in Eastern Russia.

At 5 o'clock, in the Eastern countries of Europe, Greece, Turkey, Austria, Western Russia. In Africa, at the Cape of Good Hope, and in Egypt.

At 6 o'clock, when we are getting up, in Germany and Switzerland, Italy, France, Belgium, and England.

At 7 o'clock, in Spain, Portugal, and Ireland.

At 8 o'clock, in the islands of the Atlantic, the Canaries, Cape Verde and the Azores, and in Iceland.

At 9 o'clock, in South America on the coast of Brazil.

At 10 o'clock, in North America, in Newfoundland.

At 11 o'clock, in North and South America, and the West Indies.

At 12 o'clock, in the United States to the east.

At 1 o'clock, still in North America in the Central States.

At 2 o'clock, in Mexico, and in the Rocky Mountains.

At 3 o'clock, in California.

At 4 and 5 and 6 and 7 and 8 o'clock, in the islands of the Pacific.

At 9 o'clock, in East Australia.

At 10 o'clock, in South Australia, the East Indies, and Japan.

At 11 o'clock, in West Australia, and Eastern China.

At 12 o'clock, in Western China again.

And this every day, all the year round, whether men think of our Lord's unending Sacrifice or whether they forget all about it. Oh, how true are those words of Holy Scripture that 'His delights are to be with the children of men.' When we wake in the night, and in the day-time during our work and our play, why should we not sometimes unite our intentions with those of the Sacred Heart in His continual Sacrifice of Himself for our sakes? "From the *rising of the sun till the going-down thereof,* My Name is great among the Gentiles and in *every place* there is offered to My Name a clean oblation.

Are they dry or uninteresting, these types and prophecies? No, surely, for they strengthen our faith and help us to know our Lord better. How Protestants are to be pitied, who know nothing of all this! Even pagan nations amidst the most frightful idolatry have kept this knowledge—that their gods must be worshipped by sacrifice. Wherever missioners penetrate, among the Indians of North America, or the fierce, cruel tribes of Africa; they find the offering of sacrifice, and when the missioners are Protestants the poor savages ask: "Where is your sacrifice?" Some Protestants in our own country are beginning to be sorry for the wicked laws that stopped in this dear land of ours the Sacrifice that had been offered for so many hundreds of years. They see all over England the beautiful cathedrals built for the Holy Mass, adorned so richly because of the altars there where Mass was said. They see the bare tables that have taken the altar's place, and they wish that priests stood there again as they stood in days gone by. In the cruel days of Queen Elizabeth's persecution it was made a crime to say Mass. The greater number of our English Martyrs were hunted from place to place and cruelly put to death when they were caught, for this crime only—that they were "Massing priests." And now after three hundred years, Protestant clergymen desire above all things to be thought priests, and to be able to offer the Mass for which the martyrs died. Let us pray for them, as we kneel at Mass, that God may bring them into the one true Church. Let us thank Him that we are there in safety, and show Him we are thankful by hearing Mass whenever we are able on week-days as well as on Sundays, hearing it with reverence and devotion, so that when the priest prays to Almighty God "for all here present, *whose faith and devotion are known to Thee*," that prayer may be *for us*.

A holy priest used to say: "I wonder what God has in store for us in Heaven to surpass the happiness of saying Mass." And in the private notes of retreat found after his death, he had written, "All through my Mass this morning the happy tears would flow." This was because he understood the happiness of standing at God's altar to make Him an offering worthy of Himself.

When we think who God is, and of all we owe Him, we feel a great need in our hearts to give Him something worthy of His greatness and His goodness. But we are poor, we have nothing but what He has given us. Anything worthy of Him would have to be something equal to Him. Now there is nothing—we should not like there to be anything—equal to Him out of Himself. What are we to do then? He Who sees our difficulty comes to our help. He puts Himself into our hands to be our offering. Oh, how good of Him! Now we have all we want. Now we can offer Him an adoration grander than they can offer Him in Heaven—offer Him a thanksgiving gladder than their songs of praise—offer Him what pleases Him infinitely more than our sins have displeased Him—offer Him what is of infinitely greater worth than anything we ask Him to give us. All this we can do in the Holy Mass. Well might that holy priest say, "I wonder what God has in store for us in Heaven that can surpass the happiness of saying Mass. All through my Mass this morning the happy tears would flow."

My God, and what has the Mass been to me up to now? How have I behaved at Mass whilst all this was going on?—whilst the priest was offering to God his sacrifice *and mine*, as he reminds me at the *Orate Fratres*. "Pray that my sacrifice and yours may be acceptable to God." Have I done this? Have I thought of the Mass at all as *my* sacrifice—*my* offering to God? Have I united my intention with the priest's and still more with our Lord's, as He, the invisible Priest, stands at the altar and offers Himself for me? Do I think of the four ends for which Mass is offered, and offer it sometimes for one, sometimes for another? Do I remember how much may be done during that short half hour while the priest stands at the altar? There are the intentions of the Holy Father to be prayed for, and England's conversion, and the holy souls in Purgatory, and sinners and poor pagans, and the dying. My Good Angel stands beside me with bowed head and folded wings. What a shame it would be if I were to be idle then, irreverent or wilfully distracted.

Make me, my God, remember how much there is to do, and that "mighty is the prayer that is prayed at Mass."

# VI

# THE MANNA IN THE DESERT AND THE FOOD OF ELIAS

"Manhu!" exclaimed the astonished Israelites, men, women, and children, as they came out of their tents in the early morning, and saw the white wafery flakes that covered the wilderness as far as the eye could reach. "Manhu?" *What is this?* "For they knew not what it was," says Holy Scripture. We know what it was—the figure of a better Bread to come—that most beautiful type of the Holy Eucharist, the Manna in the Desert.

The Holy Eucharist is both a Sacrifice and a Sacrament. As a Sacrifice Its chief object is the worship of God. As a Sacrament It is meant chiefly for the sanctification of man. It was as a Sacrifice we saw It yesterday, prefigured in the Sacrifice of Melchisedech. But It was also prefigured as a Sacrament, and it is as a Sacrament we must begin to study it now.

At last we have come to the direct work of our preparation. But we must go back three thousand five hundred years to find the first type of this dear Sacrament of God's love. How long He has been thinking of us and making *His* preparation. Can we take too many pains with ours?

Five hundred years have passed since Melchisedech offered his sacrifice of bread and wine. Abraham's descendants are no longer in the Promised Land.  In Jacob's time they went down into Egypt, and there, for four hundred years, they were "hated and afflicted and mocked by the Egyptians, and their life made bitter with hard works," says Holy Scripture.  Their cry went up before God and He sent them a deliverer.  The story of their deliverance you know.

Look at them now in the desert, six weeks after they have left Egypt.  The word "desert" may bring several pictures before our minds—sometimes a boundless plain of hard gravelly ground out of which dark rocks and barren mountains rise here and there, and sometimes immense plains of loose shifting sand.  Both these regions are frightfully desolate.  Except where the oases make a green patch of verdure overshadowed by palm and date-trees, there is nothing in these vast solitudes to supply travellers with food or shelter.  The Arabian Desert, through which the people of God have to pass on their way to the Promised Land, is in some parts the hard barren ground, and in others the sandy plain; both alike unproductive of anything that can serve for food.

And now the bread they brought with them out of Egypt "tied up in their cloaks" is gone, and they are hungry. Think what Moses must have felt as he looked out upon that multitude and knew there was not another meal to give them.  "Six hundred thousand men, besides children, and a mixed multitude without number with them." And not a loaf left!  Yet the heart of their brave Leader was not troubled.  It was God's people; He had brought them into the wilderness; He would provide.  But see! they are getting together in vast throngs, anxious faces and then angry ones are seen on every side.  And listen! words of discontent are heard, and then loud murmurings, and at last all the congregation of the children of Israel come to Moses and say: "Would to God we had died by the hand of the Lord in the land of Egypt, when we sat over the flesh-pots and ate bread to the full...Why have you brought us into this desert that you might destroy all the multitude with famine? And the Lord said to Moses: "Behold I will rain bread from Heaven for you...Say to the children of Israel: In the morning you shall have your fill of bread, and you shall know that I am the Lord your God."

Think with what eagerness they rose in the morning and went out to see what God had done for them.

And there it lay, that wonderful food, that "bread from heaven," covering the earth far and near. See that Hebrew mother kneeling over there, her little boy by her side. She points to heaven and shows him where that bread has come from, and makes him thank God before she puts it into his eager hands. He takes it, tastes it, looks into her face and smiles. It is his favourite food; how has she found it for him here out in the wilderness? And the food of the little child is the food of the strong man, the Levite and the Priest, the food of Moses and of Aaron. The same food, yet different to all, giving to each just what the need of each requires. Preserving from death, giving health, strength, and life, giving contentment and joy—doing this for all; and doing for each a work of its own—for the little child a different work from its work for the priest. Oh, is not the feast in the desert a beautiful type of the Feast to come, the Sacred Banquet in which Christ is received!

Our Lord has His types and figures; would you like His First Communicants to have their types too? Look at that group of innocents sitting on the ground in the midst of the manna. See them gathering it up, giving it to one another, putting it to their mouths, crowing with delight as they taste its sweetness. How little they think that it has taken the Omnipotence of God to rain down for them the delicious food that lies so plentifully all around. Now look at the altar-rails. See the First Communicants there, innocent too, for their souls have been

## The Manna in the Desert

"This is the bread which the Lord hath given you to eat." (Exodus 16:15)

washed pure and white in the Precious Blood. See the priest passing to and fro, giving the true Manna to each; see the joy in their faces; look into their hearts and see what that Divine Food is doing there. Yes, surely First Communicants may find a type of themselves in the little Hebrew children feeding joyfully on the manna in the desert on their way to the Promised Land.

The manna helped each one in that vast host in the way he needed help. It helped the strong man to fight and the little child to keep up with the rest in the day's march. It never failed them all through their forty years of weary wandering. In spite of their murmuring and wilfulness, and greater sins, it was ready for them each morning as they woke. And when the desert's border-land was reached, and enemies fierce and strong came out to fight them and keep them out of the Promised Land, Moses was not afraid. He knew that the bread which had been their strength till now would be their strength to the end. And it was so. Only when their foes were slain and the desert left behind did the manna stop, and the bread of the wilderness give place to the fair fruits of the Promised Land.

All through the forty years the children had their share in the miraculous food. They are specially mentioned in the history. In the account of the immense multitude led into the desert, there is no mention made of the women, but the children are not forgotten: "Six hundred thousand men *besides children,*" says Holy Scripture. In both the Old and New Testament we find the loving care and tenderness of our Heavenly Father for little children. When Jonas wondered that Niniveh was spared in spite of all its wickedness, Almighty God said to him, "Shall not I spare Niniveh, that great city in which there are more than a hundred thousand children, that know not their right hand from their left?"

And when our Blessed Saviour came on earth it was the same. St. Matthew and St. Mark tell us that once on a time He was "much displeased" with His disciples. Now He loved His disciples so dearly, He allowed them to come to Him so freely with their questions and difficulties, He bore so patiently with their faults, that when we hear He was much displeased with them, we wonder what could have happened. This is what happened. He had had a hard day—people coming and going from morning till night. He had been going in and out amongst then, teaching and comforting, opening the eyes of the blind here, cleansing the lepers there, sending one set home, and beginning all over again with another, and this all day long. And now evening was come and He was tired, and went aside to rest a little. But there was to be no rest for Him. Some Jewish mothers had brought a whole troop of children that He might lay His hand upon them, and pray. Now was their opportunity.

Up came the little ones, proud and pleased and smiling, and in a few minutes He was surrounded. The Apostles were indignant and tried to drive away mothers and children together. Their Master was tired, they said, and they did not want Him to be teased and troubled with children. And Jesus hearing it was much displeased, says St. Mark, and said to His disciples, "Suffer the little children to come unto Me and forbid them not...And embracing them and laying His hands upon them He blessed them." Notice that St. Matthew says as a matter of course, that He embraced the little children before He blessed them. And as He blessed them, those little Hebrew children, He thought of the multitude of little Christian children whom He would one day fold in His arms in a First Communion embrace—He thought of *me*. Yes, He loved little children. He had a welcome for all, a remedy for the needs of all, but His embrace was for His Mother, His Apostles, and the little children.

If our Lord invites guests to His Table, we could imagine

they would be Popes and Bishops, who have the government of the Church: or those who can do much harm or good to others; kings, lawgivers, and the like. Those too, perhaps, who are much afflicted and whom His loving Heart longs to comfort by His presence; the sick, the maimed, the blind, as He shows us in the Parable of the Marriage Feast. But even the kind King there makes no mention of children his invitation. Children as a rule are not expected to sit at table with their elders. But the rule at our Lord's Table is that these little guests are to be seated there as soon as they can be made to understand what that Table is. And He gives this as a very solemn charge to those who have care of them, and who can no more deprive them of their place at His Table, than the parents of a child can expose it to die of hunger. "Suffer little children to come unto Me," He says. A child has its needs and its troubles as you know. You are sad at times or out of sorts, tired, or cross, or naughty. You have an enemy who is jealous of you, an enemy so cunning and so strong that, by yourself you cannot overcome him. So our Lord wants to come to help you to drive him away. And He will not wait till you are grown up. Perhaps if you were older you would understand better what a great and grand thing Holy Communion is. But He cannot wait. He loves you too much to put it off. He knows you need His help now, and so, as soon as ever you can understand a little and really desire to get ready for Him, you are to be prepared for His Visit.

What will you do for Him in return? You can only pay Him back in love, and in desire to go to Him. But you can and will do this. We will begin, then, from this day to make more frequent acts of love and desire to receive Him. "O Jesus, true Manna, true Bread of Heaven, come and feed my soul and make it strong. Jesus, Lover of little children, I love You, I adore You, come into my heart."

It is about seven hundred years after the falling of the manna in the desert that we have to look for the second type of the Holy Eucharist as a Sacrament. We have to go to another desert to find it—a long stretch of desolate country, between Bersabee in Juda and Mount Horeb.

See that venerable man hastening forward, staff in hand. He looks neither to the right nor to the left. His face is set towards Horeb and he stays neither for food nor rest, nor shelter by the way. It is the Prophet Elias.

There have been many wonderful lives lived in this world. But among them all the life of Elias is the most wonderful. It was one chain of miracles from beginning to end. No, we must not say end, for that wonderful life is not ended yet. Where it is being lived now, God alone knows. All we know is that hidden away in some corner of creation God is keeping His servant till the end of the world. Then he is to come again and give witness to our Lord. He has already given witness to Him once, when with Moses he appeared by His side on Mount Thabor. What a day of happiness that must have been for him, when he was borne from his quiet hiding-place into the glory of the Transfiguration, there to look upon the Face of his Redeemer and talk with Him about His coming Passion and Death.

How was this most wonderful of lives—this undying life—sustained when he was upon earth? We shall see.

The Prophet lived in the days of the wicked Achab, King of Israel, and his Queen Jezebel. His holy zeal made him mock the false god Baal, which the King and Queen worshipped, and slay the four hundred and fifty prophets of Baal, who were under the protection of the Queen. In her fury she sent him word, "By this hour to-morrow I will make thy life as the life of one of them." "And Elias was afraid," says Holy Scripture, and he fled into the desert—fled with the utmost speed during a whole day. And when night came he flung himself down at the foot of a juniper-tree, weary in body and so sad at heart that he prayed death might come and take away his soul. From his troubled sleep he was aroused "by an Angel of the Lord, who touched him and said to him: Arise and eat. He looked, and behold there was at his head a hearth-cake and a vessel of water; and he ate and drank and fell asleep again. And the Angel of the Lord came again the second time and touched him and said to him: Arise, eat, for thou hast yet a great way to go. And he arose and ate and drank and walked in the strength of that food forty days and forty nights unto the Mount of God, Horeb."

As he ate that bread, a wonderful change came over him: all the aching weariness of his limbs left him and all his heaviness of heart. A giant's strength seemed given to him. On and on he journeyed, under the burning sun by day and the silent stars by night. On and on, unwearied in body, brave at heart, his eyes fixed on the distant mountain, till at last the summit was gained and he was safe. More than safe, for he was brought in some wonderful way into the Presence of God, and heard the sound of His Voice.

Oh! that wonderful food of Elias. How like the Food of which the Church sings:

> Behold, Angelic Bread from Heaven,
> True Bread, to weary pilgrims given

—the Food that supports and cheers us on our journey through the wilderness of this life, that takes us beyond the reach of our enemies, and brings us safely to the true Mount of God, to our Heavenly Country where we shall see Him, not like Elias, but face to face.

My God, I am a pilgrim like Elias; I am starting on my journey and have a long way to go. Give me the Food that will make me strong and help me to walk bravely and steadily along the road to Heaven.

I am a traveller, too, like the children of Israel, hastening through the desert to the Promised Land. Give me the true Bread from Heaven to supply all the needs of my soul.

The Manna was wonderful—so wonderful that it never lost its name. Even now we call it, like the Israelites in their first surprise: Manna, *what is this?* But the Sacred Host on our altars is more wonderful by far. Let me always remember this. As I see it passing from one to another along the line of communicants, or lifted above my head at Benediction, let my wonder and my love break out each time afresh. Let me bow down before It with the angels, crying out in my heart, Manhu! *What is This?*

And now we have done with types and prophecies. They are very beautiful and instructive, and make us long for Him Whom they foretell—just what they were meant to do. But we want Himself, we are impatient to learn about Him, not from figures—however beautiful—but by seeing Him, hearing Him, studying Him in His blessed Life on earth.

## The Food of Elias

"And he arose, and ate and drank, and walked in the strength of that food forty days and forty nights, unto the mount of God, Horeb." (3 Kings 19:8)

## VII
## "Learn of Me"

When we see a very magnificent preparation made for the reception of a sovereign, we feel sure he must be great and powerful. We get interested in him, and try to learn something about him. What, then, are we to think of that King of kings for Whose Coming God Himself made a preparation of four thousand years? In all possible ways God prepared for Him. All that He did in the world was a preparation for Him. The choice of a special nation was on His account. The privileges granted to it, and His singular protection over it, which we have been noticing, were all for His sake. The types of Him from the beginning, Adam, Abel, and Melchisedech, Isaac and Joseph, Josue and Jonas, the Paschal Lamb, the Manna, the Brazen Serpent, the Food of Elias—all were part of this magnificent preparation. The Prophets were sent to prepare His way by describing Him so precisely that men might be easily able to know Him at His coming.

How was it, then, that when He came, men not only refused to receive Him, but turned from Him with positive hatred, and handed Him over to the Gentiles to be put to a cruel and shameful death? How was this? It was because the Jews had not *prepared themselves* for His coming. God had done His part and made all things ready. But they had not done theirs, and so they were not ready. What the Jews looked for was a

King coming in power and greatness to establish an earthly kingdom—a mighty conqueror, who would deliver their nation from the Roman yoke, make them once more a free and prosperous people, and reward his followers with riches and honours. Had our Blessed Saviour come like this, He would have been welcome. But He came poor and humble, and they despised Him, saying, "Is not this the carpenter's son?" In spite of His wonderful works, they would not acknowledge Him, and when He left this world to return to His Father, out of the thousands who had heard His words and seen His miracles, there were only about five hundred who believed in Him. Does not this show us the danger of pride and wilfulness?

The Jews had no right to look for a Messiah so unlike Him, Whom the Prophets had called a worm and no man, "a Man of sorrows and acquainted with infirmity." They had been told to expect, not a great conqueror—this would only have flattered their pride—but One Who would redeem them from sin and Hell, and show them the way to Heaven. It was a Redeemer like this that all faithful Jews were expecting. But these faithful ones were few in number, compared with those who were full of dreams of an earthly royalty, and cared for nothing else. It is true that when our Lord came, many of the simpler sort, those whom the world despises, flocked alter Him and heard Him gladly. But the chief priests and the rulers, the Scribes and Pharisees, rejected and hated Him. And at last they moved "the whole people" to cry out as with one voice, "Away with Him, crucify Him. His Blood be upon us and upon our children."

Instead of wishing we had been on earth at the time our Lord came, we may well thank God we were not living then, lest we should have been amongst those who turned against Him. St. Matthew tells us that "the whole people answering said: His Blood be upon us and upon our children." We may thank Him, and with all our hearts, that our life is in these days rather than in those; that even before we could know Him Who came to save us, Holy Baptism had planted the faith in our souls; and that almost as soon as we could speak, we made our act of faith, "I believe in God the Father Almighty, Creator of Heaven and earth, and in Jesus Christ, His only Son, our Lord."

How eager we ought to be to learn all we can about this God-made-Man for love of us—Jesus Christ *our Lord*—to study Him, to listen to His teaching, to get to know what He wants of us. He set Himself a two-fold task on coming into this world—to redeem us by His Blood, and to teach us the way to Heaven. This teaching was not to be by words only, but far more by His own example. "Jesus began to do and to teach," says St. Luke. He began by *doing*, and afterwards He spent two or three of the last years of His Life in teaching. This explains what is perhaps a puzzle to some amongst us.

When we think of the short time our Blessed Saviour spent on earth, and of the great work He came to do, we wonder why He began that work so late. Why for so many years He lived unknown, occupied with little household duties and the rough carpentering of an out-of-the-way village, instead of spending His whole Life in preaching and working miracles, training His Apostles and founding His Church. Why, when His Heart was so eager, did He wait so long? The best way to answer this question is to look a little closer into those years of the Hidden Life, and see if He was really waiting all that time. We shall find perhaps, that what looks to us like delay was in reality no delay at all.

Our Lord might have come from the Hand of God a perfect man, like Adam. He need not have been a little child, and have waited so many years before showing Himself to men. As soon as He appeared in the world, He might have attracted them to Himself by His preaching and miracles. But He did not choose to do this. He had a work to do first, a work of silent teaching, quite as important in His eyes as the public preaching of His after-life. Shall we see how He could do this, how He could teach and be silent too?

There are many things about which we know little or nothing. But we do know something about our lessons. And we notice this about them—first, that when they are hard, they take a long time to learn, and are best learnt by examples—and next, that if the master's manner is winning and attractive, if he tries to make the lesson interesting, we learn not only more willingly, but more easily.

Our Blessed Lord knows all this better than we do. And see what He does. To entice us to learn what we *must* learn if we are to go to Heaven, He invites us to His school and promises to teach us Himself—not as the great God, Who spoke to the Jews from Mount Sinai in thunder and lightning—this would frighten us—but, as a little Child, lying on straw in a manger, or standing at His Mother's knee. Little helpless things win our love easily, and a tiny child attracts us at once. So He would make Himself a tiny Child. He would be a Babe to attract babies, an older Child to attract those who are older. And thus, passing through all the years of babyhood and childhood, He would sanctify them all, and leave us His example in them all. It is a Divine example, and therefore perfect. He was perfect as a Babe, and as a Child, as a Boy, and a Youth, no less than as a Man. Looking at Him in every stage of His blessed Childhood, each one of us can say, "Jesus was once just my age, and He would be my age that He might be an example to me."

It is as a Babe and a little Child that He is going to teach us our lessons now. Who will be afraid of going to school, where a little Child is Master? Who will be afraid that the lessons may be too hard? And who will not try to learn, when He teaches all the hard things by His own example? His school is in Bethlehem, Egypt, and Nazareth. We are all to go to Him

there and take our places round Him. Surely it will be sweet to learn from a little Child, Who is God as well, and can help us by His grace to learn what He teaches. If we want lessons that interest us, what can be more interesting than to watch the Child God and see how He does this or that—how He obeys, how He prays, how He suffers.

We were wondering just now why He did not begin to teach as soon as He came into the world. And now we see that this is just what He did. He did not lose one minute. He did not wait till He was grown up to say, "Learn of Me." He said it by His silent Lips and by His winning smile, as He lay quiet and patient upon the straw. He said it by the downcast Eyes and the tiny Hands so often joined in prayer, and by the little Feet that ran here and there at Mary's bidding.

We were no strangers to that little Child, Who was the joy of Mary's home. He knew and loved each one of us. He knew our faces and our voices and our characters. He knew us each by name. He knew us better than we know ourselves. Our difficulties, troubles and temptations, the wilfulness and temper, the greediness or obstinacy that make it hard for us to be good—all this He knew. And it was to help us that He spent those long years with His Blessed Mother and St. Joseph, not preaching as He might have done, not working miracles, but learning His lessons, and suffering patiently, and doing as He was told.

When we are drawing from a model, the first thing we do is to study it carefully. Then we try to imitate it. There is sure to be disappointment, if we are only beginners, and a very great deal of disappointment. But each fresh attempt will be more successful than the last. And with perseverance, we may hope for a very fair result in the end. So will it be with us in our work of studying and imitating the Holy Child. Only that here our chances are better that at our drawing. All the good-will in the world will not help us there, without a straight eye and a steady hand. But to imitate Jesus, we need not be clever. We *can* be like Him if we try. There may be many failures and disappointments, but success will come at last.

This is encouraging, you say. Yet in one way at least we are better off at our model drawing. We can have our model close to us. But Bethlehem and Nazareth are a long way off, and, somehow, it is not easy to feel much interested in what happened so very long ago. Had we been living when our Lord was on earth, it would be different.

There is some truth in this. But let us see if something cannot be done to lessen the difficulty. If we could find some way of coming nearer to our Divine Model, we certainly should see Him better, and His example would make more impression on us.

The Saints tell us of a way by which we may do this. They say that as our Blessed Saviour had us all in His mind when He was upon earth, and thought of us in what He did and taught and suffered, His Life and actions are not really past, like other events that happened hundreds of years ago. The lessons they gave us remain, and the graces they won for us remain, and by going back upon them in loving meditation, we learn the lessons and we get the grace.

So, when we are going to consider a scene of our Blessed Saviour's Life, we are not to think of it as something that happened a long time ago, and that does not concern *us*, but as taking place *now*, and concerning us so very much, that we are allowed to be there and look on. Our Lord is there *for us*, and He means us to come and learn from Him. We are to see how He looks, and hear what He says, and notice what He does.

A mother opens the door of the nursery where the children are at play. She is going on a journey, and has come to look for a companion. Who is it to be? What a rush there is, what a number of outstretched arms, what a cry of "Me, me!" Now, suppose that on the night of the Flight into Egypt, our Blessed Mother had turned to St. Joseph, and said in our hearing, "Whom shall we take with us?" Should we not have begged to go, have promised to leave everything, to do and suffer anything, if only we might be with them, promised to watch the Holy Child reverently, and learn of Him the lessons He was going to teach? This we can do now, at least in thought and in desire. And surely our hearts will bound with joy to think that by thus making the scenes of our Lord's Life present to us, we may get the fruit we should have got from them had we been there with Him.

One more thought from our model drawing. As we should never dream of simply admiring our model, without trying to copy it, or forget to compare our work with it all along, correcting our own by it, so in meditating on the Life of our Lord, we must not stop at admiration, but pass on to imitation. Nothing is easier than to say, "Ah, yes, it is all very beautiful!" and then think no more about it. What we are to do, after looking at His Life, is to look at our own, and say, "Am I like the Child Jesus? If not, I will try to be more like Him, to be like Him to-day *in this*. And I will ask Him to help me." Unless we reflect thus on ourselves, our meditations will not do us much good.

Remember, too, that whenever you feel the need of lifting up your heart to our Lord whilst you are reading, you should do so. It is only to help you to this that the book is put into your hands. It is not reading a great deal that will help you, and if, because you have stopped several times to talk to our Lord about your reading, you have no time to finish it, never mind; you have done something much better.

Oh, if we could only get thoroughly interested in our Lord's Life; And why not? For whom was it written, if not for us? Yet there are people—Catholics even—for whom the story of His

Life might never have been written. They never read it. It does not interest them. They read the life of this soldier and of that prince, the lives of the Saints, perhaps; the lives of men and women, good and bad, and are interested. Nay, they will pore for hours over lives that were never lived at all. But *His Life*, the Life of their dearest Friend, this has no interest for them.

How different it is with the Saints! The Life of Jesus is the very life of theirs. They go to it to learn what theirs should be. They look at it, and copy its beautiful virtues into their own lives, look again, and copy closer, till at last they grow to be like Him, for their lives have become little copies of His. A Saint is one who is like our Lord. All the boy Saints and the girl Saints, all the men and women Saints of the Church are like Him, *because* they have looked long and lovingly at Him, looked at His humility, at His gentleness, at His obedience, till they learned to be humble and gentle and obedient too. It took a long time with most of them. But some learned fast. The young Saints were wonderfully quick learners. We should be Saints like them if we were to do as they did. And we *must* be like them in some degree, and like the Saint of saints, if we are to be with Him for ever

To all of us our Master says, "Learn of Me. Come and look at My Life, and see if you cannot make your own a little more like it. Come to Me, men and women. Come to Me, boys and girls. Come, little children, I have a lesson for you all. And I will teach you Myself."

Our Lord could not have lived during the lifetime and beside the home of every one of us, and so have set the example of His Life before us all. But He had us in His mind and heart all through His earthly Life, and when He showed forth this virtue or that, He said to Himself, "I shall set them an example here, and gain for them the grace they will need some day." What more could He have done for us than this? Are we never to learn from that example, never to ask for that grace which is ready waiting for us! We too say to ourselves, "The things said and done there do not concern me," when I am just the person they do concern! What can we be thinking about to be so foolish and ungrateful as this! No one can help those who will not help themselves, and so St. Augustine says, "God Who made us without us, will not save us without us." Do I want Him to help me—to save me? Then I must help myself, by making use of what He has done, and taught, and suffered *for me.*

It was cold and comfortless in the stable that first Christmas night. But the Infant Jesus lay patiently in His manger, for He knew that Francis of Assisi would be coming by-and-bye to make His meditation beside Him, and that kneeling there on the straw, he would so burn with love for "the little Babe of Bethlehem," as to become a very seraph on earth.

It was sad to see the rich young man whom He loved go away sorrowful when he heard the words, "If thou wilt be perfect, go, sell what thou hast, and give to the poor,...and come, follow Me." But Jesus thought of the day when Antony, young and rich, would hear those words read in the Gospel at Mass, and taking them to himself, would make himself poor for his Master's sake—and the Sacred Heart was comforted.

Yet Francis was never at Bethlehem. It was in heart and desire only that he knelt by the manger, and saw the Babe, and learned his lesson. And Antony heard only what we hear again and again. How is it, then, that our Lord's words and example sink so deeply into some hearts, whilst they make no impression on others? Only because some prepare their hearts. They look lovingly, and listen eagerly, as He says to them, "Learn of Me," and so they see and hear what others do not, because God shows Himself to them, and speaks to them Himself. Am I one of these?

In most of the Saints we notice one of our Lord's virtues shining more brilliantly than the rest. It is the one each Saint has singled out for special imitation, the lesson each has learned best. In St. Francis of Assisi, it is His poverty; in St. Francis of Sales, His gentleness; in St. Francis Xavier, His love of souls. What am *I* going to learn of Him? What is His Life going to teach *me?* What was it that He said or did purposely *for me*—that when my turn should come, and I too could draw near to Him for my lesson, it might go home to my heart, and lead me to follow Him? I do not know yet what it was; I must look carefully for it lest I should miss it—look for it as I should look for a jewel that had been dropped in my path for me to find. I must go eagerly to my meditation, saying to myself: Perhaps He will speak to me *here*.

Dear Lord and Master, I want to do this, I ask Your grace for this. I do indeed want *to learn of You* and I will take the pains to learn. Please help me, for You know it is hard for me to fix my mind on anything but story-books and play. It goes rushing on like a race-horse, or fluttering about like a butterfly when I try to fix it on other things. I should like other people to do the work of thinking for me, and so save me the trouble of thinking for myself. But no one can think for me here. The work and the trouble must be my own, and I know it is well worth my while to go in for it heartily. I am told that to learn *how* to look at Your Life, is of such importance to the meditations that are coming, that I must be willing to take a little pains. I am willing—I will take the pains—I will read quietly and thoughtfully, trying to make the scene before me real to myself, trying to remember that it was *to teach me* that You said or did this, looking up into Your Face, feeling the love of Your Sacred Heart, listening to Your Voice saying—"*Learn of Me.*"

# VIII
## Bethlehem

Look up to-night into the starlit sky. See those points of light scattered over it in countless numbers. They are suns, most of them, with worlds like our own moving round them—worlds as large as ours, but too far off for us to see.

Just think of that! Thousands of worlds above us invisible altogether, and the huge suns round which they move—mere points of twinkling light!

Where shall we find our own little world amid this vast creation—amid

> The countless stars like golden dust
> That strew the skies at night.

Yet all creation turns to this earth of ours with wonder and admiration, for the Creator of all is coming to it to-night.

"I believe in God the Father Almighty, Maker of Heaven and earth and of all things visible and invisible. And in one Lord Jesus Christ, the only-begotten Son of God, by Whom all things were made. Who for us men and for our salvation came down from Heaven, and was conceived by the Holy Ghost of the Virgin Mary; and was made Man."

The four thousand years are ended, the years of preparation. God's time has come. It is the first Christmas night. Shall we see what the immediate preparations are? We turn first to the Holy City, the seat of the Jewish Church, where the Temple stands, where the prophecies are kept. But there are no signs of expectation in Jerusalem. In the Temple the evening sacrifice has been offered as usual, and the morning sacrifice is prepared. In Herod's palace, all as usual, every one moving about him in fear as usual, no signs of expectation, no turning out to make way for a greater King. In the palace of the High Priest, in the streets, in the talk of men—no signs of expectation. Perhaps because Jerusalem after all is not to be the birthplace of the Messiah, but little Bethlehem, six miles to the south. We will go over to Bethlehem and see the preparations there.

Bethlehem is all astir. Lights are glancing here and there in the little town, and in the caravansarai all is noise and bustle, every one trying to secure a place for himself and his beast, shelters being put up for the night, camels being unladen and tethered, shouts and cries on every side. Yet we hear no mention of the Messiah. He does not seem to be expected here. Caesar's name is in every mouth, for it is his decree that has brought together so many of David's family and crowded up the little place. But the Son of David, Christ the Prince, as Daniel called Him, the Desired of all nations—there is no talk of Him.

Disappointed, we descend the hill. Half way down there is a cave or shed, where the cattle take refuge when the nights are very bleak. It is a miserable shelter even for them. Stay, do not pass it by. This is the place which from all eternity God has chosen for Himself. When He comes at midnight, it will be here.

When we are expecting a guest of importance, we get his room ready with great care, and just at the last moment we look in to see if all is ready, if anything is forgotten.

So does God look down upon the cave at Bethlehem this Christmas night. Yes, nothing is forgotten. All is ready. The cold winds are sweeping past and sweeping in. Down the damp walls the moisture trickles to the ground. The ox and the ass are there, standing close together to get a little warmth from one another. The manger is there, and round about are a few handfuls of prickly straw. Dark and cold and comfortless it all is. All is ready.

We go back into the town. Our Lady and St. Joseph are there, and can find no room anywhere. No one can take them in. There is no unkindness; they are simply treated as tramps might be. For himself St. Joseph does not mind, but he thinks of our Lady. She is so tired and cold. Where can he take her for a shelter this bitter night? It is getting late. What is he to do? Some one had said there was an outhouse or disused stable in one of the chalk hills near the city, where they might put up for the night. He thinks they passed it on the road, and he says to our Lady, "Suppose we try to find a shelter there."

All things are in quiet silence. Night is in the midst of her course. The stars shine out brightly in the clear sky. On the hills the sheep lie huddled together, and beside them the shepherds keep watch, rough, simple men, bearing patiently the hardships of their lot.

Let us creep into the cave. There is no door, any one may go in. At first we can see nothing, but we can feel the icy coldness of the place. St. Joseph's lantern gives a faint flickering light, and after a while we grope our way up to the place where our Lady kneels. She makes us a sign to come near, nearer still— and we come up, and fall on our knees before the Crib, for God is there.

> Lo within a manger lies
> He Who built the starry skies,
> He Who throned on height sublime
> Sits amid the cherubim.

He is wrapped in swaddling-clothes. He cannot move His limbs. His tiny frame trembles with cold. His swathing-bands are damp. He has no coverlet. The straw is hard and prickly.

His eyes are full of tears, and His infant cries are cries of real pain. Poor little Babe of Bethlehem—poor indeed was there ever little babe so poor as He? Oh, who would have thought that God would come like this?

And why did He come like this? Why did God the Father make such a preparation as this for His only and well-beloved Son? It might have been so different. Our Lord might have turned Herod out of his palace and gone there. Or He might have made Himself known to holy Simeon and Anna, who were waiting for Him and would have been so glad to take Him in and give Him their very best. But He did not want the best; He wanted the worst. Why? We must try to understand why.

He has come on earth to do two things, to redeem us and to show us the way to Heaven. Both these things He will do as God—magnificently, with all the generosity of His Sacred Heart. If we are to be redeemed, it shall be with a "plentiful redemption," if we are to be taught, it shall be in the way best for us, not in the way easiest to Him.

> O bountiful salvation!
> O life eternal won!
> O plentiful redemption!
> O love of Mary's Son!

He had to teach us our catechism from the very beginning, and teach us by His own example. Now on the first page we find the question, "Of which must you take most care, of your body or of your soul?" We answer, of course, "Of my soul," and wonder why we have to learn such a very simple thing as that. But have we learned it? If we were to ask some people, "Of which must you take most care?" they would say, by their actions at least, it not by their words, "Of my Body." And so I do everything to satisfy it and make it comfortable. Whatever would give pain or trouble, I keep at arm's length; and I look out eagerly for all that it likes, for all that is warm and soft to my touch and nice to my taste, and pleasant to my sight and hearing and smell—all that is *comfortable*. Oh, that English word of ours, how much it means, how snug a place we keep for it in our hearts, how we do one and all of us love *to be comfortable!*

And because we love it, we love money which buys the things that make us comfortable. If we look around us, in the streets of great cities and out in the quiet country, what are most people thinking about? How to make money, how to get rich, that so they may be comfortable and lead an easy life. With some this desire for riches and for ease becomes so strong that it makes them commit many sins. They come to be so fond of their bodies that they can deny them nothing, not even when they are bound to deny them in order to keep from sin. The drunkard, the thief, the glutton, all sin because they listen to the body crying out for what it ought not to have.

*Now*, do we see why our Lord came poor? That He might teach us to care less for these bodies of ours and for the things that please them. He had no money. His Blessed Mother and St. Joseph were poor, very poor, and so there was nothing comfortable for Him when He came into the world—no fire to warm the swathing-bands, no curtain across the mouth of the cave to protect Him ever so little from the sharp night wind, no soft cradle or warm clothes for His little trembling limbs. We see Him lying there—looking at us, loving us, asking us to learn of Him. What are we to learn? Well, this at least—that we will not grumble when things are not just as we like, when the weather is a little too cold, or a little too hot, when our clothes or our food or things about us give us a little bit to suffer. How can we come to school here at Bethlehem and go away and grumble at the little things we have to bear?

Our Blessed Lord has another lesson for us before we leave the cave. Riches and comfort are tempting things, though they are so dangerous. The rich cling to them, the poor covet them. So He, the King of kings, would come poor to teach the rich and to comfort the poor.

And first to teach the rich. Before He came, the poor were despised by everybody. No one cared for them, no one tried to make their lot less hard. There were no hospitals for them when they were sick, no shelters for them when they grew old and helpless. Our Lord has changed all this. He has shown us that we are all one family, all children of the same Father, all going to the same Heaven. In His sight rich and poor are alike, except that the poor are more like Him. Their life is the life He chose for Himself on earth. And because of this, He expects them to be loved and helped for His sake.

He tells the rich very solemnly that they cannot spend their money just as they like—that it is wrong to spend it all on dress, or amusements, or gim-cracks, so that they have nothing left to give to the poor. Their money is only lent to them by Him, and they will have to give an account to Him of the way in which it has been spent. When the rich man in the Gospel had to give his account, he was asked why he had spent all his money in fine clothes and in feasting, and had left poor Lazarus hungry and cold at his gate. He could only answer that he did not mean to do any harm nor to be cruel, but that he had never thought of any one but himself, nor of doing good to any one. We know what his sentence was—how he was buried in Hell, where he will never have even a drop of water to cool his thirst; while Lazarus, who had been patient in his poverty, is in Heaven, comforted now and rich for ever, having all and more than all his heart can desire.

And now to come to myself. How do I behave to the poor? Do I ever do anything for them—ever save a little to give to them? What do I give in church to the poor? I may have very little to give, but I can give that. If I remember that the poor are put by our Lord in His own place, I shall treat them as I ought. I shall be ready to make little sacrifices for them now and then. At Christmas, for instance, to make or buy some clothing for them. If I come to love the poor for the sake of our Blessed Lord, to speak kindly to them, to visit them when I can, and give them with my own hands what I have to give—then I shall have learnt the second lesson the Infant Jesus teaches me as He lies on the straw in Bethlehem

Again, our Lord came poor for the sake of the poor—to comfort them by being poor with them. And so He called them as His favourites to be His first worshippers on earth. Rich and poor were called. Rich and poor, we say, putting the poor last. Up in Heaven and in the stable they say—poor and rich—the poor come first.

Long and lovingly our Lady and St. Joseph kneel beside the manger alone. Now and then our Lady takes the Holy Child and folds Him in her arms and presses her lips to His little Cheek, and tries to warm Him by holding Him close to her heart. Then she puts Him into St. Joseph's arms. Poor St. Joseph—his tears fall fast as he feels how cold He is. It is a little less cold in their arms than in the manger. But our Lady knows He wants to be there, and as she wants only what He wants, she lays Him there again. Is it because the manger reminds Him of the altar that He loves it so? His first resting-place on earth is the feeding-place of cattle. He is laid in the manger as if to be their food. His resting-place to the end of the world will be the altars of the Church, where He waits to be the food of our souls.

Suddenly there is a noise at the opening of the cave—and whispering—and the sound of heavy feet trying to come in softly—and presently first one and then another of the poor shepherds comes in. And they kneel down and tell our Lady what they have seen. How the sky was all bright with Angels singing "Glory be to God on high," and they were told to go

## The Good Tidings

"And the Angel said to them: Fear not; for behold I bring you
good tidings of great joy, that shall be to all the people:
for this day is born to you a Savior, Who is Christ the Lord,
in the city of David." (Luke 2:9-11)

over to Bethlehem and see the Saviour born for them and laid mi a manger. Our Lady listens and speaks to them sweetly of her Son, and tells them Who He is and how they must adore Him. And then she takes Him from the manger and lays Him in their rough arms, that tremble whilst they hold Him, so strong is the shepherds' faith.

When the census-taking was over and the crowds had left Bethlehem, St. Joseph took our Lady and the Holy Child into the town and hired a little house. It was there that the Magi found the Child and His Mother, as the Gospel story tells us. The shepherds were Jews, the Magi Gentiles like ourselves. You remember that God had prepared the Gentiles too to receive the Saviour. Romans and Greeks, Egyptians, Arabians, even Chinese and Hindoos were looking for a King, Who was to arise from Judea and conquer the whole world. Let us see how the Magi were called to Bethlehem.

It is one of those clear Eastern nights when the stars shine forth so gloriously. Watch that company of Persian Magi down there upon the plain. See their dark upturned faces. Those three sitting apart from the rest are kings or sheiks and priests of their nation. They are learned, thoughtful men, to whom the midnight skies are an open book in which they read wonderful lessons of the power and greatness, the beauty and providence of God. They are His servants, looking for the fulfilment of His promises. And they are talking quietly of those very promises now. But see! Suddenly they have risen from their seats, and are gazing intently towards the west. A star of unusual size and brilliancy has appeared there, a star that is a stranger to them—and they know the heavens so well. Where does it come from? What does it mean? We must look back into the past to see.

Five hundred years before, the Archangel Gabriel had appeared to the Prophet Daniel, because he was "a man of desires," and told him the exact time of our Lord's Birth. Now Daniel was head of the Persian Magi of his day, and it is very likely that he made known to them this vision and the time of the Messiah's coming. These Magi of our Lord's time may thus have learnt it from tradition. Anyway, they know the prophecy of Balaam, "A star shall arise from Jacob." This flashes upon them as they see that star to-night. They confer together; they consult their books; they make their calculations; and God at the same time enlightening their minds, they believe that the Master of the world has come and is calling them by His star. Without loss of time, they put together their most costly treasures as gifts for the new-born Child, and set out with a few faithful followers on their way to Judea. See them conversing together on the road, helping one another, encouraging one another, beguiling the weariness of the way by talking of Jerusalem, where they are to find the King, of the excitement there will be, not in the city only, but far and near, for the star must have been seen in all lands, and from all parts men will be hastening towards Jerusalem. Alas! poor Magi, how they are to be disappointed! Hear the tinkling of the camels' bells as they come along the road, the thud of their soft heavy feet. Smell the fragrance of the spices they carry.

Day after day, month after month, the travellers push bravely on, till at last the towers of Jerusalem appear in sight. Its inhabitants are living almost in the Presence of Him Whom the Magi have come so far to seek, for only a few miles to the south is Bethlehem, and the little house to which St. Joseph has removed the Child and His Mother. Yet the Magi hear nothing of Him. The business and pleasure of the city go on as usual, without any suspicion that God is so near. How often God is near us and we do not heed Him!

Suddenly, the people of Jerusalem are startled by seeing in their streets a company of noble foreigners, evidently men of rank and importance, who ask openly, "Where is He that is born King of the Jews? For we have see His star in the East and are come to adore Him." Who can these strangers be, who know so little of Herod as to put such a question, and who ask their way to the palace, that they may put it there? Surely every one has heard of the massacres and murders by which King Herod has swept away every one who could rob him of his crown. How he has put to death not the priest of the Temple only, but his good and beautiful queen, and even his own sons. Who can these men be, so fearless or so foolish as to dare to speak in Herod's capital of another King? The Gentile travellers become the talk of the city, and the King soon gets to hear of them. He can easily have them seized and put to death. But he has thought of something better than that. Of course this new-born King must be found and killed at once. Well, these men shall find Him out, and the rest will be easy work. So an order goes forth from the palace for all the chief priests and scribes of the people to assemble and declare to King Herod where Christ should be born. There is no need for consultation. All know the words of Micheas, and the answer comes at once, "In Bethlehem of Juda, for so it is written by the Prophet." Then Herod privately calling the Magi, sends them to Bethlehem, saying, "Go and diligently inquire after the Child; and when you have found Him, bring me word again, that I also may come and adore Him."

When Holy Scripture speaks of the plots of the wicked, it says, "He that sitteth in the heavens shall laugh at them," because God can defeat their plans so easily, and catch them in their own snares. See what happens here. Herod sends no one with the Magi to see where they go, or what they find, or to secure their return to him. God in His Providence, allows him to be so blinded that he never thinks of taking a precaution which would have occurred to men far less crafty and suspicious. The holy Magi, too simple and trusting to suspect his evil designs, thank him for the trouble he has taken for them, and set out again on their journey, puzzled indeed and disappointed, yet not disconcerted by the strange indifference of Jerusalem. Not a priest cares to go with them, no one offers to show them the way. See them passing with their caravan out of the Jaffa Gate and taking the road to Bethlehem. God loves to prepare surprises for His friends, and He has two for the Magi now. All at once the star shines out again in the darkening sky, and goes before them until it comes and stands over the place where the Child is. "And seeing the star, they rejoiced with exceeding great joy." But where is it resting? Is this little humble house the palace they are seeking? Is the King of kings to be found here? They go in, and find the Child with Mary His Mother, and—oh, magnificent gift of faith!—falling down they adore Him. There are no attendants round Him; there is none of the luxury and splendour for which they looked, and yet, without a moment's hesitation, a moment's disappointment, falling down they adore Him. And opening their treasures, they offer Him gifts, gold, frankincense, and myrrh; gold, because He is their King; incense, because He is their God; myrrh, because He is the Redeemer Who is to die for man.

See them there, drinking in the silent teaching of the Divine Child. He does not speak, except to their hearts. But as He looks lovingly upon them, He shows them what He thinks of earthly goods, and honours, and that, to be great and rich in His sight, they must think like Him. He means them in after years to spread the knowledge of Him, and so He gives them their lessons now, as they worship Him on Mary's knee. How long they stay there, bowed down before Him, pouring out their hearts to Him—content—oh, more than content to have come so far *for this*.

High on Your Throne in Heaven, my God, You are great and exceedingly to be feared: low in the manger and on the altar, You are little and exceedingly to be loved. I desire to love You there with all my heart and soul and mind and strength. I should like to have knelt at the manger between Your Blessed Mother and St. Joseph, to have adored You, to have had You put into my arms. But I need not wish for this. In a few days I shall be happier still. I shall go to the altar, and there You will be given, not into my arms merely, but into my heart. I shall adore You; I shall love You; I shall have You for my very own.

Give me a strong faith in Your Real Presence. Give me a firm hope that You will do much for me when You come. Give me a tender love for You, O little Babe of Bethlehem, so full of love for me.

And you, dear Mother Mary, who prepared the first resting-place for God on earth, who prepared the manger for Him on Christmas night, and your own pure heart, again and again, to receive Him in Holy Communion, prepare mine for Him now—and make haste, Mother dear, for the time is short.

# IX
## Egypt

The Church calls us all travellers "mourning and weeping in this valley of tears." Not only those who are poor, or sick, or hungry, or cold, who have no treats to look forward to, and no one to be kind to them; but those who are high up in this world—people we think must be very happy because they have plenty of money, and grand houses, and carriages, and servants, dainty food, and fine clothes; because they can spend their time as they like, and amuse themselves whilst others work for them—even these have their troubles, and many of them in the midst of their riches and honours lead such sad lives that it would make us sad if we could know them. The children travellers have their troubles too, very real and hard to bear. They want someone to help them along. And there is One Who has come on purpose to help them. The little Traveller, Who began His journey at Bethlehem on Christmas night, will be like His fellow-travellers all the way. If they are to be hungry and thirsty and cold, weary and heavy laden, He will be so too. None shall find their road harder than His. None shall begin to suffer sooner; none shall suffer more. "Learn of Me," He seems to say, as He looks up to us from the prickly straw. As soon as He begins to live He begins to suffer, and He will suffer more and more as His life goes on—more in Egypt, where we are going to follow Him now, than in the cave at Bethlehem—more in the mysteries of His Passion than in those of His Infancy.

See the holy Kings as they prepare to take their leave of the Child and His Mother. The little Feet have been kissed for the last time; for the last time she has laid the little Hands in blessing on their heads; He has given them His last look. They will have to live upon that look all their lives through, for they will never meet Him again in this world. The next time they see His Face it will be in His glory. The next time they see those Lips, so silent now, He will speak to them, and thank them for their visit to Him when He was a little uncrowned King on earth. Meantime they have had to get the graces they will need for the life that is before them—graces for themselves, graces for those they love, for those whom they have to bring to the knowledge and love of Jesus. All this they asked, and all this, with the grace of laying down their lives for Him at last, was given to them as they knelt bowed down before Him there. Their time of audience has been short, but oh, how full of grace and blessing! If in our lives there was to be but one visit to the Blessed Sacrament—what a visit it would be.

They must get back to Herod now. He seemed anxious to see them again, and to come for his turn of adoration; they must not keep him waiting. What risk there seems to be for God's plans, for that Divine Life which is to be saved now, that it may be given for us later by the more cruel death of the Cross. But we know that with God's providence guarding and guiding all things, there can be no such thing as risk. He is watching and waiting, ready to interfere at the right moment. If the Kings knew the danger to which they are going to expose the Holy Child, how horrified they would be. They do not know; Mary and Joseph do not know. Only the Child Himself knows of His danger, and His Heart is calm—all things are in the hands of His Father, and no man can disturb or alter His Father's designs.

The Kings are just starting on their homeward journey, when their plans are suddenly changed by an order given them in sleep not to return to Herod. Asking no questions, they at once do as they are told and go back into their country another way.

Herod is counting the hours till their return. He is getting old now, and must know that long before this Child can become a dangerous rival, death will have taken from him the kingdom, to keep which he had committed so many crimes. No matter, he will hold it as long as he can, and sweep away every one from whom he has anything to fear, even the world's long promised Messiah.

The Kings are far on their way from Bethlehem and still he watches and waits. He is a fox, as our Lord called his son, another Herod. But his cunning is at fault for once, and he is being caught in his own trap. The hours go by, and he begins to feel uneasy. Was his plan not so clever after all? Can it be that those simple-looking strangers are tricking him? Unable at last to bear the suspense, he makes inquiries at Bethlehem, and learns that they have left, and no one knows where they will be by this time. Then his rage breaks out, as Herod's rage is wont to do, in an act of reckless violence and cruelty. He gives orders for a general slaughter of the boys of Bethlehem of two years old and under, and the orders are to be carried out at once, say the officials, for the King is "exceeding angry."

Meanwhile all is peaceful in Joseph's little home. He and our Lady have watched the Kings going away, and the rest of the day has been spent in quiet thankfulness to God for the public honour done to the Divine Child. Night comes, and the three are sleeping. A few hours more, and Herod's soldiers will be let loose on the little town. *Now* God's time has come. An Angel of the Lord appears in sleep to Joseph, saying, "Arise, and take the Child and His Mother and fly into Egypt: and be there until I shall tell thee. For it will come to pass that Herod will seek the Child to destroy Him." Not a word as to the road they are to take, or where or how they are to live in Egypt—whether their stay there is to be for weeks, or months, or years—whether they should take all they have or leave everything behind. "Be there until I shall tell thee." This is all St. Joseph is told, and he does not ask for more. Had he been like us, he would have asked: "Why go to Egypt—why at night?" How much simpler it would be to take Herod out of life—it would be a mercy to all his subjects. Or why not blind his messengers that they may not see the Child? All this St. Joseph might have asked had he been like us. But St. Joseph *was* St. Joseph, and he had learned to look at God's Will as reason enough for all that happens and for all that he was told to do. And so he asks no questions, but does what God tells him to do, does it instantly, does it cheerfully, provides for his poor family as well as he can in this short notice, and trusts to God for the rest. O blessed Joseph, if we could only be like you here!

Let us go with the Holy Travellers in their Flight, seeing what they see, feeling what they suffer, noticing what they do, and coming back all the better for having been in their company. The thought to be uppermost in our minds all the way is the thought of our Lord's Divinity; we are to remind ourselves again and again that the little Child we see before us is always and everywhere God.

The Angel has told St. Joseph, and Joseph has told Mary, and she, after awaking her Divine Child and wrapping Him in such poor things as she has to protect Him from the cold, has laid Him down again whilst she makes her few preparations for their hasty flight. See Him following her about the room with His meek Eyes, content to be left lying there till she is ready, content to be taken up and carried out into the night, content to be passed about from her arms to Joseph's during that weary journey—and all the while He is God.

See the Blessed Three making their way south, trusting to God's care rather than to any effort of their own to escape the dangers that threaten them. Herod will soon hear of their flight, and they must pass through the very heart of his dominions before they can reach the borderland and be safe from pursuit. Look into St. Joseph's grave and beautiful face. It is full of care, and yet how peaceful. Care there may well be, for are not God's greatest treasures entrusted to his keeping? Yet, just because they are God's treasures, there is no cause for anxiety. He will provide. Look at the Child and His Mother. She is very young, not sixteen, and her little Babe is in His first year. How hard it is for them! Yet how sweet and patient they are; how resigned to God's Will. How trustingly they look up to St. Joseph to care for them and protect them:

> Thou to the pilgrim art father and guide,
> And Jesus and Mary felt safe by thy side;
> Ah, blessed St. Joseph, how safe should I be,
> Sweet Spouse of our Lady, if thou wert with me.

Their way lies first through the hill country of Judea, along rough roads, then where there is no road at all, and at last across the upper part of the desert, that very desert where the children of Israel had wandered long ago. The long sandy waste is not without its dangers even for caravans—how much more for three unprotected travellers such as these!

Painters love to show us the Holy Travellers accompanied on their way by angels, and cheered with heavenly music. And fanciful legends tell how the fierce creatures of the wilderness, lions and panthers, came bounding forward to pay homage in their own way to the Divine Child, now crouching down at His feet, now, gentle as lambs, gambolling around Him. They

## The Flight into Egypt

"Who arose and took the Child and His Mother by night, and retired into Egypt." (St. Matt. ii. 14.)

tell how the red sand grew green, and flowers sprang up in His path. How the tall palms bowed before Him and offered their refreshing fruit. How water bubbled up and roads grew shorter. And how, when the fugitives entered Egypt, idols fell down and broke as the Child passed. But art and legend, with all their beautiful imaginings, are not so beautiful as the simple Gospel story. The Church has never sanctioned these fanciful accounts, and she would have us think of the Flight into Egypt as a very stern reality indeed. It meant being friendless and footsore: plodding wearily day after day over the waste of burning sand, scorched by the blazing sun at noon, and chilled by the cold desert winds and dews at night.

The Saints see many Divine reasons for Egypt having been chosen as the place of refuge for the Holy family at this time. It was safe, because not under the government of Herod, and because amid its multitudes three insignificant strangers might well pass unnoticed. But there were other reasons too. Here Abraham and Isaac had found a refuge in times of famine, and the people of God had sojourned for four hundred years. Here the ten plagues had fallen in punishment of Pharoah's obstinacy, and his host had been destroyed in the passage of the Red Sea. When lying on his deathbed in this idolatrous land, Jacob had looked forward to the coming of Him Who should be sent. Now that He was come at last, what could be more fitting than that He should visit this land of Egypt, in which His ancestors had lived, and which was so full of memories of the early history of God's people. He came too to fulfil the prophecy, "Out of Egypt have I called My Son." And lastly, He came to sanctify by His Presence a land which was to become so famous in the Church and so fruitful in Saints. Our Lord came to Egypt to bless it. All its future glories—its doctors and its hermit saints, those who in its populous cities would defend His

Divinity like Athanasius, or in its deserts and caves sanctify themselves in such multitudes as to make it a very land of Saints—all these were present to the mind of the Babe as He was borne over that heathen land. All of these He blessed, for all of these He prayed. And the Saints tell us it was His Presence and His prayer that produced the rich harvest of holiness which Egypt bore later on.

If you look at a map of ancient Africa, you will find Memphis in the north of Egypt. Tradition says it was there, at the entry of the city, that the Holy Family lived first. A very old church, built in memory of the Blessed Three, is still to be seen; the Coptic Christians go there to pray, and show visitors to the crypt, the three arcades sacred to Jesus, Mary, and Joseph. Another tradition seems to say that the Holy Family lived for a time in the neighbourhood of Heliopolis in the Thebaid. Nowhere else in the world were there so many Jews dwelling among the heathen as in Egypt. They were rich, powerful, and respected by their neighbours, and though they lived in a land given up to idolatry, great numbers were faithful to the law of God. So much so, that in many of the cities and towns, our Lady and St. Joseph would find the synagogues to which they had been accustomed in Judea and Galilee. It is noticed that wherever the Jews settle they look after the poor of their own nation. And we may well believe it was to provide the Holy Family with the help it needed, that God chose Egypt as its home during the time of exile. Yet because St. Joseph was so poor, the Blessed Three must have lived in a very poor little house, and have had much to suffer. Even necessaries, such as they might have had in their own land, not unfrequently failed them here. The food was coarse and scanty, and St. Joseph had to work hard to provide that. See our Lady trying to make ends meet in her little home. See how satisfied St. Joseph and the Holy Child are with everything, and how they all take inconvenience and discomfort as a matter of course.

Will the servants complain when the King and His court put up with all manner of make-shifts? Among His servants, some have many privations and inconveniences in their daily life, and some have fewer. Will those who have many fret under them when they think: My King was worse off than I am? And those who have few, will they grumble when now and then He gives them some little resemblance to Himself, gives them a taste of what was His daily bread? When now and then things are not quite to their liking, not quite so good or so comfortable as usual; when they cannot afford this or that which they see others have—will they grumble then? No, we are not going to grumble. We want to be like our Lord. We are looking at Him in the different mysteries of His Life that we may learn to be like Him, that knowing Him more clearly we may come to love Him more dearly and follow Him more nearly. This is St. Ignatius' prayer. It would be hard to find a better or more beautiful one, so we will learn it and say it often: O Lord and Master, let me know Thee more intimately, that so I may love Thee more intensely, and follow Thee more closely. Here, in the mystery of Thy Flight into Egypt, know and love and follow Thee in Thy meekness.

Looking into that holy house in Egypt, what do we see? Often enough, a little Babe lying in a corner whilst His Mother does the work of the house and makes the small place neat and tidy. She cannot be always in adoration before Him, nor is He always folded in her arms. Whilst Joseph goes about seeking employment, Mary has to work hard at home, for she has no servant. The Babe waits patiently in His corner till she has time to attend to Him. Sometimes He stretches out His little Arms to be taken up into hers, and sometimes lying in her lap, He plays with her hair or watches her fingers as they spin—

and all the while He is God. Watch the Holy Child taking His first tottering steps, clinging to Mary's hand or dress. Soon He is able to do little things to help her. He can open and shut the door; hold the skeins for her to wind, pick up her distaff when it falls, and take a message to St. Joseph at his work.

And what of poor Bethlehem all this time, Bethlehem which we left on the night of the Flight? It has given to the Church the first Christian martyrs in the innocent children who were put to death because they were of our Lord's age, and He was supposed to be among them. Herod's cruel order did not take long to execute, and the streets of Bethlehem were soon flowing with blood, whilst the air was filled with the wailing of the inconsolable mothers. Up and down the streets, and in and out of the houses went the soldiers, in search of their poor little victims, seizing them wherever they came upon them, and slaughtering many who were not included in the decree. Think of the sufferings of the children, think of the agony of the mothers. It was the mothers rather than the children that the pitying Prophet thought of when seeing this massacre more than five hundred years before, he had said: "A voice in Rama was heard, lamentation and great mourning, Rachel bewailing her children and would not be comforted, because they are not." The number of those thus sacrificed to Herod's fury is not known. The soldiers' orders were to slay not only the children of Bethlehem, but those "in all the borders thereof, from two years old and under." From Herod's calculations, our Lord could scarcely be more than a year old. But it was well to make quite sure. He should not escape this time. And what did it matter if in the slaughter of the children a few unnecessary hundreds perished, so long as the Child born in the cave that December night was got rid of.

To some of us the thought may come: *why did God allow*

*this terrible slaughter, when He could so easily have prevented it?* We will try to learn why. We know that whatever God does is perfect. He can do nothing that is not infinitely wise and good and just. If then, we sometimes ask why He does this or that, why He permits this evil or sends this trial, it can only be that we are seeking in all reverence to learn some of the Divine reasons which are not plain to us at first sight. We may thus ask how it was He allowed so many lives to be sacrificed in this frightful massacre of the Innocents. One of His reasons we shall best understand by seeing what the Holy Innocents themselves think of His designs over them. Whilst their poor mothers are filling the air with lamentations over the lives so cruelly and so early taken, they are rejoicing in the crowns so quickly won. In a short time our Lord will have fetched them from Limbo, and they will be waving their little palms in triumph before the throne of God. God might indeed have sent an Angel from Heaven to strike down the wicked King, or to destroy his soldiers as He destroyed the army of Sennacherib. But had He done this, where would that troop of children be now? Certainly not among the ranks of the martyrs, venerated and invoked by the whole Church. Many Saints believe that the use of reason was given to them, so that with full knowledge, willingly and lovingly, they might make the sacrifice of their lives to God. But in any case, God only took what as Creator and Lord was His, and they were immensely the gainers by His taking from them an earthly life to give them a heavenly life instead.

Those who persecute the Church of God or His Saints are frequently cut off by death in some sudden and awful manner. Herod the Great is an example of this. He had openly persecuted the Saint of Saints, the Son of God Himself, and his death is one of the most fearful on record. It seems likely that it took place not long after the Flight into Egypt, and it was hailed all over the land he had ruled with an outburst of joy.

And now the time of exile was over, and the Angel came again to St. Joseph. "Arise," he said, "and take the Child and His Mother, and go into the land of Israel. For they are dead that sought the life of the Child." It was night as before, and He rose at once as before, and taking the Child and His Mother, crossed the wilderness again, and came and dwelt in a city of Galilee called Nazareth. Here our Lord spent the greater part of His earthly life, and here we must follow Him and study Him.

O Babe of Bethlehem, You are indeed the Lamb of God, the Prince of Peace. You could have struck down proud Herod when he sought Your Life, but You chose to fly before him as if You were too weak to resist. Bears tore in pieces the boys who mocked Eliseus. Angels and horses with chariots of fire were seen guarding him, and the men who came to seize him were struck with blindness. Lions let loose upon Your Saints have licked their feet. Spiders have swiftly spun a web across their path and hidden their hiding-place. Birds have fed them. Fire has refused to touch them. Waters have walled them round, or sprung up to quench their thirst. But when a wicked king raised his arm against You Yourself, O Mighty God, You fled before him. You Who worked such wonders for Your Saints, worked none for Yourself, to teach me that it is a greater thing to conquer malice by meekness than to escape from it by miracle.

O my most meek Lord, make my heart like Yours. By all it cost You to teach me this lesson of meekness, by all the heat and cold, the hunger and thirst and weariness You endured with those You loved best on earth, when You had to fly for Your Life across the desert—make my heart like Yours. Check the angry words on my lips; take away the hot feeling from my heart when people vex me and things go wrong. Help me then to think of You, gentle and patient, and to try with Your grace to be patient and gentle too.

"Jesus, meek and humble of Heart, make my heart like unto Thine."

> Teach, O teach us, Holy Child,
> By Thy Face so meek and mild,
> Teach us to resemble Thee
> In Thy sweet humility.

# X
# Nazareth

We shall come to know our Lord better if we picture to ourselves the land in which He lived, and the city and the house that were His home for so many years. For He Who loved to call Himself the Son of Man and to be like us in all things, was like us in this, that the scenes of His Childhood had much to do with His thoughts and His words when He grew up. In His parables He loved to speak of the things He had seen at Nazareth—the lost sheep brought back to the fold, the cornfields white unto harvest, the lilies and the fig-trees. By looking then at the land in which He lived and the scenery around His home, we come to understand His thoughts, and words, and actions better, and so to know Him better and to love Him more.

Palestine is not a very large country, but it is a very wonderful one. It is called in Scripture a land flowing with milk and honey, to give us some idea of the richness of its soil and productions. Gathered together there we find the plants and fruits of other and very different climes—the walnut, olive, vine, mulberry, and fig-tree, mingling with the orange and banana, the pomegranate and palm. Scripture speaks with admiration of the cedar on Lebanon and the cypress-tree on Mount Sion, of the plane-tree in Cades and the rose-plant in Jericho, of the fair olive-tree in the fields, and the palm-tree by the waters. It seems as if Nature had brought together all her treasures to pour them out upon the land which for three-and-thirty years was to be trodden by the Feet of God Incarnate.

In our Lord's time the country was divided into three provinces: Judea in the south, Samaria in the centre, and Galilee in the north. The district east of the Jordan was called Perea. It is to Galilee we must go now, for Nazareth is there.

Galilee is full of fertile valleys and of beautiful mountains. In lower Galilee was the little town of Nazareth, nestling in a valley, in the midst of vines, olives, and fig-trees, flowery meadows and fruitful fields. Grey houses with flat roofs climbed up its steep streets. There too were the fountains for ablution, the workshops and the synagogue.

And what about the one House there about which we want to hear, the House of the Holy Family? Can we know anything about it, so as to be able to picture it to ourselves in our meditations? Yes, we can. Pilgrims visited it from the earliest times of Christianity and told us what it was like in their days. So that we can form a very good idea of the little place in which Jesus, Mary, and Joseph lived for so many years.

Nazareth, as we have seen, was in a hilly country. The hills abounded with caves which were turned to account by the people, who built in front of them. Thus the back part of their house was already made. The Holy House was built in this fashion. Tradition tells us it had belonged to St. Joachim, and that it was here that our Lady was born. On her father's death the House came to be hers. Here she received the Archangel's visit at the Annunciation. Here the Holy Family lived after the return from Egypt, and here St. Joseph died.

Soon after our Lord's Ascension that part of the House in which the Archangel Gabriel appeared to our Lady was changed into a chapel. On the spot where she knelt, an altar was erected and dedicated by St. Peter. There St. John said

Mass and our Lady assisted. Calvary was brought to Nazareth, and those who had been present at the Bloody Sacrifice—Mary Magdalen, Salome, and Mary of Cleophas—knelt with our Mother before the altar on which the Unbloody Sacrifice was offered by the Beloved Disciple.

The Holy House at Nazareth became the first church consecrated by the Apostles in honour of God and of the Blessed Virgin, and always retained the altar that St. Peter had set up. It was the first of our Lady's sanctuaries. Through three hundred years of persecution and profanation it was preserved in safety, and then when persecution ceased, St. Helen built over it a sanctuary, which was one of the most beautiful in the East. For twelve hundred years the Holy House at Nazareth was visited by saints, crusaders, and pilgrims from every land. But at the end of the twelfth century it ceased to be honoured and was exposed to profanation and destruction at the hands of the Mahommedans. It was then that, according to a widely-received tradition, God provided for it in another land a place of safety and honour. He gave His Angels charge over it to bear it up in their hands and carry it away from Galilee to a distant shore.

If you ever go to Loreto you will see on the summit of a hill, the famous church which holds the first place among our Lady's shrines, and is the most frequented sanctuary in Christendom.

Beneath the dome stands a square building of white marble enclosing the plain rough walls of a cottage. This, says tradition, is the Holy House of Nazareth.

On a stormy night in May, 1291, it was borne across the sea to Dalmatia on the Turkish coast of the Adriatic. A few years later it was again miraculously transported over the sea to Loreto, where, standing without foundations, its four walls still remain.

In the church built over and around it more than a hundred Masses are said daily, and from sunrise to sunset the pilgrims come and go in a perpetual stream. Forty thousand have been seen praying there on one single day. They go round the Holy House upon their knees in such numbers that they have worn a furrow all round it. St. Aloysius, St. Stanislaus, St. Francis Xavier, St. Charles Borromeo, and other Saints too numerous to mention, Popes and Bishops, kings, men and women of every degree, rich and poor, have knelt within these holy walls. Princesses have asked to sweep the floor upon their knees. More than fifty silver lamps burn there night and day, and on the altar we read in letters of gold: "Here the Word was made Flesh and dwelt among us." And here every Saturday is sung before the Blessed Sacrament during Benediction that dear Litany of Loreto, which takes its name from the sanctuary that was our Lady's home.

When we say the Holy House was translated to Italy from Palestine, we mean that portion of the House which was built up in front of the cave. And thus the Holy Places are divided between the East and the West. The East retains the Holy Caves at Nazareth and Bethlehem—The Sacred Chamber of the Incarnation God has given to the West. The East possesses the Holy Sepulchre where our Lord was laid when dead—the West has the Blessed House in which He lived.

But we should like to see the Holy House just as it was in our Lord's time. Can we do this? Not quite, perhaps. But with the help of an old pilgrim we can see a good deal. Phocas, a Greek monk, visited it about a hundred years before it was carried away to Italy, and has told us some very interesting things about it.

The Holy House was a small stone building standing in front of a cave, not in the middle of the town, but near the bottom of the hill. All the town was above it. The outer door opened at once into the room known through all ages as the Chamber of the Annunciation, where our Lady was when the

Angel was sent to her from God. Here afterwards the Holy Family lived and had their meals, and here our Lady worked with the Holy Child at her side, or sat alone pondering in her heart, as the Holy Gospel tells us. High up in the wall on the left side was a window, the only one in the House. On the opposite side, hollowed out in the wall, was a fire-place blackened with smoke—for the Nazarenes used no chimneys—and a cupboard where the eating vessels were kept on a cedar-wood shelf built into the wall. There were one or two chests for holding clothing and the rolls of the Psalms and Prophets. Straight in front of this outer door was another through which could be seen a cool grotto or cave with a flight of winding steps, twelve in number, tunnelled in the solid rock. These led up to another smaller cave, called at Nazareth, "the Virgin's kitchen." Both these caves were lighted by doorways opening out upon the slope of the hill. They were so closely joined to the building that all together they formed the House of the Holy Family.

In Palestine the houses are divided by moveable partitions into as many rooms as the family requires. Thus the same room serves for use by day and by night. The partitions are commonly of matting or curtains drawn over upright laths of wood. During the day the air can pass freely through the rooms by merely drawing back the curtains. A partition divided the room in front of the cave, which we may call the living-room of the Holy Family, into two parts; that to the left, which had the window, was our Lady's room, the other was our Lord's. Early pilgrims particularly note that our Lord's room was dark, the partition shutting out the light that came from the very small and only window. No beds were seen during the day, because they were merely mattresses rolled up and put away till night. St. Joseph's room was part of the large cave, separated off from the rest of the cave by a light screen covered with matting or curtains. The building opened into the large cave through a doorway with a cedar lintel or headpiece. Through this doorway our Lord passed backwards and forwards for nearly thirty years. The steps in the tunnelled rock exist to this day.

At Nazareth the shops are not part of the dwellings, but are situated in the Street of Bazaars, and so St. Joseph's workshop was not in the Holy House, but in the centre of the town. The site keeps the name of St. Joseph's shop; there is a chapel there where Mass is said.

No pains are too great to enable us to make the Holy House familiar to us, so that it may live in our minds and hearts, filling them with memories of Nazareth and of the Blessed Three, who lived there so many years and made it a Paradise. Let us go there often, and treading softly across the threshold—because the place on which we stand is holy ground—look reverently around us.

How neat and bright the little place is. Very poor, yet everything in its place and well cared for, from the cooking utensils ranged against the wall and the stools that bear marks of St. Joseph's mending, to our Lady's distaff and wool laid carefully together near the window. Neat and bright it is, but oh, how lowly and hidden for the lives of those Three, who have been called the Earthly Trinity. See them at prayer. See them at their daily work. See them at meals.

In the morning, after reciting the Psalms together, St. Joseph goes to the shop to work. Our Lady stays at home and takes care of the house. She grinds the corn, prepares the food, spins the wool, and weaves the garments; goes to draw water from the well and to buy her provisions in the market. Our Lord stays at home with His Blessed Mother. The Jewish child commonly learned what he had to learn in his father's house, in the synagogue, and in the workshop. In the house he was instructed in the Commandments of God and in the history of his people. In the synagogue he was taught to read the Law of

God, and in the workshop he learned a trade. After a while the Holy Child is old enough to take His share in the work of the house. He sweeps the room, helps His Mother to prepare the meals and wash the dishes. Oh, what little things for the God of Heaven and earth to be doing from morning till night—working, resting, playing, praying just as He was told—this was His life at Nazareth. See Him leaving His work or His play at a word from His Blessed Mother or St. Joseph. Hear His words, the tone of His Voice, when He speaks to them. Notice the sweetness with which he does it all. He is our example; and as at Bethlehem He taught us humility, in Egypt meekness, so at Nazareth He teaches us obedience. "Learn of Me. I have given you an example that as I have done to you, so you do also." "In Jesus children have a Divine example for their admiration and imitation," said the Great Pope Leo XIII. As He grows older, He goes out with St. Joseph to watch him at work and to help him in little ways. He can spare him somewhat by gathering up the shavings, carrying home finished work, and bringing back the money paid for it. The two come back to the House at the hours of prayer and meals.

How unselfish our Lady is. When her Divine Son was quite little she had Him always with her. But as He grows older, He is more and more in the workshop, and she is glad for it to be so—glad for St. Joseph to have Him all day before his eyes. But how glad she is to see them both coming home. How happy they all are when the day's work is done and they meet together.

See them at meals. How they lift up their hearts to God at grace. What a real prayer it is. How kind they are to each other at table. How they look after one another—leave the best for each other—Mary and Jesus caring for St. Joseph, who comes in tired from his work.

Listen to the conversation, bright and happy, yet not loud, our Lord leaving it chiefly to His Parents, but putting in His word now and then, refreshing and filling their hearts with joy at the beautiful virtues they see in Him. And He in His turn refreshed by the love of those two dear hearts, that understood Him better than any others will ever do. Every word of His Mary lays up in her heart, pondering it alone and drawing profit from it; so we ought to do when our Lord speaks to us in prayer.

Can we think quiet homely work dull and hard, when we see our Lord and His Blessed Mother contented with it for so many years? And when we know that more glory rose up to God every hour from the cottage at Nazareth than had been given to Him or ever will be given by all the adoration of angels and men?

It was not *what* they did, but the *way* in which they did it that was so pleasing to God. The little duties of home life, and of a very poor life, became great in the eyes of God, because all was done for the love of Him. The value of our Lord's every act was infinite, because He was God, and Mary and Joseph took care to imitate Him and unite all their acts with His, as we may do so easily in our morning offering, renewed again and again throughout the day:

> My God, I offer Thee this day
> All I shall think or do or say,
> Uniting it with what was done
> On earth by Jesus Christ Thy Son.

In that Holy House no duty was shirked because it was troublesome or distasteful; and on the other hand, nothing was done simply because it was pleasant. But because it was His Father's Will, the Child Jesus helped His Parents and made home happy for them and worked in the shop. It was dull uninteresting work for Him Who knew all things and could do all things, Who could have painted the most beautiful pictures and taught the wisest philosophers and written the most learned books. All His Life long He never thought of what He liked best, but of what would please His Heavenly Father and help us most. And He knew that to do grand and showy things in which we could not imitate Him would be less useful to us than to set us an example by doing little lowly duties perfectly. In this we can all imitate Him. And we will try. Instead of calling these things dry and stupid and doing them carelessly, when no one is looking and we think we shall not be found out, we will do them as well as ever we can, in union with the actions of Jesus, Mary, and Joseph, in the Holy House at Nazareth, remembering always that God is looking at us and that we must not offer Him anything done in a slovenly way, but our best always. Our best is poor enough; can we think of giving Him anything less?

And so with our obedience. We will love it for His sake and obey as He did, promptly and cheerfully. Mary and Joseph did not ask Him what it was His Will to do. They, who were infinitely beneath Him, had to command Him, to make arrangements for Him as the One Who held the least and lowest place in the House. And He was quite content. He knew Who it was that had set them over Him, and that in obeying them He obeyed His Heavenly Father, and therefore He was subject to them. What they told Him to do He did at once and in the way they wished Him to do it, and this long after the age when men think themselves obliged to obey. And I? How do I obey those who are set over me by God? Is my obedience anything like the obedience of the Holy Child Jesus? Now that I am preparing for my First Communion I will make it more like His. Nothing will please Him more than to see me preparing my heart for Him by practising cheerfully for love of Him what He practised cheerfully all those long years for love of me. It was in little things He showed His love for me. In little things I will show my love for Him.

We must not leave dear Nazareth till we have looked at the synagogue, where the Holy Family prayed so often, and the site of which is still shown to pilgrims. The Holy Family went there on the Sabbath-day for public prayer, to hear the Law read and the Prophets. Think of what passed in the Sacred Heart as our Lord sat there. Look at His upturned Face as He follows the reader through type and prophecy—seeing clearly in Melchisedech, the Paschal Lamb, the Manna in the Desert, figures of Himself. How the thought of the Bloody and Unbloody Sacrifice to come, of the Tabernacle and of First Communions is filling that dear Heart of His and making It beat fast with loving impatience. He hears the glorious names the Prophets give to the Messiah—the glorious things they say of Him. He is the King of Glory, the Light of the Gentiles, Christ the Prince, the Prince of Peace, the Wonderful, the Mighty God, the Father of the world to come. He is to redeem with a plentiful Redemption, to rise triumphantly from the dead; to take His seat at the right Hand of His Father and to rule over an everlasting Kingdom. He listens. He understands. And when the book is closed and the congregation disperses, He puts His Hand again into St. Joseph's and rejoins His Mother and goes down the village street with them again to His poor Home—"*And is subject to them.*" *And all this for me.*

"Jesus of Nazareth." This was the dear Name by which our Blessed Lord loved to be known during His earthly Life. "What have we to do with Thee, Jesus of Nazareth?" cried the devils. "Jesus of Nazareth, King of the Jews," was His title on the Cross. "I know that you seek Jesus of Nazareth," said the Angel to the Maries at the Sepulchre. "In the Name of Jesus Christ of Nazareth, I say to Thee arise," said St. Paul to the lame man at the Beautiful Gate of the Temple. And our Lord Himself, speaking to Saul, said: "I am Jesus of Nazareth, Whom thou persecutest." We see then how near and dear Nazareth is to Him. It is dear to Him as the Home of His Childhood, where the happy years with His Blessed Mother and St. Joseph were spent, dear to Him as the treasure-house where He stored up for us so many examples of the humility, meekness, and obedience He had come to teach. Shall it not be dear to us too?

O dearest Lord, I shall never wonder any more at Your holy Hidden Life at Nazareth. I shall never think You waited thirty years before You began to teach. I see You began as soon as ever You came into the world, and that You could not have taught us anywhere so well as in that little House that was Your Home for so many years. It is our school and will be to the end of the world. All the Saints have studied here. It is because they studied here that they are Saints. Aloysius and Berchmans and Stanislaus and Agnes and Imelda, all came here to learn of You. And not the Saints only, but every Catholic child must come here to school. You call us all, saying: "Come to me *all*." Though it is such a little place, there is room for us all, there is room for me. Please, dear Master, give me a place there. I do indeed want to learn the lessons You have come to teach—meekness, humility, obedience. Remember that a good master takes special care of the little and the backward ones. I am little and backward too. And oh! I am so dull. With all my wanting and trying, I am so long about it. Here have I been learning my Catechism all these years and You know how little way I have made in practising what I know. I can say it off, but when it comes to doing, You know what happens. Good Master, help me to do better. You take pains to teach not only those who are high in Your school, but those who are low down like me. The dull ones besides being taught in class are taken for private lessons and have special helps. Take me by myself and teach my heart by Your secret words. Like the little Samuel I say to You: "Speak, Lord, for thy servant heareth."

# XI
## JERUSALEM

And now our Lord was twelve years old. A Jewish boy began to feel important at this age, because he was then freed to a certain extent from the control of his parents. He was treated as a man, and could choose the trade or profession he would follow when he grew up. But His twelfth birthday made no difference in the home-life of the Holy Child, for it was His Will to be subject to His Parents until the age of thirty. In other respects, however, He showed Himself like other boys, conforming strictly to all the observances of the Mosaic Law, which now became obligatory.

The Jewish Church had, like our own, its solemn fasts, feasts, and ceremonies. The first of the legal ceremonies to be observed by a Jew on reaching the age of twelve, was the receiving of the phylacteries. These were little parchment bands inscribed with passages from Scripture, and bound with straps to the head and arms. The Pharisees wore them broader than other people, that they might seem to be more holy. Our Blessed Lord subjected Himself to this Jewish rite, and was presented by St. Joseph in the synagogue at Nazareth to receive these phylacteries, which He was henceforth to bear in all religious ceremonies.

The precept of fasting which binds a Catholic from the age of twenty-one, bound a Jew at twelve. Then, too, the pilgrimage to Jerusalem at the great yearly feasts became of obligation, so that the Child Jesus would now accompany His Parents thither for the Feast of the Passover. Women were not obliged to go. But our Lady was always glad to visit the Temple, where she had been brought up and had received so many graces. And therefore we are told that "His Parents went every year to Jerusalem at the solemn day of the Pasch." Little children were taken or left at home, as was most convenient to their parents, and thus the Child Jesus may have been taken by His Blessed Mother and St. Joseph before the Pasch, which followed His twelfth birthday. But now He is bound to go.

See them making their way down the steep street of Nazareth to join the caravan which was about to leave for the Holy City. Palestine then, as now, was infested with robbers, so that it was safer for people to travel in large companies. Thus two or three towns would unite together for the annual pilgrimages. Arrived at the starting-point, St. Joseph and our Lady part, for the men and women travel in separate companies. Our Lord, as a Child, may go with either. Before following the Blessed Travellers on the journey, we will give a little time to the study of the Holy City, trying to see it as they saw it at this Passover.

South of Galilee, where they lived, is Samaria, and south again, on gradually ascending ground, lies Judea, a land of hills and valleys, the most mountainous part being that around Jerusalem.

If we love Palestine for the sake of Jesus, those places more particularly which were dearest to Him, and where He was oftenest found, and those most of all which were the scenes of His Blessed Passion, Resurrection, and Ascension—then Jerusalem must be dear to us above all other places in that dear Land. We shall want to know something about it, above all, about its glorious Temple—the place that was known and venerated all over the world; to which even pagan princes sent

### The Paschal Lamb

"Let every man take a lamb...and it shall be a lamb without blemish... and the whole multitude shall sacrifice it in the evening. And they shall take of the blood thereof and put it upon...the upper doorpost of the houses, wherein they shall eat it." (Exodus 12:3,5-7)

their costly offerings; the one Sanctuary God chose for Himself on earth; the place where our Lady's early years were spent, and where our Lord so often came to pray. There have been few sights in this world more magnificent than Jerusalem, seen from the Mount of Olives.

Arrived at the highest point of the road, over Mount Olivet, the City suddenly appeared in view against the western sky, covering five hills with its domes and terraces, its palaces and towers. Deep valleys and inaccessible rocks surrounded it, giving it the appearance of an immense natural fortress. The grandeur of its situation, the beauty, majesty, and richness of its buildings, together with its marvellous history, made it one of the wonders of the world. There has been nothing like it elsewhere. "Only there the Lord is magnificent," Isaias had said of the first Jerusalem, "the city of perfect beauty, the joy of all the earth," And Herod's city even surpassed King Solomon's, and was unequalled in splendour by any other in the world. It was built on four hills, Ophel, Sion, Acra, and Bezetha, forming an amphitheatre round Mount Moriah, on which the Temple stood. Up and down the slopes of these four hills stretched the busy City, with its streets, markets, and bazaars. And in the centre, rising sheer up from the surrounding ravines, stood the Temple Mount, alone in its grandeur. Its beautiful courts were built on three terraces, and high above them, enclosed by marble colonnades, the Temple itself stood out, a mass of snowy marble and glittering gold. From every part of Jerusalem its dazzling walls could be seen, and the entire roofing being overlaid with gold shone out with such splendour as the rays of the Eastern sun beat upon it, that the eye could scarcely endure the blaze of light.

Ascending the Mount on his way to the Temple, the traveller came to a massive wall nearly eighty feet high. This wall, which enclosed all the sacred buildings, was strengthened by a hundred marble towers, and surrounded by marble steps on every side. Passing through one of the five gates, he entered a large quadrangle called the Court of the Gentiles, because it was open to all comers. Pagans as well as Jews crowded its vast enclosure, walking about and conversing under the tall porticoes, for this court was not considered sacred. But beyond it no Gentile might venture under pain of death.

The churches of our own land give us no idea whatever of the Temple of Jerusalem. They are large enough to contain the whole congregation, and are roofed in to protect the people from rain and cold. But the temples of the East were used almost exclusively for the priests: the people prayed outside in the open air. Moreover, the Jewish Temple was not one building, but a vast mass of buildings consisting of courts, porticoes, and rooms for the priests, as well as of the Sanctuary itself. Remembering this, we can understand how our Lord found in the Temple oxen, sheep, and doves; buyers and sellers, and the tables of money-changers. It was the Court of the Gentiles that was thus profaned, and from a house of prayer turned into a den of thieves. One of the porticoes of this Court was very beautiful. Three ranges of white marble columns rested on a pavement of many coloured stones, and upheld a roof of cedar. This was Solomon's Porch, where our Lord was walking one winter's day when the Jews took up stones to cast at Him.

On the second and higher terrace, and separated from the Court of the Gentiles by a richly-carved balustrade of stone, was the Porch of the Women, so called, not from its being set apart for the use of women only—for it seems to have been the common place for worship—but because they were not allowed to go farther except when they brought an offering for sacrifice. All they could see from the galleries where they worshipped was the Holy Place in the distance, its magnificent cedar roof bristling all over with pinnacles of gold. The Porch of the Women was reached by a flight of fourteen steps. Up these steps our Lady came as a little child of three to offer herself to God in the ceremony of the Presentation, which took place in this Porch. Here, too, she came to pray when accompanying our Lord and St. Joseph to the Temple.

Beyond this Porch of the Women, and separated from it by a balustrade and a flight of fifteen steps, was the Court of the Israelites, reserved for men.

Beyond this again, on the third and highest terrace, was the Court of the Priests. The great altar of burnt-offering stood in the midst, and the brazen laver. Behind the altar and standing out high above the terrace and colonnades, rose a square mass of white marble, its cedar roof covered with plates of gold, and glittering with golden spikes. This was the Temple itself, the dwelling-place of God. Folding-doors inlaid with gold opened into the outer chamber called the Holy Place, which contained the Table of Shew-bread, the golden seven-branched candlestick, and the Altar of Incense. Beyond this was the inner chamber, the Holy of Holies, separated from the Holy Place by a broad Babylonian curtain glowing with brilliant colours. This was the veil of the Temple which was rent from top to bottom at our Lord's Death.

And what was there behind the veil? Oh, how disappointed we are! There was nothing. The Holy of Holies was empty. All that had made the first Temple glorious was wanting to the second. A large stone on which the High Priest sprinkled the blood on the Day of Atonement was in the place where the Ark of the Covenant with the Mercy-seat had stood. For the Ark had been lost since the time of Jeremias, and with it the Tables of the Law, the rod of Aaron, the manna of the desert, and the sacred fire. Sadder still to the Jews was the absence of the visible Presence of God in the Shechinah. That white, luminous cloud which descended into the first Temple on the

Day of Dedication had never shown itself in the second. The stones of the Rational, too, which the High Priest wore on his breast, had lost their lustre and no longer made known the Will of God. And thus, notwithstanding its unheard-of richness, this second Temple was in every way inferior to the first. Nothing could supply for the absence of those wonderful signs of His Presence, which God had deigned to give to His chosen people, except that fulfilment of the prophecy of Aggeus,[1] that the glory of the second Temple should exceed that of the first, because it should be visited by Christ Himself: "The desire of all nations shall come, and I will fill this house with glory, saith the Lord of Hosts...Great shall be the glory of this last house more than of the first."

That prophecy is to be fulfilled now, for the Holy Family are nearing Jerusalem. Let us go back to where we left them.

From all the towns and villages of Palestine, pilgrims are pouring out by thousands to join the caravans starting for Jerusalem for the Feast of the Passover.

See that bright line on the white, winding road. It is the pilgrims from Nazareth in their garments of many colours. Coming down from their hilly country into the valley of Esdraelon, they fell into order there, and now, after four days' march, they are nearing the Holy City. They look tired and travel-stained. Perhaps they have had to go down into Jordan valley or even to cross the river in order to avoid the country of the Samaritans, who, you know, have always shown themselves unfriendly to the Jews, especially to those on their way to Jerusalem. Anyway, here they are. First come the men on foot, then the women and the old people, mounted upon mules and camels. The journey has been long and toilsome, but the thought of God's Temple keeps up their hearts. Weary as they

---

[1] Commonly known as Haggai.

are, a joyous song bursts from their lips, and to the sound of the flute they chant their sacred hymns. In the neighbourhood of Jerusalem the caravan halts and breaks up, and families are reunited. Fathers and mothers and children meet and finish the journey together.

What a scene it is all around Jerusalem! The slopes outside the walls are covered with tents, for Jews are flocking in by hundreds of thousands, not from every part of Palestine only, but from distant lands, "Devout men out of every nation under heaven." How large the numbers are we can gather from this, that at one feast of the Passover no fewer than two hundred and fifty-six thousand lambs were slain. The city is full to overflowing. The residents have turned every corner to account for the accommodation of the pilgrims. Many are expecting their relations and friends from the country, and while the feast lasts strangers are to be received and entertained as friends. Houses are neither hired nor let, but freely thrown open to all. A curtain hung before the entrance shows that there is still room for guests; a table spread in front of it, that strangers will still be welcome there. At last every house is full, numbers will sleep on the roofs—and still the multitudes pour in. Travellers from a distance clearly cannot expect to be housed within the City, and must be content with such shelter as they can put up outside.

But see! the pilgrims from Nazareth are beginning to climb the Mount of Olives, with weary steps, all of them, but with eager hearts and eyes. In a few moments they will see Jerusalem.

The shout of Psalms has ceased. All are in silent expectation. Now those in front have reached the point from which they catch the first sight of the Holy City and the Temple rising in all its glory on Mount Moriah. Watch their outstretched arms— and listen—David's cry of admiration is bursting from their lips: "How lovely are thy tabernacles, O Lord of Hosts!" "If I forget thee, O Jerusalem, let my right hand be forgotten...if I make not Jerusalem the beginning of my joy."

Group after group passes us. And here at last come the Blessed Three! Should we not know them anywhere? Those two, so poor, and yet so dignified, their pace not hasty, their eyes lowered, their heads turned towards the Boy of twelve, Who walks between them, each holding a Hand. They are listening to His words. Oh, that we could listen too! Hush, they are passing us—and we fall on our knees, for God is there.

Now they have reached the highest point in the road, and Mary and Joseph stand reverently on either side of Him as the Boy Messiah looks down upon Jerusalem. There beneath Him is Gethsemane. Yonder the Temple rises in all its majesty. To the left are the palaces of Herod and the High Priests. But His Eye rests on none of these things. The Temple hides from His view a lonely hill on the other side of the City and outside its walls. He moves a little to the right. Now His gaze is fixed. A smile lights up His Face and the tears trickle down His cheeks. He is looking upon Calvary.

See them going down the Mount on the other side, passing Gethsemane, crossing the brook Kedron and now climbing the steep ascent of the Temple Mount. They go up the marble steps that surround the Temple and through one of the five gates into the Court of the Gentiles. Here the noise is most disturbing, especially on the Eve of the Passover, for the oxen, sheep, and doves for the sacrifices are being sold as in a market, and the lowing of the cattle, the wrangling of merchants, and the din of many voices is heard on every side. Our Lord looks sadly around Him. He cannot bear to see His Father's House dishonoured like this. But the time has not yet come for Him to show His indignation, by driving out all these merchants, together with their merchandise. So He can only lift up His

Heart to His Father and offer Him Its love in reparation.

They have crossed the vast enclosure and are mounting the flight of steps to the Court of the Women. Here, for Mary's sake, they will stay instead of going further, as St. Joseph and our Lord could do, into the Court of Israel. Our Lady goes up into one of the raised galleries, and choosing a quiet spot from which she can see her Son in the Court below, kneels down to pray.

No need for her to strain her eyes like the other women to catch a distant sight of the golden roofs of the Jewish Holy of Holies. There below at Joseph's side is the true Holy of Holies, the Lord Who, according to the Prophet Aggeus, has come to His Temple, and filled this Second House with a glory greater than that of the First.

The Lambs are being led past Him on their way to the altar where they are to be slain. She knows the thoughts of His Heart. The Lamb of God Who is to take away the sins of the world is offering Himself to be slain. And though Simeon's sword is piercing her very soul, she joins her offering to His. She watches Him standing there with outstretched Arms, as the Jews were wont to pray. He is thinking of the Pasch to come, when in the midst of crowds such as are now thronging Jerusalem, He will hang on His Cross outside the walls, mocked, reviled, forsaken by all and rejected by the people He has come to save. And He offers Himself for it all. Men pass to and fro; the worshippers come and go: but no one notices Him. Only Mary and Joseph know that God is here present, and they adore Him with the profoundest adoration. St. Joseph kneels a little behind Him, that he may have Him before his eyes and learn from Him how to pray. See the composure, the reverence, the fervour with which our Blessed Saviour prays. Do you think that with God so near him, St. Joseph was distracted—that he looked about to see who came in and out? Oh, if we could remember when we are before the Tabernacle how near God is, how different our prayers would be!

In the evening the Holy Family eat the Paschal Supper together. During the rest of the festival—it lasts seven days—they are constantly in and out of the Temple; so glad to join in the services, Mary and Joseph so glad to have our Lord with them there. They are never tired of watching Him at prayer, and they unite their prayers with His.

The time has passed quickly, as happy times always do. And now they prepare to return home. The streets are thronged with people, for the caravans are leaving, and pilgrims have to seek out and join their own.

What bustle and confusion there is on the slopes outside the walls whilst the caravans are forming. Here is the one returning to Nazareth. The women are collecting the baggage, the men are taking down the tents, or lading or bringing up the beasts for the old people to mount. At last it starts, but the City gates have been left far behind before it gets into proper marching order. Our Lady sees the Child Jesus has not come with her, but children may go with father or mother, so she is not uneasy. He will make the journey so happy for St. Joseph, and she makes the sacrifice gladly. And St. Joseph is not uneasy either as he journeys home alone, is it not right that the Child should be with His Mother? Who else has any right to Him? And thus in their unselfishness they forget themselves and their own loss in the thought of each other's gain.

The caravans for Galilee started about mid-day, and will not halt till nightfall. As evening closes in, our Lady and St. Joseph look forward to the meeting which is to make up to them for the long lonely day. But oh, what do they feel when the meeting comes and they see that each is alone! What when they find that neither has seen anything of Jesus since they started! Where can He be? Why has He gone away?

Why has He dealt so with them?

They knew they were not worthy to have the care of Him for twelve years, but oh, why has He left them like this? Will the old days at Nazareth never come back? Will they ever see Him again? They go in and out among their kinsfolk and relations and the townsfolk from Nazareth, asking for tidings of Him. Every one is busy settling down for the night, and few have time to attend to them. Some pay no heed to them whatever. Others, touched a little by their distress, shout out their question in a rough, off-hand way. "Has anyone seen the carpenter's boy from Nazareth?—he is lost." And then they added: "It is a pity his parents did not take better care of him: he might well be lost in such a crowd." Everywhere the answer is the same. No one has seen Him. No one knows anything about Him. St. Joseph says to our Lady, "We cannot go back to the City tonight, but we will go the first thing in the morning." What a night it is for them both! Very early in the morning they are on their way back, and once more in Jerusalem they continue their search there. Three weary days they seek Him—now among the throngs that choke up the narrow streets, now in His Father's House, where those happy hours were spent with Him such a little while ago. See how patient they are, how resigned to God's Will, how kind to one another, each feeling the other's pain. And now it is the third day. Our Lady says to St. Joseph, "Suppose we try the Temple again." And they go there.

Under one of the colonnades in the Court of the Gentiles, they notice a group, such as used to gather round the doctors at the hour of teaching. They were accustomed, these Jewish Rabbis, to meet on Sabbath-days under the porticoes or in one of the lofty halls of the Temple to discuss difficult questions of the Law, the interpretations of the Prophets, the observance of ceremonies, and the like. Now that the whole world was expecting the Messiah, the signs by which He might be known were more diligently sought. These meetings also served as catechism classes for the children, as soon as they were ready for fuller religious instruction than they could get at home. At the age of five, a Jewish boy was taught certain Psalms and portions of the Law. He became what was called a *child of the Law*, that is, he was obliged to study the Law of God and learn what he was bound to as a Jew, just as a Catholic child is bound, when it comes to the use of reason, to study its Catechism and learn the practice of its religion. The Doctors used to have these children of the Law around them when they held their discussions, and they encouraged them to ask questions. There were many famous and holy men among the Doctors at this time, men who were held in reverence, not in Palestine only, but all over the world, wherever Jews were to be found. Coming up to the Holy City for the solemn feasts, and particularly for the Passover, all were anxious to see and hear these far-famed teachers, and the Sabbath-day discussions were attended by crowds of eager and attentive listeners.

Let us join the gathering to-day. A circle has been formed around a group of teachers and disciples. The teachers are seated on benches, the children are on the ground at their feet. All are listening, asking, and answering by turns, for all may speak. By the tones and gestures of all, you see at once that the discussion to-day is a very animated one. They are talking about Daniel's famous prophecy of Messiah's coming, and are calculating those mysterious weeks of years, some in one way, some in another. See that young man with the grave thoughtful face. His name is Nicodemus. He is a youth of a retiring, timid disposition, of few words, but much given to prayer. And his prayer is that the Messiah may come soon, and that he himself may be so happy as to be numbered among His disciples. You wonder if that venerable old man, a little to the left, can be holy

Simeon? No, it must be twelve years since that servant of God departed in peace. This is Hillel, the most revered of all the Jewish Doctors. He is nearly a hundred years old. But next to him is old Simeon's son, Gamaliel, "a Pharisee and Doctor of the Law, respected by all the people." The child at his feet, on whose shoulder his hand rests so lovingly, is little Saul of Tarsus, the son of a Pharisee. His home is a long way off. But his parents have sent him here to Jerusalem, and entrusted him to the care of Gamaliel to be instructed in the Law, for he is to be a Pharisee like his father.

But listen, Gamaliel is speaking. He shows that the time is come, and that at any moment the Messiah may be expected. Some differ from him, and the disputants are getting warm, when a child's voice is heard. In an instant all eyes are turned to a Boy, Who has been sitting among His companions, listening quietly to the arguments and contradictions of the doctors. He cannot be more than twelve, and this is probably His first appearance here as a child of the Law. There is a singular beauty and attractiveness about Him—the glance of His Eye, the tone of His Voice, His extreme gentleness and sweetness have already drawn to Him the hearts of His little companions, who look at Him with a wondering admiration. And now His first words to the Doctors have stopped the debate and attracted every eye to Him. He asks a question of one of them, and in reply to it asks another and another— not putting Himself forward, not as if He were teaching, not showing up their mistakes. There is nothing about Him that is not perfectly becoming in a child of twelve. He hears what they have to say, and then with marvellous skill clears up their difficulty, sets their minds right, and explains when He seems to be seeking instruction.

Each time He speaks the silence around is breathless. Little Saul there on the pavement forgets his play, and fixes his eyes full on that beautiful boyish Face. Gamaliel and all that throng of learned men, the teachers of Israel, gaze and listen in mute astonishment. Who is this Child? Where has He learned this wonderful wisdom, this familiarity with the Law and the Prophets? Now He pauses and waits for them to speak. But they only bring forward new questions to draw Him out again—it is so delightful to hear Him. Surely never child spoke as this Child! And not only has He enlightened their minds, but His words have stirred their hearts strangely and given them deep thoughts to ponder.

There is no more discussion to-day. The assembly breaks up in silence. A few remain behind. They gaze intently upon Him, but do not speak. Parents come up and claim their children. Will no one claim this wonderful Child! Oh, look at her as she comes forward with outstretched arms—His Mother, as all may see! He is too like her not to be hers—every feature of her face is His—"Hail, full of grace, *the Lord is with thee.*" "Weeping she hath wept in the night, and her tears are on her cheeks"—but see that smile now—"Hail, full of grace, *the Lord is with thee!*"

Look at the meeting—the arm thrown lovingly round her neck, the hand stretched out to St. Joseph. Hear her tender complaint: "Son, why hast Thou done so to us, behold Thy father and I have sought Thee sorrowing?" It is not a reproach. She knows Who He is, that He is free to do as He wills—that He is God. But she knows too that He is her Child and that He has given her a mother's rights over Him. She knows how they live at Nazareth together. She knows what she may say, and so she pleads with Him as a mother would plead, and tells Him of her pain: "Son, why hast Thou done so to us?" He looks into her face and smiles, and then He puts one hand into hers and the other into St. Joseph's, and as they go home together He tells them *why*.

### The Child Jesus in the Temple

"And all that heard Him were astonished at His wisdom and His answers."
(Luke 2:47)

Look at them on the road. On and on they go, with Him between them, so comforted, so happy. And at last their hilly Nazareth rises before them. And they are home again. And the peaceful life in the Holy House goes on just as before, and just as before *He is subject to them.*

# XII

# Nazareth Again
# The Hidden Life

When St. Bernard had given his monks a very long sermon one day, he used to make amends by promising them a very short one the next. We were sadly too long yesterday, so to-day we will be short.

The Holy Pilgrims had just got home when we left them. How fast our Lady and St. Joseph held their Divine Child on the way, and how He made up to them by the joy of His Blessed Presence and His sweet words for the pain of the long desolate journey on that road the day before! The Curé of Ars says that when the soul reaches Heaven, it will cry out in its joy: "My God, I have found You. I hold You fast. You shall never escape from me again—never—never." This was the cry of Mary's heart and of St. Joseph's now. He explained to them on the way home why He had left them so, and what He had meant in the Temple by His Father's business.

During those three days in Jerusalem our Lord's Heart was filled with the keenest pain at the pain of His Blessed Parents. It could not have been otherwise, for He was a *perfect* Child and loved them most tenderly. Why then did He cause them this sorrow, when He could so easily have prevented it? He could have told them that His Father's business would keep Him in Jerusalem for three days. And so they would have made their arrangements to stay in the City and wait for Him. But He had His own wise reasons for not telling them beforehand what He was going to do.

We are told that the chief virtues He came to teach us are meekness, humility, and obedience. Obedience He cared for so much, that He spent full thirty years in teaching it. But He had all of us in His mind during His earthly Life, and had to set an example to all in the different circumstances in which we find ourselves. He knew that some would be called in a very special way to be His companions and helpers in His Divine work of saving souls, and to obey this call would have to leave all other things and persons, even those dearest to them. This would be hard, so hard that they would need His Divine example to encourage them. And therefore in this mystery of the three days' loss He shows them how to put their Father's business before anything else. If they have to give pain to those nearest and dearest to them, He shows them how to bear bravely the keenness of such pain, as He did when He left His Mother and St. Joseph to seek Him sorrowing.

All the while He was teaching in the Temple and astonishing the Doctors by His wisdom and His answers, His Heart was wrung with pain. He was following His Blessed Parents in their search, pitying them, supporting them, giving them splendid graces to increase their merit, but leaving them all that time in such terrible distress. His Father's business—this was the reason of it all. This was the work of His Life. This was to come before everything else. And it was part of that business to give a lesson of detachment here. But the lesson given, how gladly He returns to His Life of obedience and subjection. His Blessed Mother and St. Joseph find Him just the same as before, as gentle, as affectionate, as reverent.

Reverence to parents is a virtue that seems to have gone out of fashion nowadays. Boys and girls think it smart to treat their

## The Fourth Commandment

"Honour thy father and thy mother." (Exodus 20:12)

parents as if they were their equals. Nay, some treat them as if they were servants—valets, whose only business in life was to honour and obey their children, slave for them, and provide for their comfort and amusement. They speak to them in a short, off-hand way, even before strangers, as if this were something to show off and be proud of. They will stand nothing in the shape of a remonstrance, much less of a reproof. Am I at all like this? How do I treat my parents? Do I try to save them trouble? Do I remember that besides love I owe them honour and obedience? Am I sorry when I have pained them? Or do I think it grand to treat them roughly and rudely, to show myself indifferent to their feelings and wishes? In tone, or word, or manner, am I troublesome, unruly or sullen, disrespectful or disobliging? If so, then I am very unlike the Child Jesus. Oh, if we could have seen His behaviour to His Blessed Mother and St. Joseph, how charmed we should have been!

Our Lord stayed behind in Jerusalem for another reason—to go to catechism. If there is a place near and dear to His Heart, it is the school; if there is a work that interests Him, it is the work that goes on there. So He went to the Temple at the hour of teaching and sat among the children and the Doctors, that He might bless the schools and the catechism classes of His Church to the end of the world. There we have to go to learn our religion—what we must do to save our souls. There He is still to be found among the children, for He has promised that where two or three are gathered together in His Name, He will be in the midst of them. Think how happy those children were, who, because they were present in that Jewish class, deserved to have the Holy Child for their companion. Yet I am happier than they were. Do I love my catechism? Do I learn it well and try to understand it, and ask for an explanation when I am puzzled? Or do I learn it just because I *have* to learn it, and sit on the bench at catechism, thinking of something else, and wishing the time were over? I must not do this, and if I have done it, I must mend now. This time of instruction is very precious; if I lose it, it will never come again, and I shall feel the loss all my life long. I can never again learn my religion as I can learn it now. Now is the time when I must be about my Father's business. What is the business of my Heavenly Father, but that I learn to know Him, love Him and serve Him, and so prepare myself to be happy with Him for ever.

The Saints tell us that our Lord had another reason still for allowing His Blessed Mother and St. Joseph to seek Him so painfully during those three days. It was to teach us by their example how we too are to seek Him, when we think we have lost Him. Not by mortal sin—we will hope there is no question of that—but in some misty way that we cannot quite make out.

There are times when everything seems wrong with us. We are fretful and discontented, or lazy, bothered with temptations of many kinds, and distracted in our prayers. We seem to have lost our Lord, and, unlike our Lady and St. Joseph, we have no heart to go and seek Him. Prayer is hard, and we think the time we have to give to it will never come to an end. And it is no good as far as we can see. Nothing comes of it. We are no better. Our Lord seems a very long way off, even when we kneel near the Tabernacle where we know He is really present, even when we try to say our prayers well. We can find nothing to say to Him, our hearts are so cold and dry. And He has nothing to say to us either. Now what are we to do when we feel like this? It is very important we should know, for it may be that we feel like this even now when we are preparing for our First Communion.

The first thing we should do is to look into our hearts and see if there is any sin that is keeping Jesus away from us. If there is any grievous sin, of course we shall know it at once. That would banish Him from our hearts altogether, and we must get rid of it as soon as possible by contrition and a good Confession. But there may be venial sins—carelessness in God's service, that is, in our prayers and in our daily duties.

Next let us see if God is asking something of us that we will not give Him. There may be some fault He wants us to correct, and we will not try, some sacrifice He has been asking a long time—a little thing perhaps, but we cannot bring ourselves to part with it. If this is so, there is only one thing for us to do—we must be brave and generous and give Him all He wants. There is no other way of finding Him and being happy in His company.

But supposing we cannot find anything like this in our hearts, and still they are dark and sad. Our Lord seems to have gone away and we do not know why. We are trying to correct our faults—our chief fault especially. We really do want to please Him, but it is no use trying. He seems to be far away and to leave us to ourselves. What are we to do then? This—we are not to lose heart one bit. We are to remember that His own Blessed Mother and St. Joseph were once seeking Him in darkness and in sorrow. He let it be so that she who was to be the Refuge of Sinners might know what it is to lose Jesus, and be able to pity all who lose Him, whether by sin or by darkness, and may help them to find Him once again. We are to remember too that our *feelings* do not count in the service of God, but that our *will* does. In spite of hard, dry prayers, of temptations and difficulties, of falls even, we are really seeking God and pleasing Him, if we try to do our best; to say our prayers as well as we can; to be kind to others even when we feel cross with everybody and with ourselves most of all; to rise at once when we fall and *not to be discouraged.* If we persevere in seeking Jesus like this, we shall find Him at last and be rewarded as Mary and Joseph were.

Two things only the Holy Scripture tells us about the Childhood of our Blessed Saviour: that He was subject to

His Parents, and that He advanced in wisdom and age and grace with God and men. It was from our Lady that St. Luke learned those details of our Lord's Birth and Childhood, which he has preserved for us in his beautiful Gospel. She pondered in her Immaculate Heart all that happened to her Son, and she told St. Luke the things she noticed specially. What was it that struck her most about the Hidden Life at Nazareth? This, that He was subject to them, and that as He grew in age He advanced in wisdom and grace before God and men. Though she saw Him perfect from the first, He seemed to grow in wisdom, the Scripture word for goodness, and in grace. At ten years old He was so holy that she could not imagine holiness like that being surpassed. Yet in another year fresh beauty had unfolded itself, and He seemed holier than before, more affectionate, more lovable.

"Advanced in grace before God *and men.*" Notice these last words. If we are really growing in God's sight, others will see it. Am I growing more obedient, more gentle, more truthful? Could my parents and those who see most of me say that there is an improvement within the last year—since I began to prepare for my First Communion? Could they say that this fault and that is being gradually corrected? It was to be my example that the Holy Child seemed to advance in wisdom and in grace, so that each day His Blessed Mother and St. Joseph loved Him more. I will try to be like Him, that He and His Blessed Mother and my good Angel may love me more.

A mother's eye is quick to notice any change in her child. When her boy comes home from college she is the first to exclaim, "How well he looks, and *how he has grown!*" Does my Blessed Mother see that all is well with me in my true life, the life of my soul this last year—since I began to think of my First Communion? Can she lay her hand on my head and say, with a smile, "My child, how you have grown!"—in kindness, in obedience, in resolution to overcome your predominant fault—"how you have grown!"

We have seen pictures of the interior of St. Joseph's shop—our Lord as a Child standing beside a plank, one knee resting on it to steady it on the trestle, in His Hand a saw with which He is cutting the plank in two. His life at Nazareth was very hard. He was a poor man's Child, and as a poor man's Child there was hard work for Him as well as for His parents. As He grew older it became harder. He was St. Joseph's assistant now, learning from him how to do the village carpentry, to make yokes and ploughs and the rough cottage furniture, learning to do it all *in St. Joseph's way*. It was a rude unskilful way we may be sure, and the clumsiest joiner nowadays would turn out more shapely work. Our Lord might well have been St. Joseph's teacher, and shown him how to do better. But that was not what He wanted. He was there in the shop to humble Himself, to be obedient, and thus to teach us something far more important than good carpentry. What He wanted was not to do the work in the best way possible, but to do it *as He was told*.

The years came and went, and our Lord and His foster-father worked on together, our Lord gradually and skilfully taking all the heavy labour for His share as age began to tell on St. Joseph and hard work became too much for him. After a while the old man was missed from his place in the workshop, and a little later came that holy and blessed death in the arms of his foster-Son. There he lay, his head pillowed on the Breast of Jesus; his failing eyes fixed on the Face of Jesus; his ears still drinking in the words of Jesus; his hands fast clasped in Mary's, and wet with her tears. One moment, and our Lord is gently preparing him for death, making with him the last acts—faith and hope and charity and resignation. Another moment, and He has spoken as Judge: "Well done, good and faithful servant," and the soul of St. Joseph is speeding to Limbo with good tidings of deliverance close at hand for the Holy Prisoners there.

> O Mary, when I come to die,
> Be thou, thy spouse, and Jesus nigh;
> When mute before the Judge I stand,
> My holy shield be Mary's hand.

And now our Lord becomes the Carpenter of Nazareth. Things were ordered at His shop in a rough matter-of-fact way. He was to make such and such a thing for so much: broken benches and carts were to be fetched and mended, and they must be done quickly, for his employers could not wait. He might be seen here and there, going where He was called for, doing such repairs as were needed in the little homes of that little place. It was work all day, all through the hot days of that sultry land. And when at last the work was carried home, what was the reward? Many and many a time the reward of the poor workman, discontent and blame. He had not done what was wanted, or He had been too slow, and so the modest pay He asked was put grudgingly into the Divine Hand.

Let us take our stand by the little cottage some morning, quite early, as the sun is rising. The door opens, and a young man comes out, There is something striking about Him, though He is dressed like a poor working man. His Face is sunburnt, and His Hands are hard and horny. Across His Shoulder is slung His bag of tools. He walks briskly along till He comes to a building in course of erection. He stops, takes down His tools, and presently we see Him at work. It is a floor that has to be laid down; the measurements have to be taken accurately; the saw and the chisel, the plane and the hammer, have to be used. He works diligently hour after hour, going home for His meals and coming back again. After a while the foreman comes round to look at His work, and though all has been done so carefully, so perfectly, he finds fault with it. So it is taken to pieces and done over again, done carefully and perfectly over again.

We look into the face of this young workman. There is something in it and in His recollected air that marks Him as a Man of God. But to be told suddenly—*that is God;* to be told suddenly—that this is the Messiah Whom the whole world is expecting—that here is the Mind of God, in which are all the treasures of wisdom—that this is the great Teacher of men, and this is the way He gives His first lesson!

Oh, is not the Hidden Life wonderful; in one sense the most wonderful part of the Three-and-Thirty Years! The Infancy is wonderful; the Passion is wonderful. But there were miracles in Bethlehem and miracles on Calvary. There were Angels singing "Glory be to God" when He was born; there were shepherds coming to adore Him, and holy Simeon and Anna, and the Magi from the East. And at His Death the sun was darkened, and the veil of the Temple was rent, and the earth quaked and the dead arose. His own world spoke for Him and proclaimed Him to be its Creator. But what was there at Nazareth? There He was the Hidden God indeed, and that for Thirty Years.

Dearest Lord, and it might have been so different. But You did not want it to be different. To be like us in all things—this is what You wanted all Your Life through. And King of Heaven though You are, You take so naturally to your hard life on earth. Not like a prince in disguise, betraying himself by his unhandiness at rough and common work, not doing it by way of condescension. But all so simply and naturally; just like one of us, who have to take things as they come; just like an elder brother taking the hardest and heaviest parts of the work for his share, to spare the younger and the weaker ones. O Lord and Master, how can we ever thank You for coming among us like this? I should love to have seen Your Holy Home. I offer

You my home. Bless it for the sake of dear Nazareth, and bless all who are in it for Mary and Joseph's sake. In a few days You will be coming into my heart. It will remind You of Your little dark room at Nazareth. Love it then and fill it with the peace and happiness Your Presence brought to Your Holy Home.

# XIII

## The School of Christ

We know what graces come to us from the Blessed Sacrament during the few minutes of Exposition. At Nazareth it was Exposition all day long, and that for Thirty Years. Think then how Mary's sinless soul, which had unfolded its beauties day by day like a flower before the sun, must have shrunk from the thought of parting with her Son. The Thirty Years had gone so fast. Could it be that the end had come and He must leave her to go out into the rough, cold world? She knew His Heart so well. It was so gentle and tender, so delicate, so devoted. Whatever was rough or coarse made It thrill with pain—how It would suffer from the rudeness of men! How It would shrink when It came near to sin! And she would not be there with her love and her reparation. And yet she was content, and more than content, that He should go. His Heart was eager, and Mary's heart was eager too. See them talking together during those last days of Nazareth. Our Lord told her all He was to do and all He was to suffer; how He was to gather disciples around Him, to preach and to teach and to die upon the Cross, And Mary said, "Behold the handmaid of the Lord; be it done, O Lord, according to Thy word."

We all know what it is to see something coming which we dread very much. The days and the hours are counted between us and our trouble. It is our first thought when we wake in the morning and our last when we go to bed at night. We can feel then for our Lady in the pain she felt at the coming separation from her Son. What will Nazareth be without Jesus? A summer's day when the sun shines out in the cloudless heavens and the birds sing, and the fields are bright with flowers—and a winter's night when the snow falls fast and the wind howls dismally over the desolate country—these are different indeed, but less different than Nazareth as it has been in the past, and Nazareth as it will be now, when He has gone away.

The last month came, the last week, the last day with Him. There was their last meal together, their last prayer side by side. And now He stands at the door to bid her farewell. See the parting between the Mother and the Son. There is no begging of Him not to leave her, no lingering in the leave-taking. The last embrace—the last look—their hearts are too full for words. See our Lord's Face, so full of suffering, of pity for His Mother, and yet so calm. And Mary, losing her very life in losing Jesus, yet giving Him up gladly for us all. See her trying to hide her sorrow that she may not add to His—trying to smile through the tears that not her bravest effort can keep back.

She watches Him as He goes down the little steep street. Now He has come to the turn in the road. He is gone, and Mary is alone. She goes back into the house. She looks around. The most wonderful relics are on every side. There in the corner are His tools brought from the shop last night and laid together in the basket. She takes them out reverently and kisses them. And now her tears fall fast. The handles are smoothed and polished by the constant touch of the Divine Hands. There is the bench on which He sat; the rough porringer His Lips have touched so often; the place on the ground where for years He took His rest at night. Here and there are bits of cottage furniture made or mended by Him. Everything speaks to her of the Divine Presence that was here so long and is gone, never to return. Look into that dear heart of hers, so sad and yet so brave. Oh, when God's Will seems hard and everything around us looks dull and weary, let us think of our Mother at Nazareth in that hour when her Son went away and left her all alone.

> O Mary! when we think of thee,
> Our hearts grow light as light can be:
> For thou hast felt as we have felt,
> And thou hast knelt as we have knelt;
> And so it is—that utterly,
> Mother of God, we trust in thee!

We should like to follow our Lord down to the ford near Jericho where, amid a crowd of sinners, He was baptised by St. John. To see Him afterwards going far away into a lonely desert, where for forty days He fasted, and prayed, and was tempted by the devil. But we must hasten on to the time when He came out of His hiding-place and showed Himself to men. Now at last the Divine Lips, silent so many years, began to teach. We have seen that He was really teaching from the first—teaching by example. But now He is going to teach by His sacred words, to open His School and to call together His first scholars. How interesting to us is the opening of this School in which we are all to take our places by-and-bye.

"From that time," says St. Matthew, "Jesus began to preach." "He taught in their synagogues," says St. Luke, "and was extolled by all...And the fame of Him went out through the whole country." Gradually a little band of disciples, or "learners," gathered round Him, and He chose from among them twelve whom He called Apostles. He was to be *their* Master in quite a special way. They were to be with him always—His private pupils, as it were. They were to be trained by Him carefully. They were to be taught plainly what was said to others in parables. They were to know the secrets of His Heart.

We must see how He drew them to Himself, and how He trained them. But first of all we will see where they lived and what kind of men they were, when our Blessed Saviour called them.

Get out the map of Palestine and find to the north-east the deep basin into which the Jordan empties itself on its way south. This is called the Sea of Galilee, the Sea of Tiberias, and the Lake of Genesareth. Galilee has no need to envy Judea in the south. For if Judea has Bethlehem and the Temple, Galilee has Nazareth and the Lake of Genesareth. Nowhere in the world has there been a spot more beautiful and more blessed than this dear little inland sea.

Let us climb one of the heights that surround it, and looking down, see what our Lord saw many a time. The Plain of Genesareth, like a beautiful garden, borders it on every side. Bethsaida, Capharnaum, and many other towns lie along the western shore; and close to the Lake are the cottages of the fishermen dotted all about. Waving cornfields and clusters of oleanders come down almost to the water's edge, and on every side the crimson flower of the laurel-rose breaks in upon the line of soft white sand. The Lake is about thirteen miles in length and ten in width. Its waters teem with fish, and sparkle with the sails of many boats, some laden with Eastern merchandise, some carrying parties of pleasure, and some bringing home the fruit of the night's fishing. Solemn mountains, with bleak, bare peaks, rise in the distance and frame in this beautiful scene.

But it is not its beauty that makes us love it as we do. It is dear to us because every line of it speaks to us of Jesus. Over its waves He passed to go to the help of His disciples in the dark, stormy night. Here is the shingly beach where He so often walked with them, and there the little creek where He taught the people from Peter's boat. Up on the rising ground are the rich harvest fields where He walked with the Twelve on the Sabbath-day; and higher still the lonely mountains where He so often spent the nights in prayer. Bethsaida to the north was the home of Peter and Andrew, of Philip and James, and John.

In its little bay was a smooth strand on which they used to bring up their boats and sit and mend their nets, or hang them out to dry. A little further south, Matthew had his toll-gatherer's office on the shore. Close by was Capharnaum, where our Lord worked so many miracles that it was called His "own City." Here was the synagogue built by the good Centurion, whose servant our Lord healed. And here too Jairus lived. Nazareth is about fourteen miles away to the south-west, and near it is Cana, the scene of our Lord's first miracle, and Naim, where He raised to life the widow's son. To the south-east of the Lake is Mount Thabor, where He was transfigured; and on the east are the lonely mountains and the grassy plain, where He first multiplied the loaves of bread.

How interesting it would be to know all about our Lord's dear Apostles, "The Twelve," as St. Mark calls them, their life before our Lord called them, and their daily life with Him. They were poor fishermen, most of them, leading lonely, laborious lives, and knowing little or nothing beyond their trade. The best hours and the likeliest spots for fishing, how to mend their nets and manage their boats in the sudden storms that swept over their beautiful Lake, this they knew and this was about all. But our Lord loves simple hearts like theirs, and He chose them, and not the great and learned, to be the teachers of the world. One by one He chose them, and told them to leave all they had—parents, wife, children, and their little homes by the Lake, and take Him, and the share He would give them in His work, in place of all. They were to leave off fishing in the Sea of Galilee to become fishers of men.

St. Andrew, who was the first called, seems to have been a disciple of St. John the Baptist. St. John loved our Lord dearly. His one desire was to prepare souls for Him and to hand over his own disciples to Him. Seeing Him pass by, the day after His Baptism, he said to Andrew and another disciple, probably John,

## The First Disciples

"And Jesus said to them: Come after Me, and I will make you to become fishers of men. And immediately, leaving their nets, they followed Him."
(Mark 1:17, 18)

the son of Zebedee, who were with him, "Behold the Lamb of God." At those words the two disciples left their master and timidly followed our Lord. He turned round and, seeing them waiting, as it were, for an invitation, said sweetly, "What seek ye?" And they answered, "Rabbi, where dwellest Thou?" He said to them, "Come and see." They came and saw where He abode and they stayed with Him that day, and it appears the following night. From what he saw and heard during that day and night, Andrew believed firmly that our Lord was the Promised Redeemer. Full of joy, he went to his brother Simon and said, "We have found the Messiah." And he brought him to Jesus.

Look at our Lord seeing Simon coming to Him, seeing for the first time His Vicar upon earth, the rock on which He was to build His Church. St. John, who describes the scene for us in his Gospel, and who seems to have been present, says: "And Jesus looking upon him said, 'Thou art Simon, the son of Jona; thou shalt be called Cephas,' which is interpreted Peter." Peter in Hebrew and in several other languages means a rock. It is the same then as if our Lord had said in English: "Thou art a rock and upon this rock." In Latin and in French it runs so: *Tu es Petrus et super hanc petram—Tu es Pierre et sur cette pierre.* It is a pity we cannot give the force of our Lord's words in our English translation.

The Apostles must have been very much struck by the way in which our Lord spoke to St. Peter on first seeing him. They would have been more struck still, they would have been perfectly amazed, to hear there would be Christians unable to see in the Gospels any signs of our Lord's preference for St. Peter and of his having been set over the rest of the Apostles. If anything was clear to them, it was the high place Peter held in his Master's sight, and the authority that was given to him. They would have thought it absurd for any Church to pretend to be the one founded by Christ that could not point to Peter as its head under Him. In their lists of the Apostles the Evangelists always name him first. St. Matthew says: "The names of the twelve Apostles are these, the first Simon, who is called Peter." When our Lord asked them a question, they waited for Peter to speak first and left him to speak for them all. They noticed that our Lord chose to teach the people from Peter's boat; that to him specially the Keys of Heaven were given; and that he was commanded to confirm the faith of all.

The day after He had called St. Peter to follow Him, our Lord went forth into Galilee, says St. John, "and He findeth Philip, And Jesus saith to him: Follow Me!" Philip had a friend called Nathaniel, and he brought him to Jesus. This Nathaniel is supposed to be the same as St. Bartholomew. He was so simple and innocent that our Lord, seeing him coming, exclaimed: "Behold an Israelite indeed in whom there is no guile." Notice how eager the Apostles are to bring all their friends to know and love our Lord. In their lists of the Apostles, the Evangelists always put these two friends together—"Philip and Bartholomew."

Walking by the Sea of Galilee, our Lord saw two brothers, James and John, sons of Zebedee, a fisherman. They were in a boat with their father, mending their nets, and He called them; and they immediately left their nets and their father and followed Him. The old man seems to have been quite willing to give them up to our Lord's service, and so was their mother, Salome.

Two more brothers were called by our Lord—St. Jude and St. James, surnamed the Less, either on account of his stature, or his youth, or because he was called later than the other St. James.

Most of the Apostles were fishermen, but Matthew the Publican was rich. The Publicans were hated and despised by the Jews, partly because they collected the taxes for the Romans, and partly because they were often covetous and unjust. Matthew was sitting one day in his office gathering the customs of goods that came by the Lake of Genesareth, when Jesus passed by. Our Lord looked at him. "Follow Me," was all He said. And without a moment's hesitation, the rich man rose up, pushed aside his heaps of gold, and taking nothing with him, went out to where our Lord was waiting for him. He knew our Blessed Saviour was poor and had not where to lay His head. But that word was enough. He would gladly be poor too, and in need of all things, if only he might be with Him.

How Thomas was called, and Simon, surnamed the Canaanean, we are not told.

One more was called. How sad it makes us to think of that call. Judas was once good and innocent, and grand graces were given him. He too gave up all he had to follow Jesus, but an evil passion, which he took no pains to correct, strengthened little by little, and—our Lord tells us what the end was: "It would have been better for him if he had never been born."

Judas was not the only one of the Twelve who had to overcome himself. They all had their faults, and some of them had big faults.

Peter was eager and generous, ready to do and dare everything for his Master. But he trusted too much in himself. He thought his love of our Lord was strong enough to bear any trial or temptation, that it was stronger than the love of all the rest. This made him neglect warning, neglect prayer, neglect to avoid the occasions of sin, and he fell into grievous sin. But how quickly he rose again, how bitterly he repented, how certain he was that his Master would forgive him and treat Him just as before! Our Lord loved that generous, trusting soul.

James and John, two favourites, were Boanerges,[1] "Sons of Thunder"—which shows us, by the way, that our Lord can love us dearly in spite of our faults. Think of the gentle St. John

---

1 See Mark 3:17. This was a nickname given them by Jesus due to their impetuousness.

having ever been a thunderer!

He and his brother could not bear to see our Lord ill-treated and dishonoured. This zeal was all well enough and quite right. But there are two ways of showing zeal—a right way and a wrong way, and theirs was the wrong way. Because the Samaritans would not let our Lord pass through their city, they wanted to call down fire from heaven to burn them all up. They wanted to set every one to rights.

The same fault is found in our Lord's disciples nowadays, and there are plenty of sons and daughters of thunder outside the Holy Land. We see, then, that they need not despair. Nay, St. Ignatius goes so far as to say that God's best servants are made out of these hot, hasty natures, when they set to work vigorously to conquer themselves. They are like volcanic soil, which is very fertile and yields rich harvests when it is quieted down and well tilled. Of course they must try, and try hard—grace will not do all. We must never excuse our violent words and behaviour by saying we could not help ourselves; we lost control over our feelings. We should not have lost it, that is all. If we drop the reins, of course the horses will run away with us. The reins are in our hands always, but they need a firm grasp at times. With God's help we are always strong enough to hold our feelings in check—with God's help, mind, which is to be had by asking for it.

The Boanerges had another fault—they wanted to be first always. They once got their mother to ask our Lord to let them sit one on His right Hand, the other on His left in His Kingdom. When the other Apostles heard this, "they were filled with indignation against the two brothers," says St. Matthew. This fault of wanting to be first, our Lord had to correct in all His Apostles.

One day, during the time of His public preaching, He took them with Him to Capharnaum. As they walked behind Him, they began to dispute among themselves which of them was the greatest, the cleverest, the favourite. He said nothing till they came to the house where they were going. Then, calling them round Him, He asked what they were talking about on the road. "But they held their peace," says St. Mark, "for in the way, they had disputed which of them should be the greatest." They did not think He had been listening, and they were ashamed of themselves—ashamed that Apostles should be caught in such silly talk.

This was the way our Lord reproved them. He took a little child and set him in the midst, and told them that unless they conquered their pride and became humble like that little child they would never get into the Kingdom of Heaven at all. They listened; they were sorry; but they were not cured yet. Even at the Last Supper, when their hearts were full of sorrow because our Lord had said one of them would betray Him, even then they began again the old quarrel, which of them was the greatest.

Before going on, I cannot help telling you that our little friend Urban was immensely interested in the Apostles. He loved them all, but St. John was the favourite. He always listened very attentively when St. John spoke, and he was put out when St. Peter, taking the lead, spoke for the rest. When he heard the Apostles telling our Lord that some people said He was John the Baptist, and others Elias, or Jeremias or one of the Prophets, and our Lord answered, "But Whom do you say that I am?" he thought St. John would be sure to answer. But he was disappointed. Simon Peter answered and said, "Thou art Christ, the Son of the living God." "Oh dear," he said, impatiently, "always Peter; why can't he give the others a chance?"

Thomas was inclined to be stubborn and contradictory. When he had once said a thing he kept to it, even when he was clearly in the wrong. He thought himself wiser than others.

THE LITTLE CHILD AND THE TWELVE

"Whosoever shall humble himself as this little child, he is the greater in the kingdom of Heaven."
(St. Matt. xviii. 4.)

He thought others were silly because they did not think as he did. He called the Resurrection an "idle tale," because he did not happen to believe it. Because he was vexed that he had not been with the rest when our Lord came, and had missed seeing Him, he would not believe that the others had seen Him. He would have further proofs and his own proofs. He kept apart from the rest, and was moody and discontented during a whole week. And all because he would not give up his own way of thinking and own himself to have been in the wrong.

Those dear, rough, warm-hearted Apostles—how our Lord loved them, in spite of their failings! He knew them all, knew them better than they knew themselves. He loved each one—Peter, brave and generous, born to rule, always coming forward, always taking the lead; John, gentle and lovable; James, retiring and quiet; Thomas, slow, but fervent and devoted. He dealt with each one as the needs of that one required. Peter got the hardest words and rebukes, because he could bear most, and our Lord was not afraid to speak plainly to him. Peter never sulked or got discouraged.

Our Lord's Apostles were, you see, very different characters. They had plenty of faults, just as we have, and yet they were going to be prepared for their First Communion, as we are. It will help us to see what our Lord did to prepare them, and what He expects of them in return. He would not do all; they had to *prepare themselves* just as we have. But He helped them. He gently pointed out their faults, and taught them to study their own natural character in order to mend what was amiss. Notice that He helped them in the way in which some of us do not like to be helped at all!

Our Lord showed no surprise at any faults, however ugly. All He wanted was that His scholars should take well what He said, should take themselves in hand and work with Him to bring themselves into shape. And this is all He wants of His scholars *now*. So you see the study of our Lord's School is a real help to us in our preparation for Holy Communion.

In the Holy Gospels we notice the faults of the Twelve coming out again and again—hot temper, selfishness, and little jealousies, grumbling and sullenness and obstinacy. It is a good thing when our faults come out, because then we can see and cure them. As long as they lie hidden, there is no chance of a cure. Doctors like to see a rash come out well all over the patient's face, though we think it looks frightful. They are afraid of diseases that never appear outwardly, because they know there is all the more mischief working within. So it is with us. There are some whose faults are all on the surface. They are so much on the surface that they are very visible. But their hearts are good and generous, and the outside ugliness will disappear in time. With others the harm is all inside; it does not come out. They look all right. They seem to be honest and truthful and industrious and pious. And all the while God, Who sees the heart, knows they are nothing of the sort. They do not get into trouble like the others, because their smooth faces and their sleek ways deceive. But a day comes when they are found out, and the sooner that day comes for them the better. With it comes their chance of being corrected and of correcting themselves.

So it was with the Twelve. Our Lord's rebukes and warnings gradually told upon them, because they were so well taken. They knew themselves to be full of faults, and they did not mind their faults being shown up even before the rest. They all loved their Master dearly and trusted Him thoroughly—all but one. Whilst the rest loved to be near our Lord; to be spoken to by Him, even when He spoke to correct; were at their ease with Him; took to Him their questions and their difficulties; woke Him up when they were in danger, trusted themselves to Him always—one kept aloof, one did not like to meet His Eye, to be alone with Him, to be noticed by Him. We never hear of Judas putting questions or difficulties like the rest. Grumbling—oh yes, when Mary Magdalen deprived his pilfering fingers of the money her costly ointment might have brought him. But answering a question when our Lord was instructing them all—joining in the conversation when He spoke to them of heavenly things—no.

It is not likely that Judas was bad when our Lord called him to be an Apostle. But, little by little, a fault small at first, but dangerous because uncorrected, got a mastery over him. He did not take it to our Lord. He did not ask Him for His help to overcome it. He stole a little at first; then more and more. Often and often our Lord must have warned him and reproved him gently. But he did not try to mend, and by degrees he came not to care for his Master's reproofs; not to care for wounding the Sacred Heart, not to care for anything or any one but himself and the money that he thought would make him happy. What the end was we all know.

Our Lord's training of the Twelve was very gentle and patient. We might have thought rebukes would have been incessant, so that it would be hard to live in His company. But it was not so. He bore with them, and though He reproved them, they were at their ease with Him. They felt He reproved them because He loved them. And His reproofs were sweetened by a Divine compassion and a wonderful patience. He was among them as one of themselves.

Those who have lived with Saints have been afraid to appear before them with sin on their souls, because God has often shown to His Saints the secrets of hearts. But our Lord's Apostles were not afraid of Him. Though they knew He read their hearts, they were not uncomfortable in His Presence. They knew Him and loved Him as the best of Masters and the truest of Friends. After three years in His School, hearing His instructions, living in His company, seeing His example, they were far from perfect. Yet He did not lose patience with them. He forgave them again and again, helped them in their efforts to do better, and encouraged them to try and try again when they failed.

And see how they repaid His teaching. Except that poor Judas, for whom He could do nothing, who would not be taught nor helped, all the rest came in the end to be what He wanted them to be, and one and all laid down their lives for Him at last. From their example we see that in our very faults there is something which may be turned to good.

When Peter had learned humility by his fall, he was ready for all things, as he said at the Last Supper, and he did indeed follow his Master to prison and to death. And the Boanerges? Again and again our Lord had to find fault with those hot tempers and that hasty speech of theirs. They were sorry each time, and told Him they would try and do better. And see what they became. St. John, by leaning on the Sacred Heart, learned to love all whom the Sacred Heart loves, and to be tender and patient with all. His Epistles are so loving that some foolish people say they could never have been written by the "Son of Thunder." Yet the thunder did not go altogether. It was kept under control, but we hear it whenever he speaks of heresy or of those who do not love our Blessed Lord. So that you see, instead of being a hindrance, his naturally fiery character helped him to serve God. He and his brother had once put their mother up to ask for the first place near our Lord. This was pride. But it was love too. And though our Lord gently reproved the pride, He rewarded the love. John alone of all the Apostles stood with His Mother beside the Cross; and James, who wanted the first place in the Kingdom, was the first of the Twelve to lay down his life for his Master, and so the first to enter there.

Let us ask our dear Master by His love for the Twelve to remember that we too belong to Him, and that we have all our place in His Sacred Heart. Like them, there are no two of us alike. But He loves us all. He wants us to let Him train us as He trained His Twelve Apostles. He will speak to our hearts. He will show us what He wants of us. He will help us when we try, He will forgive us again and again when we fall. Little by little we shall come to be like Him, if only, with the Twelve, we love Him and try to *learn of Him*.

Dear Apostles of our Lord, Peter and Andrew, James and John, Philip and Bartholomew, Thomas and Matthew, James and Jude and Simon, speak for me to Him. Remind Him that I too belong to Him, that He is my Master as well as yours. Ask Him to put into my heart what made your hearts so dear to Him. He sent Peter and John to prepare for Him the Upper Chamber, where you were all to make your First Communion. Ask Him to send Faith and Love into my Heart, to get it ready for His Coming.

St. Peter and St. John, pray for me.

## XIV
## "Who Went About Doing Good"

We have been trying to see what the Apostles were like before they were called by our Lord; during their training by Him; and when His training had done its work in their souls.

And He, our Lord and Master—what was *He* like? If we had a picture of Him, such as we have of those who are dear to us, we think it would help us to love Him, and this is what we want, this is *the* preparation for First Communion—to get the love of our Lord into our hearts. What then was He like? Oh, what we would give to have a true likeness of Him! To know what men saw, what the Apostles saw when they looked upon Jesus! What was He like? Nay, that we cannot tell, for we know He was like no one that has ever trodden—that ever will tread again—this earth of ours.

Prophets foretold that He would be "beautiful above the sons of men—excellent in form—all lovely, on Whom the Angels desire to look."

How could it be otherwise? If beauty of soul is reflected in the countenance, what must that Countenance have been which reflected the most glorious Soul that ever existed, in which the Beauty and Holiness of the Godhead shone! Adam coming straight from the Hand of God was beautiful. But the servant is not above his Lord, and we cannot doubt that Jesus, the second Adam, was far more beautiful than the first man in Paradise.

We find in the Book of Exodus a list of the costly materials provided for the construction of the Tabernacle in the wilderness—"purest gold and silver, marble, and setim wood, and precious stones, fine linen, blue and purple and scarlet twice dyed." We are told that God Himself inspired those who were to adorn His sanctuary, that both in design and in workmanship all might be perfect and befitting the Divine service. "And the Lord called by name Beseleel and Ooliab, and filled them with the Spirit of God, with wisdom and understanding and knowledge and all learning, to devise and to work in gold and silver...and to do carpenter's work and tapestry and embroidery in blue and purple and scarlet and fine linen, and to weave all things and to invent all new things."

If God so enriched the Jewish Tabernacle, and more particularly the Holy of Holies, which was to contain the Ark of the Covenant, the Tables of the Law, and that mysterious sign of His Presence, the light that streamed upwards from the Mercy-Seat, with what majesty and beauty must He have adorned the Sacred Body of Jesus, the Lord of the Covenant and the Giver of the Law, in Whom dwelt the fulness of the Godhead corporally!

Like the veil which hid the Holy of Holies from the sight of men, that Sacred Manhood concealed and yet revealed the Hidden God. His Divinity did not always dazzle the sight of men and force them to fall on their faces before Him as in the Transfiguration on Mount Thabor. There, for a few moments, It shone through its beautiful Veil and lit up His Face and Form with the glory which belonged to Him as the Son of God.

It was not always thus. He could not have done His work among men if it had been. But at all times there was a majesty about Him which made men feel that He was no mere man;

which made His Apostles, to whom the Eternal Father had revealed Him, feel that God was there—the very God by Whom all things were made. He was "beautiful above the children of men." And never had words like His been heard before. So those said who were sent by the Jewish rulers to seize Him. St. John tells us that returning as they went, the angry Pharisees said to them: "Why have you not brought Him?" And the men said: "Never did man speak like this Man." These men only experienced what all felt who drew near to our Blessed Saviour, who looked into His Face and listened to His words. The Hidden Godhead filled them with awe. The love of those who knew Him best and loved Him most, and were admitted by Him to the closest familiarity, was full of the deepest reverence, for they knew and felt that He was God.

When holy Simeon had seen the Face of Jesus, he asked to die in peace. Our Lord Himself told His Apostles that many prophets and just men had desired to see the things they saw and had not seen them, and to hear the things they heard and had not heard them. On Thabor they had a glimpse of the glory of that Divine Countenance as it is n Heaven, and the sight so satisfied their hearts that they asked to stay there always to gaze upon It.

The glory of that Face lights up the Heavenly Jerusalem. St. John says: "The City needeth not sun nor moon to shine in it, for the Lamb is the lamp thereof." That Countenance will be the joy of His Saints to all eternity. And meanwhile the one desire of all who love our Lord is to see It. "Show me Thy Face." "And after this our exile ended, show unto us the Blessed Fruit of thy womb, Jesus."

Not only men and Angels, but the Eternal Father Himself desires to see the Face of Jesus. And so, to move Him to pity and compassion for us, we say: "Look upon the Face of Thy Christ!"

We cannot know our Lord and Master as those knew Him who were privileged to see and study Him during the years of His Earthly Life; who knew the features of His Face and the tone of His Voice; who noted His ways and dealings with men. We cannot even picture Him to ourselves, for no true likeness of Him has come down to us, and the Gospels tell us very little about His exterior.

But though the Evangelists have left no description of Him, they say enough to show what the attractiveness of our Lord must have been. They speak again and again of the multitudes that thronged around Him, flocking after Him even into desert places, and forgetting their bodily needs in their desire to be near Him. "There were so many coming and going," is said in one place, "that there was not so much as time to eat bread."

Some of you perhaps will be inclined to say sadly with Urban, "Ah! cupboard love." And there is no denying that there was a great deal of this. We are told that the people followed Him because they saw the miracles He wrought on them that were diseased. Still, it was not altogether the thought of what they could get that drew them after Him, even into the wilderness. It was the gentle gravity of His beautiful Face, the sweetness of His words, the graciousness of His ways, and above all the hidden and higher beauty of His Soul and Divinity, that drew to Him the hearts of men.

Little children pressed round Him, and were glad to be taken up into His Arms and folded to His Heart. Poor Magdalen came to Him, and was not afraid to press His Sacred Feet to her lips and let her hot tears fall over them. Those who were shunned and despised by the world loved to be with Him, Who despised no one and was good to all. How proud the Twelve must have been of Him: What enthusiasm and excitement His Presence must have roused throughout the land! Think what it must have been for the people of Judea and Galilee to have One amongst them

Who could cure every disease and every infirmity; to Whom the greatest miracles cost only a word; Who walked upon the waves, and stilled the tempests, and cast out devils, and raised the dead to life; and Who used His Divine power so liberally, with such an overflow of Heavenly compassion. Up and down their beautiful land He went, doing good to all. "And Jesus went about all the cities and towns, teaching in their synagogues, and preaching the Gospel of the Kingdom, and healing every sickness, and every disease," says St. Matthew. Our Lord's own account of these wonders is: "The blind see, the lame walk, the lepers are cleansed, the deaf hear, the dead rise again, the poor have the Gospel preached to them." "And there came to Him great multitudes," says St. Matthew again, "having with them the dumb, the blind, the lame, the maimed, and many others: and they cast them down at His Feet and He healed them." St. Mark tells us. "And when it was evening, after sunset, they brought all to Him that were diseased, and that were possessed with devils. And all the City was gathered together at the door...And all wondered and glorified God, saying: We never saw the like...And it was heard that He was in the house; and many came together, so that there was no room, no, not even at the door...So that now He could not openly go into the City, but was without in desert places: and they flocked to Him from all sides...And Jesus retired with His disciples to the sea: and a great multitude followed Him from Galilee and Judea, and from Jerusalem, and from Idumea, and from beyond the Jordan: and they about Tyre and Sidon, a great multitude, hearing the things which He did, came to Him. For He healed many; so that they pressed upon Him for to touch Him, as many as had evils...And running through that whole country, they began to carry about in beds those that were sick, where they heard He was. And whithersoever He entered, into towns, or into villages, or cities, they laid the sick in the streets, and besought Him that they might touch but the hem of His garment: and as many as touched Him were made whole."

How they all longed for Him to come their way! What wonder that when the news was spread that He was nearing any town or village, men, women, and children left all they were about and flocked out to meet Him. "Multitude," and "a great multitude," are the words the Evangelists use, when they speak of the crowds that went after Him. There would be two multitudes meeting. That from the place He was leaving, was all joy and gratitude. Their blind saw, their lepers were cleansed, and their lame were "walking and leaping and praising God."

See them, plenty of such are in the crowd around Him now. In vain He tells them to keep their cure quiet. The more He tells them, the more they publish and blaze it abroad. On all sides the air resounds with the cry, "He hath done all things well, He hath made the deaf to hear and the dumb to speak." What a joyous multitude it is! And there will be the same joy presently in the town to which He is coming. Messengers run on before to prepare the people for Him. If the sun is down, the sick must be brought into the streets, and He will lay His Hands on every one of them and heal them. If they cannot come to Him, He will go to them, for He has never been known to refuse a cure, or to turn a deaf ear to any prayer. The townsfolk turn out to meet Him, and as they mix with the on-comers and hear all the wonderful things these have to tell, the eagerness and expectation grow every instant more intense.

He moves along slowly, for the people throng about Him on all sides. The Apostles try to keep them off, but it is no use. In vain He retires into wild and desert highlands. Up the hill slopes they follow, bringing all manner of dumb, and blind, and lame, and lay them down at His Feet that He may heal them.

One day He meets a sad procession at the gates of Naim. They are carrying to the grave the only son of an aged mother, and she is a widow. And the Lord seeing her is moved with compassion, and says to her, "Weep not." Who but He would dare to say such words? "Weep not." She looks up wonderingly into His Face. Oh, the tender pity of the Eyes that meet those red eyes of hers! It is more than she can bear. Her heart is breaking; she cannot speak; but she keeps her eyes fixed upon Him, and lays her hands in His. He draws near to the bier: "Young man, I say to thee, arise!" And see, he that was dead sits up and begins to speak. Stupefied and frightened, the mother creeps closer to Jesus, and the colour in her cheeks comes and goes. But her hands are still in His, and she does not faint or fall. A moment He waits, for her heart is beating fast. And now He gently brings her forward and leads her to her son, and draws her arms around his neck, and blesses them and leaves them there together.

There is an open space round Him to-day—those must be lepers He is healing—the crowd always makes way *for them*. They are objects of horror and disgust. Turned out of towns and villages, they must live how and where they can. They must not enter the homes of other men, nor drink at the public fountains, for they taint all they touch, and poison the very air they breathe. Why does He not cure them from a distance? Why does He let them come so near Him? See, they are kneeling on His robe! He need not touch those hideous sores. But He seems to like to lay His Hand upon them; more merciful than His Prophet of old—to touch with His Hand the place of the leprosy, and so to heal it. The people wonder why. It is always so, they say, when lepers come. He is kind to all, but there is always a special smile and welcome for them. Others may have to wait; sometimes there is a question; sometimes even a reproof. But He never keeps a leper waiting, *his* prayer is heard at once. Is it because leprosy is a figure of sin? And

He, the Physician of our souls, wants to show us how tenderly He will treat us, how readily He will hear us whenever we come to Him and show Him the wounds of our souls. "Lord, if Thou wilt, Thou canst make me clean." And stretching forth His Hand, He touches him and says, "I will, be thou made clean,"

See Him standing there near the sea, a great multitude around Him. Suddenly a whispered word passes from mouth to mouth. A man is making his way forward, and the pitying crowd gives place. It is Jairus, ruler of the synagogue. All know why he is here. But why did he not come sooner? Is it not too late now? His voice is thick and husky as, falling down at our Lord's Feet, he says: "Lord, my daughter is at the point of death, but come, lay Thy Hand upon her that she may be safe and live." And while he is speaking a servant comes up and says, "Thy daughter is dead, trouble Him not." Jesus looks at him kindly, and saying, "Fear not, believe only and she shall be safe," bids him lead the way to the house. At the door they find the wailing minstrels and all the noisy grief usual in Jewish mourning. Our Lord says quietly, "Give place, for the maid is not dead, but sleepeth." And they laugh Him to scorn. It is no place for laughter, but they laugh *at that*, knowing that she is dead. He will have no one to follow Him into the silent room but the father, with Peter, James, and John. The mother takes Him to the bed. There she lies, a child of twelve. Is it true that children have no need to think of death? The soul is gone, but not into Eternity, for its time of trial is not yet over. It is one of the very few who are to pass a second time through the gates of death. He Who is looking down upon the still face is God. He is holding the soul on the brink of Eternity. At His bidding it is to return to finish its course of probation, then it will come to Him for judgment. How quiet the room is! Not a sound but the mother's stifled sobs. The Apostles hold their breath as they wait for Him to speak. He is God, and He speaks as

God: "*Talitha, cumi!* Damsel, I say to thee, arise!" Instantly the limbs stir; the face flushes with life and health; she opens her eyes—and rises immediately—and walks. See the awe-stricken faces of those two as they fall down before Him. For a while He leaves them there at His Feet, bewildered and speechless. Now He touches them. He makes them a sign, and they go up, the mother first and then the father, for a long embrace. He watches them through His tears. And now, bidding them take care of her and give her something to eat, He lays His Hand tenderly on the child's head, and passes again into the crowd.

So His days are spent amid every sort of human suffering and wretchedness. He is thronged on every side. He is at every one's beck, going here and there as He is wanted. No one notices how tired He looks. He is footsore and weary, weary in body, more weary still in heart. He does not grudge those eager crowds His toilsome days any more than He grudges them His gifts. But to think they should be ungrateful for it all! It is *that* that makes His Heart so sore. He sees into all hearts, and knows all that is to come. He knows there are many there who will soon forget the touch of His healing Hands, and turn against Him the very gifts He has restored to them. There are many singing "Hosanna to the Son of David" now, who will one day cry, "Away with Him, crucify Him."

What wonder that when the shades of night begin to fall, and the last suppliant has left Him satisfied, He turns His weary glance away from earth and seeks the Face of His Father in prayer. He sends the Apostles home. They have had a hard day and are tired. But they are so happy, they have been all day with Him, working for Him, under His Eye. What more could they want? They would willingly be with Him now, but He sends them home to rest. *He* has no longer any home, and no one thinks of offering Him a shelter. They have left Him on the mountain-side, where He will spend the night, and the first of them in the Temple to-morrow morning will find Him there.

See our Lord alone on the Mountain-side—alone with the Father. Only the Father could understand the Sacred Human Heart of His Son, and it is in prayer to the Father that It finds Its rest. He carries the whole world in His Heart. He has to pray for all—for all the sick on whom He has laid His Hands that day; for all the sinners He has brought to repentance; for all the sorrowing hearts He has soothed; for His dear Apostles. And not for them only among His disciples, but for all who through their word shall believe in Him; for us, therefore, for each one of us. We have all had our place in that Sacred Heart. We have all had our share in that Divine prayer by night on the mountain-side. He knows us all by name. He knows our dangers and our troubles and His designs over us. All our life lies stretched out before Him there, and His prayer has won for us all the graces we need: pardon for past sin, grace for the future, and perseverance to the end. Let us turn with confidence to that prayer of Jesus for us when we feel the worthlessness of our own.

O Lord and Master, if I could have seen You there by night in prayer *for me!* If, like so many, I could have knelt at Your Feet, and held the hem of Your garment in my hands and kissed it—how happy I should have been! I think then I should have been satisfied. But this would not have satisfied You, O Lover of my soul. You will give me, not the hem of Your garment, but Yourself. You will come to me Body and Blood and Soul and Divinity, all that You have and are, to satisfy Yourself and me—Your love, and the needs of my poor soul. Come then, Lord Jesus, come! But before You come, prepare my soul for Your Holy Presence. Let me bring to You all its needs and miseries, as in Judea and Galilee they brought to You their sick. And do for me what You did for them.  Look with pity on my wounds and weaknesses: lay Your Blessed Hands on every one of them and heal them.

> Jesus, Jesus, come to me,
> O how much I long for Thee:
> Come, Thou of all friends the best,
> Take possession of my breast,
> Earnestly I cry to Thee,
> Jesus, Jesus, come to me!

# XV
# Feeding of the Five Thousand

The Twelve had their holidays from time to time. Their daily life in our Lord's company was not an easy life. There was hard work, poor food, long journeying. They did not mind it one bit, for it was *with Him*. His society sweetened everything to them. They had no thought for their own ease and comfort. But He was thoughtful for them and now and again He took them off by themselves and gave them a treat. Their treat was to be in some quiet place alone with Him, to have Him all to themselves, the multitude far away. There on a grassy plain or on some hill-side, they sat at His Feet, looking up into His Face, listening to the tones of His voice, drinking in every word, *learning Him* better and better. But what they liked best of all was to be with Him out on the Lake; they were safest there; the people could not get at Him.

So they were glad one morning when He said to them, "Come aside into a desert place and rest a little." Off they set to get Peter's boat ready—He always used Peter's boat—and in a short time they were all on the shore. See Peter steadying the boat as our Lord gets in, getting in after Him, all the others getting in and taking their places. Generally our Lord is at the rudder, but Peter is to steer to-day. He has put our Lord's place where he can see Him, and John is next to Him as usual. The boat is pushed off, the water gets deeper and deeper, the clear blue water of that beautiful lake. How still it is; only the fresh morning breeze coming down between the mountains, and the pleasant splash of the oar. Our Lord begins to speak, and their eyes are fixed upon Him. See the oars held straight out over the water, and dripping, as the rowers bend forward to catch every word. When our Lord stops speaking, they ask explanations. They are ignorant men and dull, as their questions often show; but He is patient with them and explains to them again and again.

Let us get out the map and follow the boat. You see that Bethsaida, Capharnaum, and all the towns by the Lake are on the western shore; the eastern is a country almost uninhabited, some parts covered with grassy plains, in others barren and dreary. Sailing eastward then, they would come to what three of the Evangelists call a desert place. They have been so engrossed by our Lord's Presence and conversation that they have attended to nothing else. But suddenly one of them points to the shore. The people who are always on our Lord's track have found out that He is in the boat, and they are making their way round by the head of the Lake to meet it at the point for which it is steering. Our Lord's Eye has been following them all along, and He says to Peter: "Put into that little creek." The Apostles look at each other in dismay—are they not going to have their quiet day with Him after all? Might they not go further down where the multitude could not come? But our Lord tells them that those who work for Him must not be selfish. There are many in that crowd who want His help; who have come a long way to find Him; who are bringing their sick with them. There are many in need of comfort, and all of instruction. His disciples must be ready to sacrifice their own rest and pleasure for the good of souls. At once they throw their wills into His and the boat is run into the creek. Such a welcome as it gets there! The men lay hold of it and moor it fast.

See our Lord getting out and going into the crowd drawn up to receive Him, "a great multitude having with them the dumb, the blind, the lame, the maimed, and many others, and they cast them down at His Feet." See Him going in and out among them laying His Hands on them, healing them all, so that the dumb speak, the lame walk, the blind see. Hear the shouts of joyful praise on every side. See how the newly healed press upon Him; they kiss the hem of His robe, they kiss His Feet, they seize the Blessed Hands that have worked their cure and cover them with kisses. They scarcely know what they are doing, they are wild in their new found happiness. He gives Himself up to the people. He is at every one's call. He is taken here and there, wherever there are sick who cannot come to Him. And it is not the sick only who want Him. In that vast crowd there are sadder faces than the pale, pinched faces of the sick. There are sores and wounds more painful than those on which He had laid His healing Hand. Many a bruised, many a breaking heart is there, whose secret pain no touch has ever reached to heal or soothe. Our Lord's Face looks so kind, His ways are so gentle and so gracious, that all who are unhappy long to speak to Him and get perhaps a word of comfort from His Lips. They come up to Him timidly, one here and one there, and are welcomed with a smile. He knows their long sad story before they tell it. But He likes to hear it from themselves. Just as He likes us to bring our troubles to Him in the Tabernacle now. He bends down His ear to listen, He does not hurry them. He lets them tell it all. And then He speaks—a few words only—but they go deep into their hearts and reach the trouble which was never reached ere this. Their tears fall fast, but they are not like the tears they shed a while ago. Those who know them wonder to see them go away with that peaceful look on their faces. And who has ever seen them smile like that before?

At last our Lord's work of healing and comforting is done, and He tells the Apostles to get the people ready for an instruction. He will go a little higher up the mount and they are to come to Him there. See the Twelve arranging the people. "You in front sit down here at His Feet; make a larger ring—so. You behind kneel. And a third row can stand. All must keep close together to lose no room. Those who are too far off to hear the Master can see Him at least, and He will have them by-and-bye."

Our Lord seats Himself on a bit of projecting rock. He looks down with compassion on this vast multitude, "wandering like sheep not having a shepherd," and He begins to teach them many things. He tells the people that the poor are blessed if only they are content to want the good things of this world and to wait for those of Heaven. He tells them that those are blessed who are kind and forgiving. Those too, whose life is hard and sad, for the time will come when they will be comforted, and God will wipe away the tears from their eyes. He speaks to them of the Kingdom of God. He explains by parables. His words are simple and strong, and go straight to their hearts. And as they rise to go away, they say to one another, "Never did man speak like this Man."

Now another set is to come up and be formed in the same way. Our Lord begins all over again with them. The Apostles stand round Him as before. All eyes are fixed upon Him as before.

These are moved off and another set comes, and another and another. Now He rises and goes among the people. And they come round Him freely, with eager petitions once more. Will He not come to their village? They have some sick at home who could not be brought all this way. He listens, and quiets, and satisfies them. He will be coming their way by-and-bye, and meantime they must cheer and encourage their sick by telling them all they have seen to-day.

The afternoon comes and the evening. The short Eastern day will soon be ended. The Apostles come to Him and say, "This is a desert-place, and the hour is now passed. Send away the multitudes, that going into the towns they may buy themselves victuals." He says to them, "They have no need to go; give you them to eat." They answer Him, "Let us go and buy bread for two hundred pence, and we will give them to eat." Andrew says, "There is a boy here that hath five barley loaves and two fishes, but what are these among so many?" Our Lord tells them to make all the multitude sit down in companies upon the green grass, by hundreds and by fifties.

Look into His Sacred Heart. See His joy at what He is going to do. He is going to relieve the need of those who love Him, and have followed Him so trustfully into the wilderness. And yet it is not this feeding of the hungry multitude that is making Him so glad. What then? Of what is He thinking as He looks down upon that moving mass of men, women, and children? He is thinking of a far greater hunger, the hunger of the soul, which He will soon appease by a Bread which shall be Himself. He is thinking of the Feast He has prepared to the end of the world for those who follow Him. It, too, will be given in the desert; it will be unexpected; it will be for His followers only and be prepared by Himself; it will be multiplied in a miraculous manner to satisfy the needs of all; bestowed with lavish generosity, yet remaining undiminished to the end; it will be distributed by Him through His ministers: it will be satisfying and delightful though given under a simple form, and will be a Food giving strength and gladness, opening the eyes of all to know Him, and kindling a personal and enthusiastic love of Him in the hearts of many.

The feast in the desert is a type of the Sacred Banquet in which Christ is received, and a beautiful type it is. Look at the scene—the Apostles getting all the people into order: a hundred there, fifty there. Their bright garments form patches of colour on the grass, making the groups look like so many flower beds. See the little boy coming up to our Lord and giving Him his loaves. See the eyes of all that multitude fixed on our Blessed Saviour as He takes the loaves and the fishes, and looking up to heaven, blesses and breaks the loaves, and gives them with the fishes to His disciples to set before the people. As the Apostles break the bread it multiplies in their hands. Look at all the hands stretched out to receive it. See the Apostles pressing the people to take all they want—there is plenty. See them going to their Master for more—from the rising ground where He stands, our Lord seeing that all are provided—a company out there has had none yet—this one is ready for some more—the Apostles so pleased with their work, so glad to hear the people's grateful thanks and all they say of their Master, so proud to be His disciples. The crowds are very hungry: they have had nothing all day.

But at last they are satisfied. St. Matthew says, "the number of them that did eat was five thousand, besides women *and children.*" Giving an account a little later of another multiplication of loaves for another multitude of four thousand, he says, "*besides children and women.*" He was not likely to leave out the children, who add so much to the splendour of the miracle. Those who have had to provide children's treats know what those words "besides children" mean, and understand how St. Matthew felt he had said all that need be said of our Lord's generosity when he had said that *they* were satisfied. Twelve baskets are filled with the fragments that are over, and on these fragments our Lord and the Apostles dine.

The multitude looks on. For some time there has been a consultation among the men: "Surely this is the Prophet that is to come into the world. Let us go and take Him by force and make Him King." They wait till He and the Apostles have

## The Feeding of the Five Thousand

"And looking up to Heaven, He blessed, and brake, and gave the loaves to His disciples, and His disciples to the multitudes."
(Matt 14:19)

finished their poor meal, and then they come forward with a great cry: "Hosanna to the Son of David! Hosanna to our King!" He is surrounded. They have Him fast. The enthusiasm spreads. Men and women press round Him. The children behind take up the cry: "Hosanna to the Son of David!" All over that grassy plain that shout rises and swells. The Apostles look on and listen with exulting hearts. At last the Kingdom has come. It was for this He brought them here. Oh, how glad they are now that they came. But their delight is soon at an end. Our Lord tells them to go at once down to the boat, and cross over to Capharnaum again, whilst He stays to dismiss the people. What! leave Him just now? Might they not stay to help Him—Peter, at least, and James and John? No, they are all to go. They leave Him reluctantly, go slowly down to the shore and put out to sea. What a pity! All was going so well. Why would He not let them stay?

Our Lord calms the excited crowd. He tells them He does not want to be made King now. They must go quietly to their homes, and think of all He has told them to-day. At last they listen to Him and He dismisses them, troop after troop, till all are gone, and He is alone. Think how tired He must be. With weary Feet He climbs the mountainside to find His rest with the Father—in prayer.

The hours pass, and now the wind is rising. It sweeps in gusts round this unsheltered height. It chills Him, but does not disturb His prayer. There is His Church to be founded and guarded and prospered through all ages by that prayer of His. There are His Sacraments to be instituted—His Vicar upon earth to be protected and guided—His Saints to be trained—His Martyrs to be supported—His little ones to be cared for and brought to know and love Hun.

Hark, how the storm is raging. See the great waves upon the lake that was so still a while ago. The moon is up, but the clouds fly fast across her face, and her fitful light only adds to the wildness of the scene. Oh, look at the waves down there! What will become of boats on the Lake?

He rises from His prayer; it is time to go to His Apostles. See Him going down the mountainside and standing by the shore. See the majesty with which He gathers His robe around Him and steps forth on to the waves. Now the moon shines out suddenly and throws His shadow forward on the waters. Now all is dark, and the wind howls, and the waves rise high around Him. The Apostles are far out at sea, making no way, for the wind is against them. Peter has ordered the sail to be taken in, and they are all of them baling the water out of the boat. She cannot hold out much longer. Oh, if their Master were only here! Suddenly there is a cry from one of them. A Form is walking over the waves and coming straight to them. It must be an apparition, and they all cry out with fear. But a Voice comes across the waters and is heard above the tumult of the storm: "Be of good heart. It is I, fear ye not." At once Peter cries out, "Lord, if it be Thou, bid me come to Thee upon the waters." And Jesus says, "Come." See St. Peter getting out of the boat, putting one foot upon the sea, and now the other, feeling it firm beneath him. The waters bear him up, and he walks boldly on to Jesus. But now a gust of wind brings a great wave towards him; he turns round to look at it—he loses sight of Jesus—he is afraid—he begins to sink. "Lord, save me," he cries as he is going down. And Jesus at once stretches out His Hand and takes hold of him, and brings him, wet and terrified and clinging close to his Master, to the boat. The rest have been leaning over the side of the boat watching all. And they take our Lord and St. Peter in. And the wind ceases, and presently the ship is at the land to which they are going.

My soul, dear Lord, is like that changeful lake. Sometimes it is still and happy like the lake lying in the sunshine, the blue sky above, the blue waves below, and only sights and sounds of peace around.

Sometimes Your service seems sweet and easy. It is not hard to be good then. And as I kneel before the Tabernacle at Mass or Benediction, I can feel that You are there and that You love me.

And then quite suddenly comes a storm. Something vexes me, and at once my temper or my bad passions rise. Everything looks black and dismal, and I lose sight of You. O dear Master, be near me always. Be near me in the sunshine. Be nearer still in the storm. I am safe always if You are there. When I am in danger, when temptation comes, remind me to call on You like Peter: "Lord, save me, I perish;" and stretch forth Your Hand and save me.

# XVI
## The Promise of the Eucharist

"And presently the ship was at the land to which they were going." That land was the sea-shore of Capharnaum, from which they had pushed off so joyfully a few hours before in expectation of a whole holiday alone with their Master. How different the day had turned out! Holidays often turn out very differently from what we expect. Our Lord has, many a time, lessons for us which we had not looked for, and which are not quite to our taste. Something happens that does not fit in with the plans for enjoyment we had made for ourselves. Disappointment comes to us as to the Twelve. What are we to do then? As the Apostles did. Were they upset? No. They trusted themselves entirely to their dear Master. They let Him have His own way with them, and they were beginning to find out that His way was, after all, the happiest and the best.

There is no harm in making plans for enjoying ourselves—praying for a fine day when we are going out for a picnic—and at all times asking God for what we want, even for the least things. Only if He happens to want something else, we must be ready to give up our plans and come into His.

The Apostles lost nothing, but gained a great deal by doing this. If they had had their Master all to themselves that bright sunny day, would they have come to know and love Him half as well as when they saw Him going in and out among the sick and sorrowful, or listened to His tender words; or watched Him blessing and multiplying the bread; or coming to them in the dark night across the stormy sea?

But we must go back to the multitude whom we left on the eastern shore of the lake. They do not seem to have been in any hurry to get home. Indeed, some of them must have lingered about the spot where the miracle had taken place, in hopes of being with our Lord again next day. Surprised and disappointed at not finding Him in the morning, "they took shipping," says St. John, "and came to Capharnaum seeking for Jesus." And when they had found Him they said to Him: "Rabbi, when camest Thou hither?" Jesus answered them and said, "Amen, amen, I say to you, you seek Me...because you did eat of the loaves and were filled. Labour not for the meat which perisheth, but for that which endureth unto life everlasting, which the Son of Man will give you."

At last our Lord was going to speak to men of the Blessed Eucharist. See how near it lay to His Heart, how it rose to His lips at once.

He, Who was promised to us in Paradise, had promised Himself not merely one visit to us after four thousand years, but many and many a visit, even to the end of the world. He would come not only to the people of one time and of one land, but to His followers of all time and of every land. And He had invented a way in which this was to be done. It was a very wonderful way, and so He had to prepare the minds of men for it. You remember how they were prepared for His coming on earth by types and figures. So were they prepared for His still more wonderful coming to the souls of men in Holy Communion. The Manna in the desert, the Food of Elias, and lastly, the bread multiplied to feed five thousand in the wilderness—these were all types of the Holy Eucharist as a Sacrament, striking and beautiful figures of a reality to come. With all this preparatory instruction men would be ready, or ought to be ready, to believe what He was going to say to them now.

It was to be the first instruction to the Twelve about their First Communion. One of them, the dear St. John, tells us all about it, and repeats for us the very words our Lord said. We must listen attentively, for these words were spoken for us too.

Of all the instructions for our First Communion, this one, given by the Lips of our Lord Himself, is the most solemn and impressive. All the circumstances are important. The words themselves, and the effect of the words, the listeners, the time, the place, have all to be noticed. The listeners, as we have seen, were a great crowd of people that thronged about our Lord the day after the miracle in the wilderness. They had been with Him then. They had seen what He had done. They had followed Him back to Capharnaum, some by water, some round the shores of the lake. Their minds were full of the miracle; they could think of nothing else, talk of nothing else. All were eager to see and hear again the wonder-working young Prophet. Surely He could be no other than the long-expected Messiah. Every eye was fixed upon Him. His every gesture was noted. They would hang upon every word. His time had come.

Whilst all stood round in breathless silence, our Lord told them that besides the meat that perishes, there is a meat that endures unto life everlasting, which He, the Son of Man, would give them—a true Bread from Heaven given by His Father—a Bread coming down from Heaven and giving life to the world. And He told them that He Himself was this Bread, the Bread of Life. "Labour not," He said, "for the meat which perisheth, but for that which endureth unto life everlasting, which the Son of Man will give you." By the meat which perishes our

Lord meant any kind of food for the body. We are to care less for this than for the Food He is going to provide for the soul to bring it to everlasting life. Of this Divine Food the priest says when giving Holy Communion: "May the Body of our Lord Jesus Christ preserve thy soul to life everlasting."

They said, therefore, to Him: "Our fathers did eat manna in the desert, as it is written: He gave them bread from Heaven to eat."

You see they were thinking only of the bread that feeds the body. Our Lord wanted to show them that the soul too needs its food, or it will die, and that the soul is something so great, so noble, that it must have a very grand and noble food provided for it. If God sent down such delicious bread in the desert to feed the bodies which were to die, He would certainly provide something greater for the souls which are never to die.

Then Jesus said to them: "Amen, amen, I say to you, Moses gave you not bread from Heaven, but My Father giveth you the true Bread from Heaven. For the Bread of God is that which cometh down from Heaven and giveth life to the world. They said therefore unto Him: Lord, give us always this bread." They do not yet know what this wonderful Bread is, but our Lord has said enough to make them desire it.

"And Jesus said to them: I am the Bread of Life, he that cometh to Me shall not hunger; and he that believeth in Me shall never thirst...The Jews therefore murmured at Him because He had said, I am the Living Bread which came down from Heaven...Jesus therefore answered and said to them: Murmur not among yourselves...I am the Bread of Life. Your fathers did eat manna in the desert and are dead. This is the Bread which cometh down from Heaven, that if any man eat of it he may not die. I am the Living Bread which came down from Heaven. If any man eat of this Bread he shall live for ever: and the Bread that I will give is My Flesh for the life of the world,"

"The Jews therefore strove among themselves saying: How can this Man give us His Flesh to eat? Then Jesus said to them: Amen, amen, I say unto you, except you eat the Flesh of the Son of Man and drink His Blood, you shall not have life in you. He that eateth My Flesh and drinketh My Blood hath everlasting life, and I will raise him up at the last day. For My Flesh is meat indeed, and My Blood is drink indeed. He that eateth My Flesh and drinketh My Blood abideth in Me and I in him. As the living Father hath sent Me and I live by the Father, so he that eateth Me the same also shall live by Me. This is the Bread that came down from Heaven. Not as your fathers did eat manna and are dead. He that eateth this Bread shall live for ever...Many therefore of His disciples hearing it said: This saying is hard, and who can hear it?...After this many of His disciples went back and walked no more with Him. Then Jesus said to the Twelve: Will you also go away? And Simon Peter answered Him: Lord, to whom shall we go? Thou hast the words of eternal life."

Now was not this strange? The Jews had just been praying, "Lord, give us always this bread." And directly after, because they could not understand *how* our Lord could be "Living Bread," they began to murmur.

There are some children—none of you, of course—who get cross and grumble the moment something comes in a lesson which they cannot understand. They forget how very small their minds are, how little they know of anything at all. And so when the least bit of a difficulty has to be mastered, they are impatient and begin to complain, just as these foolish Jews did here. A sensible child says to itself, "I cannot understand this, certainly. But I will wait and listen to what my master has to say about it. He knows what he is talking about; it is quite clear to him; no doubt it will be clear to me by-and-bye if I only have patience." Ought not these Jews to have said this?

Mind, many of them were our Lord's disciples, St. John tells us so expressly. They looked upon Him as their Master and the promised Messiah. And He had just given them abundant proof that He was God. He had multiplied the bread the day before on purpose to prepare them for what He was saying now. They ought to have believed what He was saying on His word, the word of God. Did He not know what He was saying? Was it their place to murmur?

They said this saying was hard to understand. Of course it was. But did our Lord ask them to understand it? He did not mean it to be *understood*. He meant it to be *believed*.

If, instead of grumbling to one another and saying, "How *can* this Man give us His Flesh to eat?" they had turned to their Master and asked reverently, "Lord, how *will* you give us Your Flesh to eat?" or if they had cried out with the man who was reproved for his want of faith, "Lord, I believe, help Thou my unbelief," our Lord would have come to their help, and they would have remained with Him as His disciples. But they were too proud to do this. They would not believe unless they could first see and understand. Is that *believing*?

They understood our Lord to mean exactly what He said—that the very Living Flesh they saw before them was to be given to them—otherwise they would have had no difficulty. And because they could not see *how* He could do this, "many of His disciples went back and walked no more with Him."

Now it is very important to notice how our Lord met this difficulty of theirs. He saw into their minds. He knew exactly the sense in which His words had been taken, and He knew what would follow from their being taken in their plain and literal sense. If these men had made a mistake, if they had misunderstood Him, He would have been bound in justice and in charity to set them right. How anxious a good teacher is that the children should understand him aright. How carefully he chooses his words so that there may be no possibility of mistake. How he questions them to find out if they have seized his meaning exactly. This is because he cannot see into their minds and know the sense in which his words have been taken. Our Lord saw into the minds of His hearers always, He knew exactly the sense in which His words would be taken, for He was God. And yet, to show how anxious He was to have His teaching grasped, His instructions were full of questions. St. Matthew tells us He said one day to His Apostles, "Have you understood all these things?" They say to Him. "Yes."

He saw into the minds, not only of those men who were listening to Him in the synagogue of Capharnaum, but of all who should ever hear of this Mystery. He knew the tremendous importance of being rightly understood, and He was able to choose such words as would exactly express what He meant to say. Who could suppose that He would not choose the best and most fitting to convey His true meaning? He did choose such words. And when He saw His words were taken literally, that is, were taken to mean that He would give to men for their food the very body they saw before them—instead of changing anything He had said, He added other words that were stronger still, "Amen, amen, I say unto you"—this was a very solemn expression among the Jews—"unless you eat the Flesh of the Son of Man and drink His Blood, you shall not have life in you. He that eateth My Flesh and drinketh My Blood hath everlasting life, and I will raise him up in the last day. For My Flesh is meat *indeed* and My Blood is drink *indeed*." Thus did our Lord show unmistakably that the sense in which He had been understood was the sense in which He meant and willed to be understood.

To us His meaning is plain enough. Plainer still, if possible, it must have been to those who saw the majesty and the authority with which He spoke, who heard those solemn words: "Amen, amen, I say to you, My Flesh is meat *indeed* and My Blood is drink *indeed*." There was no mistaking Him, and murmuring at such a hard saying, many of those who, up to now, had hung upon His words went away and walked no more with Him.

Now just think. He saw them going away. He knew it was because of the sense in which they had taken His words. If they had mistaken His meaning, would He not have called them back and explained; have set their minds right; told them He was only speaking figuratively; and so have kept as His disciples those dear souls which He was going to lose? Most surely He would have done so. But He did nothing of the kind, for there was nothing to explain. He could not speak more plainly. They would not believe. He must let them go.

Look at the Twelve standing round Him, silent, thoughtful, reverent. They will carry those words of His to the uttermost parts of the earth, and wherever they are heard, the true disciples of Jesus will adore as very God the Bread that is His Flesh indeed. And this as long as the Catholic Church shall teach, as long as the world shall last. If His words were not rightly understood, such adoration would be idolatry. Will He allow this? Will He let His Church make such a mistake, if it is a mistake? Nay, will He give rise to it by His own words? "Thou hast spoken so clearly, O Lord," cried St. Augustine, "that if I could be mistaken in my belief, Thou wouldst Thyself be the cause of my mistake." To say this would be blasphemy. Yet this is what comes of denying the Real Presence.

All those who stood round our Lord that day had to choose between two things, either they must bow down their souls before Him in unquestioning faith, or they must go away and walk no more with Him. Which was it to be? "After this many of His disciples went back and walked no more with Him." O Sacred Heart! And this is what has come of promising men that wondrous Gift, devised with so much love, desired with such eager expectation.

Sadly our Lord turned to His Apostles and said, "Will you also go away?" St. John is eager to tell us that at once, "Simon Peter answered Him, Lord, to whom shall we go? Thou hast the words of eternal life. And we have believed and have known that Thou art the Christ, the Son of God."

A little Protestant, five years old, was listening for the first time to the story of the Last Supper. "And Jesus took bread and blessed and broke and said, This is My Body. This is My Blood." Noticing the look of reverence in the thoughtful face beside her, the mother hastened to explain that these words were only figurative. Of course our Lord did not really mean that the bread was His Body and the wine His Blood. "And why did He say what He did not mean?" said the child in an injured tone. But He *did* mean it, He *must* have meant it, she thought. And from that day till another many years after when she was received into the Holy Catholic Church, nothing could shake her belief in the Real Presence which our Lord had declared so plainly.

"This *is* My Body." These words of our Lord are so plain that for more than a thousand years, no one ever thought of denying the Real Presence. Then a wicked man called Berengarius dared to say that our Lord did not mean the Blessed Sacrament to be His true Body, but only a figure of His Body. He taught this new doctrine for many years. But he was afraid to die in his heresy and appear before our Lord as Judge, after having denied His Real Presence beneath the sacramental veils. So before his death he retracted his error, that is, he drew back and unsaid his wicked words. We may hope our Lord had mercy on him. But it is a terrible thing to teach others wrong: we never know where the evil may stop.

Berengarius had been dead five hundred years when his heresy was revived by the men who invented the Protestant religion in the sixteenth century. Of these, Luther and Calvin were the chief. They denied more doctrines taught by our Lord and His Church than any of the heretics who had gone before them, and Calvin taught, among other errors, that our Lord is not really present in the Blessed Sacrament. This Luther, bad though he was, could never bring himself to do. On the contrary, he had no patience with those who denied the Real Presence. He said that our Lord's words: "This *is* My Body," are so plain that no child of seven could make a mistake about them, and that the Calvinists ought to be ashamed of themselves for being so stupid.

You know perhaps that hundreds of Calvinists were converted by the learning and gentleness of the great St. Francis of Sales. But you may not know how a baby Saint took part in the work of confounding heresy and stood up as a champion of our Lord in the Blessed Sacrament.

Suppose we transport ourselves into a rambling old house in one of the principal streets of Dijon, and watch what is passing in one of the rooms there.

You see those two seated by the window. One is the President Frémyot, whom the world will remember as the father of St. Jane Frances de Chantal. In days when many are falling away from the Faith, he is a staunch Catholic and insists upon his children being well instructed in their religion. His visitor is a Calvinist gentleman of rank.

It would be rude to listen to what they are saying, and if we did, the probability is we should not understand the old French of three hundred years ago. The discussion is evidently a warm one, and from the words that reach us every now and then we should say the subject is the Real Presence of our Lord in the Holy Eucharist.

Somebody, however, is listening and understanding too. The President's little daughter Jane has left her dolls on the floor, and for the last ten minutes has been standing beside her father's chair. How intently she is watching the speakers. She is only five, but her intelligent face and burning cheeks show that she knows what they are talking about and that she does not approve. Listen! she is going to have her say. "But, my lord, we *must* believe that Jesus Christ is present in the Blessed Sacrament, because He said it Himself. If you do not believe it, you make Him a liar." My lord was not expecting this. He is taken aback and tries, with a smile it is true, but with no little secret annoyance, to put down his small antagonist. But in vain. Jane will not be put down. She knows her Catechism well, and meets his arguments with wise and ready replies. Ah, now he remembers an unanswerable argument—he wonders he had not thought of it before. Diving into the depths of a capacious pocket, he produces a packet of sweets, and with a courtly bow offers them for her acceptance.

She accepts them indeed—takes them in her pinafore, and marching straight to the fireplace, throws them into the flames, saying, "Look, my lord, that is how heretics will be burnt in the fire of Hell, because they do not believe what our Lord says."

"I thank Thee, O Father, Lord of Heaven and earth, because Thou hast hidden these things from the wise and prudent and revealed them unto babes."

O Lord and Master, I cannot bear to think of the pain those disciples gave to Your Sacred Heart that day at Capharnaum. They ought to have been so grateful and so glad. And instead of this, they would not believe Your words and went away and walked no more with You. I cannot bear to think that there are many who will not believe Your words now. And many who, though they believe, pain Your Heart by their coldness and neglect. Let me not be like one of these. Let my prayer be, "Lord, give us always this Bread." Give me the Living Bread that I may live for ever. Give me the Bread that is Your Flesh, that I may have life in me, that I may live by You, that You may raise me up at the Last Day.

"Lord, give us always this Bread."

# XVII

## "Will you also go away? Lord, to whom shall we go?"

It is St. John, the Apostle of love, who tells us of the promise of the Eucharist, the Gift of Love. And he tells us something very interesting about the place where the promise was made.

You remember that the people came over to Capharnaum from the other side of the Lake in their eagerness to find our Lord, and that He began at once to speak to them of what was so near to His Heart. But to show them that the subject of that day's instruction was more than usually solemn and important, He did not gather them round Him in the open air, as was His custom, but led the way to the synagogue, where, as St. John expressly tells us, this discourse was delivered.

The synagogue of Capharnaum was built by a Gentile—the Roman Centurion who came to our Lord for the cure of his servant. Its style and richness of ornament showed the generosity of the giver, and won for him the gratitude of the Jews. When he was in trouble they pleaded for him to our Lord, saying, "He is worthy that Thou shouldst do this for him, for he loveth our nation and he hath built us a synagogue."

This gift of the good Centurion, built in our Lord's "own city," has long been a heap of ruins. But even the ruins speak of the Blessed Sacrament. A Jewish synagogue had generally some sacred symbol—the seven-branched candlestick or the pot of manna—carved on the lintel over the door. Now, wonderful to tell, the lintel of this synagogue has been found among the ruins of the building, which still exist; and what is more wonderful still, it has carved on it not only a pot of manna, but a flowing pattern of vine leaves and clusters of grapes. Is not this the very stones crying out to remind us of the Sacrament of Love? You need not, of course, be told that the humble prayer, "Lord, I am not worthy that Thou shouldst enter under my roof," which the Church puts upon the lips of her children before Holy Communion, is the prayer of this good Centurion.

We know that the Apostles were accustomed to ask our Lord in private for the explanation of anything in His public instruction which they had not understood. It may be, therefore, that when alone with Him after this memorable day at Capharnaum, they asked Him to tell them more about the wonderful Gift He had just promised. Certain it is that at one time or other, either now or later on, He unfolded to them the wonders of the Blessed Eucharist. What did He teach them about It? Just what the Church teaches us. And to this we must come now.

The first thing we have to note about the Blessed Sacrament is that It exceeds all the other sacraments in dignity, as It gives not grace only, but Jesus Christ Himself, the Giver of all grace. This is so clear that we need not stop to examine it.

Urban, our First Communicant, thought a good deal about everything that came under his notice, though he could not always bring out his ideas clearly—you see he was only a little boy. Because he was thoughtful and found things out for himself, he was apt at times to get impatient when his masters or his books took the trouble to explain what to him was perfectly clear. And so when he was told that "the Blessed Sacrament exceeds all the others in dignity *because*"—he broke in sharply with "Why, of course It does; It doesn't deserve to be named with the rest." Then, after a moment's thought, he added, slowly: "Do you know—I think perhaps some day they will take It away from the others and put It—*quite by Itself*."

The chief dogmas or truths respecting the Holy Eucharist are these three:

1. The Real Presence.
2. Transubstantiation.
3. That Christ is present as a whole under each of the species, and in every part of the species.

1. That Jesus Christ is really and truly present in the Holy Eucharist—that is, not in figure, but substantially—*Himself*, Body and Blood and Soul and Divinity, is clear from three texts of Holy Scripture:

First, as we have seen from the solemn words spoken in the synagogue of Capharnaum and preserved for us by St. John in the sixth chapter of his Gospel.

Secondly, from the words of Institution at the Last Supper. Let us watch the scene. Our Lord is seated with His Apostles for the last time. He has eaten with them the Paschal Lamb. He is fulfilling every type and every prophecy. And now whilst all look on in silence and in awe, He takes bread and wine, and blesses them, and gives them to the Apostles, saying: "This is My Body; this is My Blood. Take and eat; take and drink."

"*This*"—the substance which I hold in My Hand,

"*is*"—really is, not reminds you of,

"*My Body*"—My Flesh and Blood that I promised you—that shall be given and shed for you.

Our Lord is instituting something to fulfill the types of the Manna and the Paschal Lamb. The fulfilment must be a reality, not another figure. And it must be greater than the figure. It is His last great act of love before His Death. We must expect something wonderful and mysterious. His words could not be of doubtful meaning or misleading. When He said, "This is My Body," He knew the whole Church to the end of the world would take these words literally and would *adore* the sacred species.

Thirdly, from St. Paul's words in his Epistle to the Corinthians. He had heard that some of his converts at Corinth had been guilty of a terrible sin and sacrilege by going to Communion without that necessary preparation which is required—the state of grace. He wrote to them in reproof, and his words are very solemn and very terrible. "I hear that when you come together into one place, it is not now to eat the Lord's Supper. For every one taketh before his own supper to eat. And one indeed is hungry, and another is drunk... What shall I say to you? Do I praise you? In this I praise you not...The Chalice of Benediction which we bless, is It not the Communion of the Blood of Christ? And the Bread which we break, is It not the partaking of the Body of the Lord?...For I have received of the Lord that which also I delivered unto you, that the Lord Jesus the same night in which He was betrayed, took bread and giving thanks, broke, and said: Take ye and eat, this is My Body which shall be delivered for you; this do for the commemoration of Me. In like manner also the chalice after He had supped, saying: This is the New Testament in My Blood; this do, as often as you shall drink, for the commemoration of Me. For as often as you shall eat this Bread and drink the Chalice, you shall show the Death of the Lord until He come. Therefore, whosoever shall eat this Bread or drink the Chalice of the Lord unworthily, shall be guilty of the Body and of the Blood of the Lord. But let a man prove himself, and so let him eat of that Bread and drink of the Chalice. For he that eateth and drinketh unworthily, eateth and drinketh judgment to himself, not discerning the Body of the Lord."

Now, can anyone say that St. Paul is here speaking figuratively? "The Chalice we bless, is *It* not the Blood of Christ? The Bread we eat, is *It* not the Body of the Lord?" He speaks of the guilt of eating this Bread and drinking this Chalice of the Lord *unworthily*. No one can eat mere bread or drink mere wine unworthily. If this bread and wine were merely a representation of our Lord's Body and Blood, it might indeed be received with a want of reverence, but it could not be received unworthily, so as to make the communicant guilty of the Body and Blood of the Lord—could it?

St. Paul goes on to say that before going to Communion a man must "prove himself"—that is, examine himself to see if he is in a state of grace. "And so"—when he is thus prepared, "let him eat of that Bread and drink of the Chalice." "*That* Bread"—see how reverently the Apostle speaks.

Lastly come those terrible words: "He that eateth and drinketh unworthily, eateth and drinketh judgment to himself"—that is, earns his own damnation for so frightful a sacrilege. "Not discerning the Body of the Lord." See how the Real Presence is proved again and again. To discern a thing is to perceive and recognize it—we do not discern what is not there.

A Presbyterian minister lay dying. He had been a good man. He had lived up to the light God had given him, and taught his people what was right as far as he knew it himself. And now he was going to his account. Round his bed stood other ministers of the Protestant Church of Scotland and his sorrowing friends. Plenty of people, but, oh, how little help. None of the means at hand by which the Church comforts and strengthens and defends her children at their last hour. No holy water sprinkled on the bed to keep off the Evil One. No Sacraments to cleanse and soothe the trembling soul. No tender words bringing Jesus, Mary, and Joseph there to assist it in its last agony, that it might depart with them in peace. Some dry, hard speeches—they could scarcely be called prayers—long readings about Noah and Jonas and the Hebrew children—these were the last sounds the soul was to hear as it passed out of this world. It did *not* hear them. For a long time the dying man lay still, so still, some thought the end had come; when, suddenly, he opened his eyes wide and fixed them on something that he seemed to see in the air above him. It could not have been anything terrifying, for there was no sign of fear in his face. But there was awe and profoundest reverence. The spectators held their breath. He seemed to be listening, as if some one unseen to all but himself were instructing him, and there were signs as if he accepted all he heard. Gradually a look of astonishment came over his countenance, and recovering for a minute the use of speech, he said in amazement, "Seven! I always thought there were only two." Another long pause, and the room was still as death. Again he listened—again he bowed his head. Then came a look of intense surprise, and awe and reverence and faith and love spoke out in tones that thrilled through every heart: "Really present! Really present! Had I known *that*, I would have preached it to the whole world." The eyes closed, the head fell back—he was dead.

2. We go on now to the next great truth respecting the Blessed Sacrament—Transubstantiation.

To understand the meaning of this hard word we must take it to pieces. *Trans* means a taking *across* or change. When you translate an exercise into French or Latin, you take it across, that is, change it from one language into another. *Transubstantiation* is the change of one substance into another. "But what is the substance that is changed?" Ah, that is a hard question. I am afraid you would not understand the answer, but we can try. In all bodies, that is, in everything around us, there are two things to be noted; there is the thing itself, and there is what our senses perceive about it—the shape, colour, length, breadth, smoothness, by which we know it and distinguish it from other things. The thing itself is called the *substance*; what our senses perceive about it are called the *appearances*, or *accidents*, or *species*. These appearances are all we can perceive of a thing; the substance we never see—it is invisible. "But if I break a nut and find the kernel, I have come to the substance of the nut and can see it?" No, you have only come to new appearances—the appearances of the kernel. You are as far as ever from finding or seeing any substance.

The appearances cleave to the substance, that is, they are fixed in it, we cannot separate them from it. You cannot lift the colour or the smell from that cedar pencil you are holding.

Yet the substance and appearances are distinct, and if we cannot separate them, *God can*. When He does it, a miracle takes place—and this miracle is taking place on every altar, at every Mass.

"A miracle at every Mass!" Yes, and not one miracle only. Let us see what happens at Mass. When the priest says the words of consecration, the whole substance of the bread is changed into the Body of Christ, and the whole substance of the wine into His Blood. The Body and Blood are not there *together* with the bread and wine, but the substances of the bread and wine are *changed*. This is Transubstantiation.

Does this seem wonderful? Yet it is not more wonderful to change one substance into another than to create a new substance altogether. In the Mystery of the Altar we know of the change by faith only. But there was a transubstantiation at the marriage-feast of Cana, of which the guests knew by their senses also. The waiters were called in every direction to relate what had taken place. They told everybody that there had been a wonderful change. They were quite sure it was water they poured into those great water-pots. And Jesus of Nazareth had changed it into wine.

One of our Lord's reasons for working this miracle was to make the miracle at Mass easier to our belief. One was a type of the other. But as usual, the type was less wonderful than the fulfilment. At Cana the accidents or appearances of the water went away with the substance of the water, and the new substance of the wine brought its own accidents with it—the colour, the smell, the taste of wine. But at the Consecration it is not so. The substance of the bread and the substance of the wine are changed into the Body and into the Blood of Christ. But the accidents of the bread and wine remain, separated from their substances. The colour and taste and smell of bread and wine are there without the substances to which they belong— these are entirely gone. Moreover, the substance of our Lord's Body and the substance of His Blood which have come in place of the substances of bread and wine have come without their own proper accidents or appearances. If it were not so, we should see Him as Man on the altar after the Consecration. The sight of Him hereafter is to be the reward reserved for our faith now, as He has promised. In the meantime we have in the Blessed Sacrament all that is good for us to have now— our Lord Himself, the true Body and Blood of Jesus Christ, together with His Soul and Divinity under the appearances of bread and wine.

Bowed down before the altar, St. Louis, King of France, was hearing Mass. Around him there was the shuffling of feet moving towards a distant part of the church. But the King never looked up to see what was going on. Presently one of his attendants touched him. A miracle had taken place at the other end of the church. At another altar where Mass was being said a beautiful Child had been seen in the priest's hands since the Consecration. Would not his Majesty go and see? "Let those go who must see to believe," said St. Louis, "I would rather be one of those to whom our Lord says, 'Blessed are they who have not seen and have believed.'" And bowing down his head again, he went on with his acts of faith.

Urban showed the greatest contempt for those who have any difficulty in believing what God has revealed, and who ask, "*How* God can do this and that?" "How stupid of them," he said, "don't they know that God is incomprehensible and that if they could understand Him and what He does, He wouldn't be God? Why, there is the corn growing, they can't even understand such a simple thing as that!"

3. The third truth about the Blessed Sacrament comes naturally out of the others. Christ is present, whole and entire, under each species or appearance, and in every part of the species, because by the words of consecration the Body and Blood of Christ become present in the Host and in the Chalice as He is when these words are uttered. He is now in Heaven, in a glorified state. A glorified body cannot undergo any change. It is indivisible—where one part is, the whole must be. It is true that the words, "This is My Body" signify only that the Body is present. But It is a living human Body, which has therefore a human Soul dwelling in It and contains human Blood. And because by the Hypostatic Union, our Lord's two natures are inseparable, wherever the Human Nature is there the Divine Nature will be.

The words of St. Paul which we have considered just now show this truth very clearly. He says, "Whosoever shall eat this Bread *or* drink the Chalice of the Lord unworthily, shall be guilty of the Body *and* Blood of the Lord." Because the Lord is there whole and entire under each species.

This being so, we see that the laity are not deprived of anything by the law of the Church which allows them to receive this Sacrament under one kind only. In early times they used to receive the Sacred Blood in the chalice also. But we can easily understand how the fear of accidents and other reasons have moved the Church to alter her practice in this respect. All therefore who communicate—even priests, except when they are saying Mass, receive under one kind only.

The effects of this Divine Sacrament we must study another day.

My God, I wonder why You love us so much. You like to be with us. You work miracle upon miracle to come to us, as if You could not be happy without us. I wonder why, for I know You are quite happy by Yourself. I should have thought that far away in Your beautiful Heaven You would have forgotten all about us, or at least that You would wait till we got to Heaven to give Yourself to us. But You cannot wait. You come to fetch us home. You will be our Companion all the way. I wonder why.

And there is another thing I wonder. I wonder why we love You so little—why we care so little to be with You, when we cannot be happy by ourselves. We need You to make us happy. We need You to help us to be good; to care for us; to comfort us; to give us all we want. And yet we forget You so—at least I do. I wonder how it is.

David cried out, "How lovely are Thy tabernacles, O Lord of Hosts!" I know a good many of Your Tabernacles, and one at least I know very well. Do I think it lovely to be kneeling there before You? Do I long for You like the little Imelda who drew You into her heart when she was quite small by her loving desires? Remember, dear Lord, that You promised to draw *all* hearts to Yourself when You should be lifted up. Please keep

Your promise, and whenever You are lifted above my head at Mass or Benediction, draw my heart to Yourself.

# XVIII
## The Last Supper

A year has passed since the promise at Capharnaum, and as yet the Great Gift has not been given. Our Lord's work on earth is nearly done. The Thirty Years of the Hidden Life with their silent lessons; the Three Years of the Public Life with their incessant toil and teaching and miracles; the training of the Apostles; the Divine Example given to men—all is nearly over—the last week of His Life on earth has come.

It is Thursday. Four days ago there was the people's last burst of joyous praise. The wonderful miracle of the raising of Lazarus was in every mouth, and, hearing that our Lord was going up to Jerusalem from Bethany, a very great multitude went out from the City to meet Him, carrying branches of palms, strewing their garments on His way, and making the air resound with their shouts and acclamations.

On reaching Jerusalem, He went to the Temple, "and there came to Him the blind and the lame, and He healed them." A few days more and His teaching in the Temple would come to an end. Was there to be no public honour shown to "the Son in His own House"—to the Son of God in that beautiful and glorious House which His Presence had glorified so many times? There had been the silent homage of Simeon and Anna, of His Blessed Mother and St. Joseph. But was there to be no public glory given to Him within its walls? It would have been sad to think that there was none. Yet, but for the little children of Jerusalem there would have been none.

The hatred of His enemies was so well known, that no one now dared to shelter Him, much less show Him any marks of reverence and honour. The children alone were not afraid. They gathered round Him as He sat healing in the Temple. They watched Him laying His Hands on the eyes of the blind, putting His Fingers into the ears of the deaf, and at each fresh cure a shout of praise went up from those innocent hearts, "Hosanna to the Son of David! Hosanna to the Son of David!" There was no silencing them. Not the cross faces of the Pharisees, nor the angry words of the Chief Priests, nor the threatening gestures of the Scribes, who from behind the pillars shook their fists at them—could stop those shouts of praise. They had their Benediction service all to themselves— their songs of joy before the Son of God there present Whom no one else would honour. The wrathful Pharisees told our Lord to stop the children making that noise in the Temple. But He took the children's part, and said if they were silenced the very stones would cry out. Dear little children of Jerusalem! To you we owe it, that just once those glorious Temple-Courts were filled with the praises of the Son of God made Man.

Each night our Lord was obliged to leave Jerusalem and seek from His friends at Bethany a shelter for the night. Bethany was about a mile from Jerusalem, and there, as you know, lived Martha and Mary and their brother Lazarus, whom our Lord had raised to life. He was at Bethany this Thursday, the day of unleavened bread, when the Paschal lamb had to be killed. Calling Peter and John, He sent them into Jerusalem, saying, "Go and prepare for us the Pasch, that we may eat. But they said: Where wilt Thou that we prepare? And He said to them: Behold, as you go into the city there shall meet you a man carrying a pitcher of water; follow him into the house where he entereth in. And you shall say to the good man of the house: Where is the guest-chamber, where I may eat the Pasch with My disciples? And he will show you a large dining-room furnished, and there prepare."

See Peter and John setting off together. Bethany is the place where the Paschal lambs are reared. They are being driven by hundreds into the City, and the Apostles hear them bleating as they pass them on the road. This is just such a Passover as that to which Mary and Joseph brought the Holy Child when He was twelve years old—the caravans arriving and breaking up, the hill-side covered with tents, the noise, the bustle, the concourse of people increasing every moment. Now Peter and John are entering the City. They must look about them carefully, not to miss the man they are seeking. See, here he is turning down this street. They turn, too, and follow him. What a motley throng it is!—Jews, not only from every part of Palestine, but from Persia and Arabia and Egypt, Pharisees and Sadducees, Roman soldiers and Greeks, merchants, students, rabbis, and peasants. Here they meet the head of a family hurrying forward to buy the lamb and take it to the Temple to be sacrificed; here they pass a house whose curtained entrance shows that guests may yet find a lodging within. Over there are pilgrims going up the outer staircase which leads from the street to the roof or to the guest-chamber. At this street corner they find the crowd respectfully giving way before a Pharisee who is standing there to say his prayers. Wherever there is a break in the houses, the Temple can be seen—its roof one blaze of light.

Following closely on the steps of their unconscious guide, the two thread their way through the narrow streets, past splendid palaces, and busy markets, and noisy bazaars. Now he has stopped in front of a house on Mount Sion, and is going with his pitcher up the outer staircase. The Apostles do not follow him farther. They have to speak to the owner of the house, and must go in by the door that opens on the street. He looks pleased when Peter gives the Master's message, and takes them upstairs to the guest-chamber. Peter goes off to buy the lamb, leaving John to prepare the room.

Let us look around this room which is to be hallowed by such wonderful mysteries. Here, to-night, the holiest of all the Sacraments will be instituted. Here the first Mass will be said, the first Priests ordained, and the first of First Communicants receive their Lord. Everything about it is of interest to us. Let us look at it as the Beloved Disciple moves here and there, and see what he sees. A large upper room furnished. Pictures do not give us a good idea of the room and its furniture. In the centre is a low semi-circular table. Round it, and raised only a little distance from the floor, are couches with cushions for the head and arms. Lamps, carpets, and mats, pitchers of water and basins for washing hands are about the room. The couches will hold two persons or even three. Guests do not sit as we do, but recline on the left arm, which rests on the table or on a cushion. The head leans on the left hand, the right hand is thus free to reach the food. St. John looks at the couches and makes his arrangements. There—in the centre—shall be the Master's place, and his own place shall be next Him. Peter and Andrew on the couch to the left. Judas near the Master on the right. The rest in pairs around.

When Peter comes in, the two go together to see to the preparation of the lamb, for the Law requires the greatest care to be taken in all that concerns it. It must be a lamb of a year old and without blemish. Not a bone must be broken. It is to be roasted at the fire, eaten with unleavened bread and wild lettuce, and the whole must be consumed. When all that has to be provided is ready, the two Apostles go out to meet our Lord. He comes into the City towards evening, and through the crowded streets makes His way to the Upper Room with the Twelve.

No—one has slipped away and is on his road to the Chief Priests. He has already made his bargain with them. For thirty pieces of silver, about £4 of our money,[1] he is to betray his Master into their hands, when there is no crowd of people about that might stand up for Him and rescue Him.

Judas tells the Chief Priests that to-night will be a good opportunity. His Master is going to eat the Pasch in the City, but he heard Him say He would afterwards go as usual to the Garden of Gethsemane to pray. They must be ready to seize Him there. He will go back to Him now, eat the Pasch with Him, and then come back for them. When He is in prayer in the Garden, they must go up quietly and take Him. "But how shall we know Him in the dark?" "The moon will be bright and I will lead you to where He will be under the olive-trees. I will go up and kiss Him and call Him Master, so you will know Him. You cannot mistake the Man, He is kingly and beautiful—there is no one else like Him. Hold Him fast and lead Him away carefully—there will be no one near to help Him."

Having made his arrangements with the Chief Priests, Judas hurries to the Supper-room. They have all taken their places. He slinks in, and hiding his money-bag in his sleeve, lest any one should notice how full it is, looks round the room for his place. It is near his Master, and as he comes up to take it, his eyes meet the Eyes of Jesus. Our Lord looks at Him gently and sorrowfully. He knows where He has been; He sees the bag, but He says nothing.

Let us look again at the Supper-room, lit up now by the white light of the Paschal moon.[2] Our Lord is there with the

---

1  This would correspond to roughly $600 today.
2  Since the Jewish calendar was based on the lunar cycle, Passover always fell during a full moon.

Twelve around Him. It is His last night with them. He knows that by this time to-morrow He will have given His life for the redemption of the world and be lying in His grave, and that His little flock will be scattered like sheep who have lost their shepherd. John is resting his head on his Master's Breast. On the table are the roasted lamb, the unleavened bread, the dish of bitter herbs, the wine and the wine-cups. You remember that the Jews were ordered to eat the Pasch as they ate it the night they came out of Egypt—in the dress of travellers, in haste, with shoes on their feet and staves in their hands. But in later times they seem to have eaten the Pasch reclining on couches as at an ordinary supper.

The repast began with a solemn act of thanksgiving made by the father or head of the company. This done, all drank of a cup of wine. Afterwards they washed their hands. Then a child, or the youngest there, was to rise and ask the meaning of this solemn service and how this night was different from all others. Why they might eat unleavened bread only? Why only bitter herbs? The father was to reply by relating in words suited to the child's capacity the whole history of the people of God, from Abraham to the deliverance from Egypt and the giving of the Law, and the more fully he explained it all, the better. Then some psalms were sung; there was another washing of hands; and the Paschal lamb was eaten with the unleavened bread and bitter herbs. The ordinary supper followed.

The youngest at the Last Supper is St. John. Think what our Lord's thoughts will be when the Beloved Disciple asks Him why this night is different from all others—when He tells the Apostles about the sprinkling of the blood of the Paschal Lamb; about the Manna in the desert; about the Brazen Serpent being lifted up.

At the washing of the hands our Lord rises, and to the surprise of all, lays aside His garments, and having taken a towel, girds Himself. Then He pours water into a basin and begins to wash the feet of His Apostles and to wipe them with the towel wherewith He is girded. He comes to St. Peter. Peter knows Who it is that is kneeling before him. He draws up his feet quickly and exclaims, "Lord, dost Thou wash my feet?" Jesus says to him: "What I do, thou knowest not now, but thou shalt know hereafter." Peter only answers more resolutely than before, "Thou shalt never wash my feet." Our Lord knows how to frighten him: "If I wash thee not, thou shalt have no part with Me."

No part with his Master! Oh, look at poor St. Peter now, holding out both hands and crying, "Lord, not only my feet, but also my hands and my head."

Our Lord washes his feet and then goes round to the rest. See Him kneeling at the feet of Judas—taking them into His Hands, pressing them to His Lips. See Him looking into the face of Judas—trying to touch his heart—offering him grace and forgiveness still. It is no use. Judas will not meet His Eye, and he will not have His grace. What more can the Sacred Heart do?

It was to show us the purity of soul with which we ought to draw near to His Holy Table that our Lord washed the feet of His Apostles. He wanted us to see that before we venture there, not only greater sins but lesser stains ought to be washed away.

Look at our Lord sitting down again after the washing of the feet. He is tired in Body and troubled in Soul. His Apostles are His friends, and He tells them why He is troubled. "Amen, amen, I say to you; one of you shall betray Me." See how thunderstruck they all are, with what consternation they look at one another, wondering who it can be, each one asking, tremblingly, "Is it I, Lord?" And He says, "One of the Twelve who dippeth with Me his hand in the dish." This is to show Judas He knows all that is passing in his heart. Still Judas shuts his heart and pretends not to understand.

## The Washing of the Feet

"He began to wash the feet of His disciples and to wipe them with the towel wherewith He was girded." (John 13:5.)

Our Lord's love has made Him try to win back His miserable Apostle by marks of the tenderest affection; now the same love tries to frighten him and so to save him still. For an instant the countenance of the meek Lamb of God is changed. In tones that strike terror into the hearts of all the innocent ones there, He says, "Woe to that man by whom the Son of Man shall be betrayed. It were better for him if that man had not been born." It is another grace unheeded, another warning lost.

Instead of entering into himself, and throwing himself at our Lord's Feet at those awful words, Judas is looking round at the faces of his companions. His only fear is the fear of being found out. He does not mind what God thinks of him, but he does mind being disgraced before the rest. He had not asked with the rest, "Is it I, Lord?" But this had not been noticed. Each one was afraid for himself, and so no one had thought of Judas. See how kind and charitable they must have been, never to have noticed his faults and how different he was from the rest. See too the charity of our Blessed Lord, Who had never said anything which could have led others to suspect Judas. What would have happened if Peter or the Boanerges had found him out! Afraid of being found out by them now, he asks—asks after this awful warning, "Is it I, Lord?" In a voice so low that the others cannot hear, our Lord answers, "Thou hast said it."

And now the time has come for our Divine Lord to keep His promise and give us His best Gift by instituting the Blessed Sacrament. All that He could give us He had given, and this best Gift—His Body and Blood and Soul and Divinity—He is to give us to-night, on the eve of His Death. Well may St. John begin his account of the institution of the Blessed Sacrament by those words: "Jesus having loved His own who were in the world, He loved them unto the end."

They do not know, those dear Apostles, what He has in store

for them. But they feel their Master is different to-night from what they have ever known Him to be before. All through the supper-time He has been different. He has treated them not as disciples, but as friends, to whom He could speak freely of His troubles, who have a right to know the secrets of His Heart. "You are they who have continued with Me in My temptations." Never before has He shown Himself so loving. Never have His words been so tender. "As the Father hath loved me, I also have loved you. Abide in My love. Little children, yet a little while I am with you...Let not your heart be troubled...I go to prepare a place for you. I will not leave you orphans, I will come to you." Never has His Heart been poured out to them like this before. They feel as if they had never known Him till now. Their hearts go out to Him with a vehement love. It is as if He were drawing them out of themselves to make them one with Him.

They do not know their First Communion is so near, that in a few moments the first Mass will have been said and they will have received their dear Master into their hearts. But He knows, and He has been preparing them all through this supper-time, calling forth acts of *faith* in Him, acts of *trust* in Him, acts of *love* for Him—the acts before Communion. Acts of *sorrow* that they have ever grieved Him, acts of *humility*, for He has said one of them is to betray Him and they do not know who it is. And acts of *desire* to be with Him always, to have Him always with them, to be united with Him always by the deepest and the tenderest love. Just the very acts by which *we* are preparing ourselves to receive Him and which ought to be more frequent and more fervent now that the time is so near.

Supper is finished, but He does not rise to go. See, He has taken into His Hands one of the small loaves of unleavened bread that have been left. He is looking at it. He blesses it. He breaks it. He is speaking over it: "Take ye and eat; This is My Body." Every eye is fixed upon Him. To every soul there comes a flash of light. This, then, is the Gift He promised that day at Capharnaum. This is the Living Bread from Heaven—the Bread that is His Flesh—the Flesh He is to give for the life of the world. Yes, there is the light in His Eyes, the glow on His Face they saw that day at Capharnaum, Those Hands that multiplied bread in the desert have worked a greater miracle here.

"*This is My Body.*" The moment of their First Communion has come. They fall on their knees. To each and all He gives a portion of that consecrated Bread. They receive It into their heart, knowing well what It is. They believe. They adore. See them with bowed heads and joined hands, as they make their thanksgiving in the silent room. They have received what we receive, the Body and Blood, the Soul and Divinity of Jesus Christ under the appearance of bread.

But hush! He is speaking again and they look up, "Drink ye all of this. For this is My Blood of the New Testament which shall be shed for you and for many unto remission of sins." He has spoken these words over the Chalice before Him. And now He passes It round to them and they all drink of It, receiving—not more than before—not more than we receive, but under another appearance, the appearance of wine. He gives them, as He promised, His Body and Blood, that they may have life in them.

And He gives them power to do what He has done: to change bread into His Body, and wine into His Blood, and to pass on the same power to the priests of His Church to the end of the world, that so not they only, but all who believe in Him, may have life in Him, and be raised up by him at the Last Day. "*Do this,*" thus instituting both a Sacrament and a Sacrifice, and do it "*for a commemoration of Me.*" Oh, those tender words! Friends when they are parting look about for some keepsake to remind them of each other when they are far apart. Our Lord was going away from us, going to die for us. He wanted to give us some keepsake to remind us of Him.

What had He that was good enough for us—that was worthy of Himself? One thing only.

Had we been in that Supper-room and had He asked us what He should leave us now He was going away, should we not have cried out: "Stay with us, Lord; stay with us!" And if He had told us that it was expedient for us that He should go, that He might save us by His Death and go up to Heaven to prepare a place for us, should we not still have cried out, "Find out some other way of saving us, O Lord, but do not leave us—we cannot do without You. We cannot follow You into Your Kingdom, for how shall we know the way? And how can we abide in Your love as You have bidden us, we who are so weak? Stay with us, O Lord."

And He did find out a way—not to avoid dying for us, that He was determined to do—but to die for us, and go to prepare a place for us, remaining with us always: "I will not leave you orphans, I will come to you." No one but God could do this. But He was God. "Greater love than this no man hath, that a man lay down his life for his friends." But greater love than this He had for us, for each one of us, poor and little though we are. He was as anxious to stay, nay, more anxious a great deal than we could be to keep Him—and he *has* stayed. He invented this wonderful means of being with us, not in one place only as He was then, but in thousands of tabernacles all the world over. Thus He keeps His promise, "Behold I am with you all days even to the end of the world." His best Gift is Himself, less than this He would not give us, more He could not give. He gives us Himself, on just one condition—that His Gift, the Blessed Sacrament, should be to us a remembrance of Him, especially when we are present at Mass, where His Death for us is shown, and in Holy Communion, when we receive Him into our hearts.

And this was how the Twelve made their First Communion

in that Upper Chamber in Jerusalem. No, not the Twelve, we cannot call them any more by that dear name. They are the Eleven now. One has left the Supper-room, never to return. He has left, carrying our Lord away with him in his heart to go and sell Him to His enemies. Oh, what bitter sorrow that one is causing our Blessed Lord! To think that among His Twelve, one should be found to betray Him! Only twelve First Communicants—and one of them a traitor! His Heart is so wrung with anguish at this betrayal that He goes back upon it again and again. "Amen, amen, I say to you, one *of you* shall betray Me." And a little after, "Behold the hand of him that betrayeth Me is with Me on the table." Not all the joy of His First Communion, to which He has looked forward for so long, can make up to our Lord for the loss of that poor miserable Apostle whom He has tried so hard to save. The agony of His Soul shows itself in His Countenance and in the tones of His voice. The Apostles see it and wish they could help Him. It needs all their loyal love to bring comfort to His Sacred Heart.

When Urban came to this meditation and saw the Beloved Disciple making his thanksgiving with his head on his Master's Breast, he said, "How happy St. John was! He had our Lord within and without, within to speak to his heart, without to speak to his mortal ears."

> Dear Saint! I stand far off
> With vilest sin opprest;
> O, may I dare, like thee,
> To lean upon His Breast.
>
> O teach me, dear St. John!
> The secrets Christ taught thee!
> The beatings of His Heart
> And how It beat for me.

And now we bid farewell to the Supper-room, the scene of such tremendous mysteries. One more look at our Lord and Master as He sits there in the midst of the Eleven. The next time we see Him here, it will be after His battle and His victory. The Lamb will have redeemed the sheep. The Innocent One will have reconciled sinners with the Father. But oh, at what a cost! For to save us, He must first pass through the red sea of His own Blood.

One more look at the King in His Beauty, the Fairest of the sons of men, before our sins have battered out of Him the likeness of man and made Him a worm and no man. One more look at His beautiful Face while yet it is beautiful, before our sins have defiled it and made it a fearful sight to see.

He rises. He is leaving the Supper-room. He is going to torments and to Death—*for me*. I throw myself on my face before Him. Farewell, O my Saviour and my Redeemer! Nay, how dare I say farewell to Him? I know how it is going to fare with Him—I know to what He is going—to what my sins will bring Him. I cannot say farewell to You, dear Lord. He raises me up, He speaks to me tenderly, He tells me to weep not for Him, but for my sins. He is glad to suffer and give His Life for me, if only I will let Him save me by His Death—if only I will profit by His Blood.

# XIX
## Calvary

When our Lord wished to make the Samaritan woman desire greatly the living water He had so great a desire to give her, He said, "If thou didst know the gift of God!" So He says to each one of us now: "O child, if you did but know what the Gift is which I left you at My Last Supper—what it cost Me to purchase It for you—you would be grateful for It; you would desire It eagerly; you would try to give Me back love for love."

We measure the worth of a thing by its cost. That was a precious cup of water which David sacrificed in his thirst when he was at war with the Philistines. You remember how often he had to fight those obstinate enemies of the Jewish people. Holy Scripture says that once "when the men of Israel were gone away, he stood and smote the Philistines till his hand was weary, and grew stiff with the sword."

And once his own little city, Bethlehem, called in later times the "City of David," was in the hands of the enemy. They had a strong army drawn around it, so that no one could go in or out. "And David was then in a hold," says the Scripture, "and there was a garrison of the Philistines then in Bethlehem. And David longed and said: "Oh, that some man would give me a drink of the water out of the cistern that is in Bethlehem by the gate." And three of his "valiant men broke through the camp of the Philistines and drew water out of the cistern of Bethlehem, that was by the gate, and brought it to David. But he would not drink,...saying: Shall I drink the blood of these men, who went at the peril of their lives? Therefore he would not drink." See how he prized that costly cup of water. He called it, "the blood of these men."

Our Lord has paid a greater price to bestow spiritual food upon us. He has given, in very truth, His own Blood. The cost was Calvary. Pointing to Calvary, St. Paul says *to us*: "You are bought with a great price." Pointing to Calvary, we may surely say of the Precious Food of our souls: "O Divine Eucharist, O Gift of God, truly *You* were bought with a great price! "

What that price was we can never know in this life. But we may learn some little by climbing the hill of Calvary in company with the Divine Victim and the Mother of Sorrows—keeping close to her all the while—trying to see what she saw—to feel what she felt—to love and compassionate Him with her.

> Let me mingle tears with thee,
> Mourning Him Who mourned for me,
> All the days that I may live.

Oh, the outcries and the curses and the blasphemies that are rending the Mother's heart, as she waits here at the corner of the street to see her Son pass by on His way to His Death! Since midnight, John has been coming and going to and fro, from the Garden, and the Courts, and the Pretorium, bringing her word of all that has befallen Him—how pale He looked in the moonlight when He rose from His three hours' prayer and went forth to meet His enemies—how awful He was in His Majesty when He cast them on their faces before Him—how He let them rise and approach Him again, and how meekly He received the traitor's kiss—how they bound His Hands behind His back and led Him away, and how all, even Peter, had forsaken Him. How in the palace of Annas He had been struck in the Face, and in Herod's been mocked as a fool, and

### David and the Three Valiant Men

"David would not drink...Saying...shall I drink the blood of these men that went at the peril of their lives? Therefore he would not drink."
(2 Kings 23:16,17)

in Pilate's been mocked again and spit upon and crowned with thorns. Of the scourging John could not speak to her, only he said that when it was over, the Lord had fallen on the pavement in a pool of His own Blood.

Hark! the cries are getting louder: the procession is coming up this way. See the eager sight-seers in every doorway, on every roof, as well as in the streets, the packed streets of this Paschal-time. The greater number have been waiting since the time of the condemnation—about eleven—and it must be nearly twelve now.

Listen to the words that fall on the Mother's ear: "So the impostor has been found out at last, Blessed be the Lord God of Israel! He will have His deserts now. He had nothing to say for Himself when He was brought before the judges. His disciples, too, all fled away and left Him—a pitiful set they must be! King of the Jews indeed! Why, the whole people cried out, 'Away with Him, crucify Him!' when Pilate showed Him to them from the balcony an hour ago. Well, there will be an end of Him now and of all the disturbances He has been making in the country during the past three years!"

The noise grows louder. They are coming now. Boys run on before, shouting and laughing. Some of them were in the Temple five days ago crying, "Hosanna to the Son of David!" Here are the trumpeters and the herald who have to proclaim the sentence at the corner of every street. They are followed by men and children carrying the crosses of the thieves, ladders, cords, hammers, and nails. Next come the thieves, and now a whole troop of Scribes and Pharisees and Chief Priests, all with their eyes fixed on the spot where the throng is thickest. He must be there, but we cannot see Him, the crowd is too dense.

Now there is a break and we can see within the circle. What is it that we see—what is it that this vast multitude has come out to see? One with bare and bleeding Feet, bowed down and staggering under the weight of a long, heavy Cross. He is torn and bruised and weary. Since supper last night He has had neither food, nor drink, nor sleep. He is tortured with a burning thirst from loss of Blood. His right Hand tries to steady the Cross upon His shoulder, His left to gather His long robe from under His Feet. He is so weak and His steps are so tottering, that stumbling over it just now, He fell upon His Face. He has reached the place where we are standing. He knows who is to meet Him here. He lifts His Head. He raises His Eyes to hers. O poor Mother! Is *this* your Son? Is this the Blessed Fruit of your womb, Jesus? Is this He on Whom the Angels desire to look, Whom we saw a little while ago, "beautiful above the sons of men?" There is no beauty in Him, nor comeliness, that we should be desirous of Him. Who has dared to lay hands on Him and treat Him so shamefully that He is become a worm and no man?

Hush! Let us look on in silence to see what she sees, to feel what she feels, to see and feel *with her*.

She sees the Blood trickling down upon His Forehead from the thorns that have been beaten into His Head. She sees His Eyes all full of Blood. She sees His Checks disfigured with bruises, filthy with spittle, swollen with blows. She sees the marks of the scourges on His neck. She sees His Hair matted, His raiment dyed with His Blood. She sees how our sins have defiled and disfigured the Lord of Glory, how from Head to Foot He is covered with the hideous marks *of my sins*.

> O let me feel it was my sin
>  As though no other sins there were,
> Which was for Him Who bears the world
>  A load that He could scarcely bear.

With a wild cry of grief Magdalen has thrown herself at His Feet. But no cry escapes from the Mother's broken heart. She is quite still. Only the blinding tears, only the white quivering lips tell the agony of her soul. It is but an instant that she stands there face to face with her Son, but her eye has noted all. And now they thrust her aside; He is lost to sight again; the order is given to move on. She makes a sign to John to follow her, and in another moment she is in the midst of the swaying crowd, driven, pushed, borne along on her road to Calvary. She is making—first among us all—the Way of the Cross.

> With Mary now we follow Christ,
> He mounts the Hill of Woe,
> And bears His heavy Cross along,
> With fainting steps and slow.
> Can we relieve His weary Limbs,
> Or ease His racking pain?
> Oh yes, if we will show Him now
> He did not die in vain.

Presently there is a stoppage. Those in front say He is dying. The Chief Priests fear they will never get Him to Calvary, and they are forcing a Cyrenean stranger to carry His Cross. He is dying? *Oh, that it might be so* would be Mary's prayer, if her heart and her will were less one with His. But she prays as He has taught her to pray, with perfect resignation to the Will of God: "Abba, Father, all things are possible to Thee. If Thou wilt, remove this chalice from Him—nevertheless not as I will, but as Thou wilt."

A little further on, the procession stops again, but only for a moment. A noble lady has made her way through the crowd, and in spite of the soldiers who guard Him, has offered our Lord a veil with which to wipe the Blood and the filth from His Face. He has taken it gratefully and returned it to her, and now she is hastening back to her house with the greatest of relics to be guarded and venerated by the Church to the end of time.

Here, in this narrow street, there is another and a longer halt. He has fallen again. His Mother hears the cries all round Him. She knows how cruel His guards will be to make Him rise and go on, and her tears burst forth afresh. Those around see her tears and hear her broken sobs. They point at her as "the Mother of the Galilean." They whisper and they stare, but no one is kind or compassionate, no one has a word of comfort for her.

How lonely our Lord is in His Passion! Where are those whom He has fed, and taught, and cured, and comforted? Where are the five hundred disciples, many of whom, in a few weeks, will be passing through these very streets to see Him ascend in glory? Where are all these now? "Many are willing to rejoice with Jesus, few are willing to suffer for Him." "I looked about, and there was none to help. I sought and there was none to give aid. I have trodden the wine-press alone, and… there is not a man with Me." Only the faithful John. In the Jewish Council there was none to speak for Him, though He has His friends and disciples there. Joseph of Arimathea and Nicodemus, who in a few hours will come forward so boldly, are afraid to own him now. The Apostles are hiding.

No, there is not a man with Him. Yet He is not quite alone. If men fall away and fail Him, the women are faithful to the last. There, following close upon His footsteps, are the dear brave women of Jerusalem, openly bewailing and lamenting Him. Their little babes are in their arms. We are glad to think that the little children He has loved and blessed are following Him right up to Calvary. He turns round to speak to the weeping women. His words are words of solemn, very solemn warning. There are times when He has words like these for those whom He loves most. They must not be afraid to hear them, but take them and lay them up in their hearts.

Another fall upon the rising ground, and Calvary is reached at last. The Roman soldiers ride to and fro to drive back the immense crowd. None may follow Him now but those who have to carry out the sentence. The executioners throw Him down on the Cross and tell Him to stretch out His Hands and

Feet that they may take the measure for the holes. Now He may go and wait till they are ready for Him. Pity our Lord as He stands trembling in the cold wind until His Cross is ready.

St. John takes our Lady to a little distance. If only he could take her where she would not hear! She goes where he leads. She cannot see her Son, but He is over there and the executioners are round Him preparing Him for His Death. Now He is on the ground and they are kneeling beside Him. Oh, the agony with which her heart is waiting for the first sound. There it is—the first stroke of the hammer—and another, and another. The Divine Victim is offering Himself upon the Altar of the Cross. And Mary unites her offering with His: "Thy Will be done on earth as it is in Heaven. Be it done unto Him according to Thy Will."

He is nailed to the Cross. They bring it to the place prepared for it. They let it fall into the hole with a great jerk and make it fast with blocks of wood driven in all round. Now at last His enemies are satisfied. And whilst the Roman soldiers sit around and watch Him, they come up and mock Him in His agonizing pain.

How dark it is getting! Is this night that is coming on? Yes—darkness is creeping up over the sky—midnight darkness at noon is covering the whole world. The earth quakes—the rocks are rent and the veil of the Temple is torn from the top even to the bottom—the graves are opening, the bodies of the Saints are rising. Fear is creeping into the hearts of men—the centurion and the soldiers that are with him watching Jesus, are sore afraid and say, "Indeed this is the Son of God." And all the multitude of them that are come together to this sight, and see the things that are done, return, striking their breasts.

The mockers fall away from the Cross. And now Mary makes a sign to John to lead her there. She knows where she is to stand. She knows what she has to do. In the quiet days at Nazareth He told her all. She is to be there—the Mother beside her Son, the Queen of Martyrs at the right Hand of the King. She is to assist at this Bloody Sacrifice and unite her offering with that of the Great High Priest, Who is Himself the Priest and Victim.

> Through her heart His sorrow sharing
> All His bitter anguish bearing
> Now at length the sword has passed.

Let us look into the Sacred Heart and see what is passing there. We should have thought that now at least He had done all He could do for us, that He could only hang there patiently and die. How hard it is for us, when we are in pain, to think of anything else. But He, on that bed of pain, has His great work to do, the work for which He came into the world. He must forget Himself and make haste to reconcile the world with the Father. He must offer Himself for the four ends of Sacrifice. He must pay the four debts which, as God's creatures and sinful creatures, we owe to Him.

And so—looking over all time from the beginning—seeing the Sacrifices of the Old Law, which through two thousand years have drawn all their value from this Sacrifice of His, He offers Himself: First, for God's honour and glory. Secondly, in thanksgiving for all the benefits He ever has or ever will bestow upon us. Thirdly, to obtain pardon for all sinners, from Adam, and His dear Magdalen on whose head the Precious Blood is falling, to the last sinner, to the least little child who will come to Him in His Sacraments to have that Precious Blood applied to their souls. And, fourthly, to obtain all graces and blessings for those whom He has loved more than His own Life.

There from His Cross, He looks down upon the world He has come to save—upon the land where His earthly Life amongst us has been spent. He thinks of Bethlehem, and dear Nazareth, and of the lessons He has given us there. He thinks of the streets of Jerusalem, and of the Temple, of the synagogues, the

Lake, the hill-sides and the cornfields where He has preached and taught. He thinks of the prayers and tears and sufferings of His Life, and the torments of His Death by which such merits have been gained, such graces won for us. The price is paid. He has them ready for us. All we have to do is to ask for them. See the graces He is giving freely from His Cross now.

All through the agony of those Three Hours, while His Body is racked with fiercest pain, His Heart is at work for us. Poor sinners are Its first thought, because their need is greatest. Whilst the executioners were driving the nails through His Hands and Feet, a cry was going up for those cruel men, and not for them alone, but for all who should crucify Him again by sin—"*Father, forgive them, for they know not what they do.*" See the fruit of that dying prayer—

A sinner is going to be forgiven now. Just in time, our Lord saves the poor penitent thief at His side. One cry to His Sacred Heart: "Lord, remember me," and instantly the answer comes: "*Amen, I say to thee, this day thou shalt be with Me in Paradise.*" Grace goes forth from that Sacred Heart; the Precious Blood cleanses him from every stain; and now he is waiting patiently by his Master's side—with Him on the Cross, to be with Him in Paradise before the day is done.

"*Woman, behold thy son...Behold thy Mother.*" Our Lord's thoughts turn next to those whom He is leaving orphans, to the children of His Church to the end of time. He is always giving to us, but His best gifts He has kept till the end. Last night in the Supper-room it was the gift of Himself in the Holy Eucharist—what can He have left to give us now? He knows we shall want a Refuge in our sinfulness, a Comfort in our afflictions, a Help in all our needs. And so He gives us

His Mother to be our Mother, and puts into her heart for each one of us a Mother's tenderness and love. "Woman, behold thy son," as if He had given up *to us* the right to call her "Mother." Looking down from the Cross, His failing eyes see the hands of John being laid in the hands of Mary. He lays our hearts there too, to be kept for Him. And Mary opens her heart to all, making the exchange He asks—giving up the Child Who is the life of her life, for the sake of the children who are costing her this bitter death.

Another long silence:

> See! how the nails those Hands
> And Feet so tender rend;
> See! down His Face and Neck and Breast
> His sacred Blood descend.

The blood trickles down more slowly—the body droops lower—the limbs get whiter and whiter—the great Wounds widen—the eyes grow glazed and dim.

And the Soul of Christ and His blessed human Heart—what of them? Is it with Him as it is with us, who suffer less as the end draws near, because our senses become clouded with the film of death? No, it is not so with Him. The fierce tortures of crucifixion that are making every limb and nerve throb with intense pain, leave His Soul undulled up to the end. Up to the end He knows, and therefore feels as acutely as when the nails were driven in nearly three hours ago.

What, then, are the thoughts of that wonderful Soul as He hangs there so patient and so still? Oh, listen to that cry: "*My God, My God, why hast Thou forsaken Me?*" Can those words be the words of the Son of God? Yes, for the Father looks on Him now, not as the Son of His love, but as the Victim of sin on Whose head all His hatred of sin is to be poured out. He is not sin, but He is in the likeness of sin, and so the Father's face is turned away from Him. From the beginning of His

Passion, when He accepted His Father's Will under the olive-trees; all through the Scourging, the Crowning with Thorns, and the Way of the Cross; when He has been doing all He can to repair the Father's honour, to win back His dear creatures for Him, to pay the enormous price the Father asks; all this time His Soul has been plunged in a darkness and a horror thicker than the black night on Calvary. Oh, those awful words in the mouth of the Son of God, "My God, My God, why hast Thou forsaken Me?"

This cry was to let us know what we could not have known, what we could scarcely have suspected, had we not been told. We can hold our crucifix before us and go, one by one, over the wounds of that mangled body, compassionating our Lord for each. But we forget too often that the sufferings which we can, as it were, see, were not the greatest our Lord had to bear. The pain in His Soul and in His Heart were worse by far. It was to win our tender pity for these that the Soul and the Heart of our Lord were thus unveiled to us in His Passion. Thus only could we come to know how much He has loved us.

As we hang over the death-bed of those we love, how we long to follow their thoughts, to catch a word or a sign that may let us into those secrets of the end of which we know so little. Is any deathbed what that Cross on Calvary is to us! Can any last words interest us so intensely as the words that go out into the darkness there!

Listen; the parched lips open once more—with greater difficulty now—and from them comes that meek complaint, yet not so much a complaint as a revelation to us of His Heart: "*I thirst.*"

Of all the deaths the cruelty of man has invented, crucifixion is perhaps the worst. And amongst the tortures of that most awful death the fiercest is the torment of thirst. The crucified turn their eyes hither and thither as if to beseech the bystanders to give them a drink of water. All other pains are forgotten in the pain of that burning thirst. And Jesus says, "I thirst"—not to complain, not to get relief, but to win from us a little sympathy, a little sorrow as we think of the thirst of that parched tongue, and the far greater thirst of that Sacred Heart for the sinners whom all His sufferings will not save.

Silence once again. The end has nearly come. The Redeemer's thoughts have turned away from Himself and travelled back to His redeemed. He thinks of the Promise in Paradise and the work that was given to Him there. He has done it all. He has not spared Himself a single task. He has not grudged us a single pang. He has not shrunk back from a single sacrifice. All the types are accomplished. All the prophecies are fulfilled. The world has been redeemed with a plentiful redemption—"*All is finished!*"

The end has come. It is the hour for His last lesson. He has taught us how to live. He must teach us how to die. He must teach us that what we have to do in that hour of darkness and of terror—when all things of this earth are falling away from us—is to cast ourselves with faith and hope and love into the arms of Him Whose creatures we are. If "it is a fearful thing to fall into the Hands of the Living God," it is sweet and safe to return to the hands of our Heavenly Father, Who for the sake of our Elder Brother has forgiven us and is waiting to receive us "as most dear children"—"*Father, into Thy Hands I commend my Spirit.*"

The end has come. All is silent around the Cross. His Mother and His disciple are looking up into His face as they have looked these last three hours. Magdalen has raised her head for the first time and is looking too. The limbs droop.

The head falls forward on the breast. The lips part. The Soul has gone forth to the Father. The Sacred Heart is still—Jesus having loved His own who were in the world, has loved them to the end.

But the end is not yet. A little while before His Passion our Lord was telling His Apostles of the signs which are to precede His Second Coming at the Last Day. And He said to them, "Fear ye not...the end is not yet." A little after He said: "Look up and lift up your heads, because your redemption is at hand." Surely when we have seen Him die on Calvary we shall say He has loved us to the end. "But the end is not yet." The great Sacrifice is completed. The one great Sacrifice has been offered on Calvary; there can never be another. But what our Lord *did once* on Calvary He will do again, though in a different manner, to the end of the world, for He is a Priest *for ever* according to the order of Melchisedech. And therefore, from the rising of the sun to the going down thereof—that is, in every place throughout the whole world—He will offer that sacrifice which is a memorial of His Sacrifice on Calvary, and is "to show the Death of the Lord until He come"—that Sacrifice which is a memorial Sacrifice, not another Sacrifice, the very same as the Sacrifice on Calvary, with the same Priest and Victim—which is a representation of Calvary and a continuation of Calvary.

And thus our great High Priest stands for ever at our altars—no longer dying really, but seeming to die—no longer offering Himself visibly, but offering Himself invisibly by the ministry of His priests—no longer actually shedding His Blood, but offering Himself in an unbloody manner, and seeming to shed His Blood; the Lamb, "standing as it were slain"—not now paying the price of our redemption, but applying that Redemption to our souls.

Just because its worth is infinite, the merits of the Sacrifice of

Calvary can be applied unceasingly. Just because it was offered once *for all*, the graces it purchased must be brought within the reach of all. Magdalen was not the only sinner who needed the touch of the Precious Blood. We all need to kneel under the Cross and feel our Lord above us procuring pardon for our sins, offering Himself for us in adoration and thanksgiving, and to obtain for us all the graces and blessings He has purchased for us. Our Lord could not have us all around Him on Calvary, and therefore Calvary is set up near the homes of every one of us. We can all "go with confidence to the throne of grace," and get the very helps, the very graces our Lord bought for us long ago on Calvary.

And get that which is the grandest of graces—the greatest of helps—the Giver of grace Himself. It is to Calvary with its bloody Sacrifice offered once, and to Calvary perpetually renewed in an unbloody manner on our altars, that we owe our Lord in the Blessed Sacrament and in Communion. His bitter Passion and Death was the price He paid to bring us this gift of Himself.

Of course, it was possible for Him to give us His Body and Blood without the fearful death on Calvary, just as it was possible for Him to redeem us without Calvary. But the slaying of the victim naturally precedes the consumption of the victim, and in the design of God, the Sacrifice of the Cross was the price of the infinite boon of the Blessed Eucharist. In other words, without Calvary there would have been no Eucharist, and it is only through the renewal of the Sacrifice of Calvary that the Sacramental Presence comes into being upon our altars.

In some of the sacrifices of the Old Law, the victim, after being slain and offered to God, was consumed by the priests and the offerers. And thus it is with the great Sacrifice of our altars. St. Paul says: "Now all these things happened to them in figure," under that Law which was "a shadow of the good things to come...God providing some better things for us."

The end is not yet. The Church has to be supported and guided by the lifting up of the daily Sacrifice; and by the daily Bread provided for her children at the altar of sacrifice. When the last fruits of the Sacrifice upon Calvary have been gathered, and applied by the last Mass to the last of the elect, then the end will come. Then we may lift up our heads, for the great Redemption will be at hand. Then "the Son of Man...shall come in the glory of His Father with the holy Angels." Then Jesus, having loved His own who were in the world, will have loved them unto the end.

# Part the Second:

# Our Preparation for Meeting Our Lord in Holy Communion

# XX
# Our Enemies Abroad

Communion is the meeting of two. We have seen our Lord's preparation for meeting *us*. We must look now to our preparation for meeting *Him*.

Before a King can enter his capital two things must be done—his enemies must be turned out, and his friends must be within to furnish and adorn the palace. We have long been asking our King to enrich our souls with the gifts and ornaments of His grace, and to send His friends the Angels and Saints to help on the preparations. But the first thing to be done is to see who are the King's enemies there, and how we have to deal with them.

Our soul has its enemies, against which we must fight all the days of our life, the Catechism says.

Hatred of God, and envy, have made the devil our enemy. We have done him no harm, that he should hate us as he does; and our ruin, at which he works so hard, can bring him no manner of good. But God loves us. This is the secret of his enmity. God, Who has cast him off, has shown mercy to us, and we are to have the thrones which he and his companions lost through pride. It is to be revenged on God, by spoiling His plan, that the devil is determined we shall never reach those thrones if he can help it.

Now he can only prevent it and harm us by *tempting* us, or *trying* to get us to commit sin: temptation means trying. He cannot *make* us sin. Some people think temptation and sin are the same thing. This is silly, for no one *tries* to do what is already done. Or they think that because the devil is so strong and cunning, they have no chance against him. This is silly, too. For sin depends on our will, which the devil cannot touch. He can get thoughts into our mind, but he is quite powerless when it comes to our will. He is like a thief trying to get into a house where a servant has been left in charge by his master. If the servant is faithful, he will shut the door promptly in the thief's face. It is his own fault if he does not. And suppose the thief goes on knocking—this does not oblige the servant to let him in. The knocking is very troublesome; that cannot be helped. But all the knocking in the world will not open the door. As long as we say "No," the temptation can do us no harm. It may go on teasing us, but there is no reason why it should frighten us in the very least, still less why it should cast us down.

Sometimes the devil knocks very loud, as if he would bring the house down, and sometimes He whispers in a soft voice and begs to be let in. When we feel within us a tremendous disturbance—a violent storm of pride, or anger, or jealousy—this is the devil knocking loud. When it is the desire of some pleasure that entices us, such as indulging sloth, or greediness, or vanity, it is the devil knocking softly. Our friend Urban had his own way of answering the soft knocks. "Shall I tell you how the devil tempts me?" he said. "He comes to me and says, 'Do this, dearie, it will make you happy.' And I say, 'No, I won't, I positively won't.' That is giving him a punch on his head, isn't it—his great ugly head, that is always contriving sin."

Sometimes the devil attacks us by proposing what is plainly sinful—thoughts against faith, or hope, or purity, or humility. At other times he hides his wicked designs, whispering to us that such or such a thing is no sin at all, or only a venial sin. If he can get us to be careless about venial sin, and to harden our conscience by those dangerous words, *"only a venial sin,"* he will come some day with a strong temptation to mortal sin, and we shall be overcome.

The devil has no chance with the fervent. So he tries to cool their fervour by getting them to be careless about prayer and the sacraments. This done, the way is open to him, and he begins to attack them by all sorts of temptations. We are not ignorant of his plans, and as to be forewarned is to be forearmed, we must lay this up in our memory for our whole lifetime—that all falls from fervour begin by a neglect of prayer. A more useful piece of knowledge we could scarcely have.

Though the devil is so strong and so cunning, he would have little chance of overthrowing us if it were not for the enemy within our own hearts, with whom he is in league. What a general fears more than any number of outside foes, is a traitor in the camp. And what we have most to fear is not the devil, but our own corrupt inclinations and passions, which, as the Catechism tells us, are the most dangerous of all our enemies.

Beset by such enemies within and without, it is plain we cannot expect to be free from temptation. What, then, we have to see to, is that we do not increase our danger by bringing temptation upon ourselves; and that when it comes, we meet it as we ought.

We must not bring temptation upon ourselves, for "he that loves the danger," says Holy Scripture, "shall perish in it." Things that often occasion temptation and lead to sin are called the occasions of sin. Perhaps the most common of these are *bad or foolish companions, bad books, curiosity, and idleness.* These things are the devil's agents, or instruments, that he makes use of to help him in his evil work; they are all enemies of the King, and must be turned out of His palace before He comes.

What our *companions* and books are, that we shall be, so it is of the utmost importance that we choose them wisely. Good companions will help us by their example, and confirm us in our good resolutions. Bad or foolish companions will soon rob us of whatever good we have. We shall come to be ashamed of our practices of devotion, and give them up through human respect, which means caring more for what others think and say of us than of what God thinks. We shall fear the ridicule of these companions more than we fear to offend God. The question with us will no longer be, "What will *God* think of this?" but, "What will *So-and-so* think and say?" The hold we have let others get upon us will soon become so strong that we shall be afraid to do anything that they do not like. We shall not dare to resist them even when our conscience cries loud, and warns us of our danger. Oh, what a slavery this is!

It is no uncommon thing nowadays to hear boys and girls proclaiming their rights loudly. They are not going to be sat upon—they will stand up for themselves and be independent. An excellent resolution this, where human respect is concerned! No, indeed—why should we let others sit upon us when they want to make us do what is wrong!

"I don't care what they say; I won't do it." Do you ever catch yourself saying that, when some order goes against the grain? Do you ever find the proud feeling rising—"Why should I knock under to others when I am in the right?" If you do, just keep those words and that feeling safely bottled up, you will want them by-and-bye. By-and-bye some of those about you will want you to do what is wrong. You are going to tell them you cannot, when the thought comes, "Oh! but what will they say?" Now, then, for those bottled-up feelings: *I don't care what they say; I won't do it. Why should I knock under to them when I am in the right?* Here you are making a *safe* use of your independence—*safe* and *grand*—the use made of it by God's grandest Saints!

We must watch the beginnings of our friendships, and when we find we are getting to like certain people, ask ourselves, "Will they do me good or harm? Will they help me to love and serve God better, or will they hinder me?" Our conscience and our common-sense will give us a faithful answer, and we must do as they tell us. It is not necessary that companions should be bad for us to avoid them. It is enough that they are silly, or idle, sly, or careless in spiritual duties. "Birds of a feather flock together." If we find ourselves attracted to such as these, is it not a rather unpleasant revelation about ourselves, and can we afford to get more like them by making them our friends?

We must take care, then, not to be led away from our duty by example or by ridicule. Whilst we are young we have to learn to overcome human respect in small things. Later on we shall have to overcome it in big things; we shall have to guard ourselves against the world—that is, "the society of those who love the vanities, riches, and pleasures of this world better than God." The struggle with the world will be much easier for us if we learn whilst we are young to go on our way towards Heaven without minding what the giddy and the thoughtless say about us.

It is God Who is to judge us. The great thing is to satisfy *Him*, and to obey our conscience, which is His Voice speaking within us. It will be no excuse at our Judgment to say, "Such a one did this or that," when our conscience told us it was wrong to do it. On the other hand, what will it matter when we stand before Him there, and see the smile on His blessed lips, that long, long ago some one down there in that little bit of a thing called the world, laughed at us for not doing as others did, and for caring more to please God than to please them? Oh, what will that matter *then*!

Whilst we take care to guard ourselves against human respect and the bad example of others, let us beware of being ourselves an occasion of harm to any one. Our Lord's words are very awful: "He that shall scandalize one of these little ones that believe in Me, it were better for him that a millstone should be hanged about his neck, and that he should be drowned in the depth of the sea. Woe to the world because of scandals. For it must needs be that scandals come: but nevertheless woe to that man by whom the scandal cometh." We shall have enough to do, when we stand before the judgment-seat of God, to answer for our own sins. How terrible it would be if, besides these, the sins of others were to be laid to our account—if the Angel Guardians of souls whom we have harmed were to appear there as witnesses against us! Oh, let us fear to do the devil's work by being to any one an occasion of even the least sin, but rather do all we can by good example to help others, that their Angels may be our friends and plead for us when the awful hour of our Judgment comes.

And now about *books*. It is quite necessary you should understand that you are not to read everything you can get hold of—every book, every newspaper you find lying about. This does not mean, of course, that these are all bad. But things that are not bad—indeed, things that are very good—may not be good *for you*. In many books, and in newspapers particularly, there are plenty of things that are meant for grown up people only; and children have no more business to meddle with them than they have to taste the pink stuff on father's mantelpiece, that looks so nice. Some of the stuff there is *poison!*

"It's a great shame," thought Harry, as he climbed up to the sideboard, "that grown-up people should keep all the mustard for themselves. If it's nice to them, it will be nice to me; and if nobody will give it to me, I will take it." So he seized the cruet and helped himself to a good spoonful of the "nice yellow stuff."

Perhaps it was as well that he did, for he learned that day what he had never been able to understand before—that it is safer for little boys to do as they are told, and not to meddle with what is not meant for them.

Books may be bad for us, then, without being bad in themselves. But some are bad in themselves, and these—because of His love for us—the King counts among His worst enemies. The harm they may do us is so deadly, that the devil himself could not hurt us more. Books bought at railway-stalls, or procured from lending libraries, taken up anywhere and read without discretion or advice; newspapers got to while away the time on a journey—how often these have robbed a child of its faith, of its peace, of the friendship of God. It is seldom safe to read books of which we know nothing, books of fiction especially. Yet how many of us think of asking advice about our reading? Perhaps we should be afraid to ask it, lest a friendly voice should warn us of danger. It is often curiosity that leads us to read whatever comes in our way, and this brings us to a third occasion of sin that we must guard against—a third enemy of the King, and a very mean one.

*Curiosity*, which makes us want to know what does not concern us; what we are not meant to know; and what in many cases we feel we ought not to know, is a habit which grows as fast as a poisonous weed. We must pluck it up as soon as we perceive it, or it will take deep root and be very hard to destroy. It is so dangerous a habit, that there is no telling where it may lead us. It will make us pry into the secrets of others, read what we have no business to read, and inquire about things which will only make us miserable when we know them.

The first temptation to Eve in Paradise was to eat the forbidden fruit, that so she might come to know good *and evil*. What in the world was she thinking of to let such a motive as that tempt her! She already knew good. All that was good for her to know God had told her. And to want to know evil! Can we imagine greater folly? As if God did not know what was best for her when He gave her the knowledge of good only. As if the knowledge of what was bad could make her happier. Oh, that wretched curiosity which made her want to know what in His love He had kept from her! Poor, silly Eve—and poor, silly children of Eve, who are caught as easily as she was, and find out, to their cost, when it is too late, what misery the knowledge of evil brings! Supposing any one were to say to us: "You know what it is to have a good home and kind parents, to be well clothed and fed. But you do not know what it is to be cold and hungry, to be cuffed and beaten, and made miserable every hour of the day and night." Which of us would want this experience? Which of us would pine for what we had not got?

Curiosity and *idleness* generally go together, as some of us know perhaps by our own experience. Both are really among the King's *enemies at home*, but they are so often found in company with His *enemies abroad*, and they work so much mischief in league with them, that we may consider them as the same camp and speak of them in the same place.

It is impossible to exaggerate the danger of idleness. As long as we are well employed, the devil finds no room for his temptations; he can only put them into empty places. But the moment he sees us lolling about doing nothing, or, which is the same thing, doing nothing to the purpose, he pounces upon us as his lawful prey. Idleness is so completely his field, is so exactly suited to his evil work, that to be doing nothing is almost to invite him to come with his temptations. We must always have our head or our hands usefully occupied, if we want to keep him at a distance. Play-time and holidays are no exception to this rule. They are times for rest from school work, but not times for idleness. In playtime, and in the holidays, and when school life is over, and our time is more or less at our own disposal, idleness must always be feared and shunned.

It is well to have a hobby—some favourite pursuit, which is at once useful and pleasant—to fall back upon in our leisure time. Some children show very early a taste for natural history, or botany, or music, or drawing, or carving. We should cultivate such tastes. God has given them to us for wise and loving ends, to be employed in His service, and to keep us out of mischief. A child with a useful hobby is rarely seen idle. Some boys have a turn for chemistry or joinery. And girls, besides what employs their head, have always the resource of needlework for their hands. If they knew how much a skilful needle can do for the service of God directly, by repairing altar linen, or supplying what is necessary for poor missions: and indirectly, by making clothes for His poor, they would all resolve to have this among their other resources for leisure moments.

We should try too to acquire a taste for useful reading, to take an interest in books that improve our mind, as well as in those that simply amuse us. Story-books, and, later on, good and safe novels, may do us valuable service by resting our head, and making us fit for serious application afterwards. But they should be our recreation, not our occupation. We should take them as we take our meals—temperately—and to recruit our strength, not simply for pleasure and self-indulgence. An immoderate use of them, like greediness in food, would harm instead of helping us.

We can scarcely exaggerate the value of an intelligent habit of reading, and it is well worth our while to take pains to acquire it. Good books inform and elevate our minds; they take our thoughts away from ourselves, and make us wiser and better. How much that will improve us in every way, we may learn from books of science or history, biography, or travel. Spiritual books are the food of the soul, giving it health and strength. From them we get counsel and encouragement, and impressions, to last, it may be, through eternity. Many of the Saints, like St. Augustine and St. Ignatius, owe the height of sanctity and glory which they have reached, to the thoughtful reading of a good book.

To get good, not harm, from our intercourse with books, our choice of them, as we have said, must be wise and happy. Advice, when we can get it, is always useful. But there is one counsellor whose guidance we may always have: As we close a book, let us ask ourselves what it has done for us; a silent voice within will tell us whether good has come to us, or harm.

If we can make ourselves happy in the companionship of good and useful books, we have found the most helpful of all resources for our leisure hours. We may add, by-the-bye, that a capital act of self-denial is to determine beforehand how long we should give to our reading, and to close our book when the time is up. To be able to stop short at an exciting or interesting part shows no little power of self-control, and is an admirable exercise of mortification. Some are the slaves of their books, or rather of their self-indulgence. Once engrossed in them, no call of duty, no appeal of charity can make itself heard. The little ones may want amusing, father or mother need a helping hand, but nothing moves them. Curled up in their chair, they follow the fortunes of their heroes and heroines, and when they are compelled at last to leave them, it is only to turn cross and discontented to the humdrum duties of their daily life, and make themselves disagreeable to everybody. Clearly this is not using books with moderation, but defeating the very end our reading should have in view.

We seem to have strayed a long way from our subject, and some things that have been said are perhaps beyond our present needs. But the employment of our time, and above all this question of our reading, are matters of such importance, that it is well to have a word of warning in time. Lay up in your memory what has been said. You may not want it now, but in all probability you will want it later. All your life long, your heart is to be the palace of our Lord, and all your life long you must guard it against His enemies.

And now we are all thoroughly tired. Shall we refresh ourselves, as we have every right to do, by taking three stories to-day instead of one? They all teach the same lesson: how God should be served by the brave and faithful discharge of duty, and how such fidelity is often rewarded by great and unexpected results.

One evening a party of young men were gathered together in a room of one of the Colleges at Oxford. The wine had gone round freely, and the conversation was becoming less and less edifying. At length a Catholic present felt he could no longer keep silence. At any cost he must speak, or he would be sharing in what his conscience told him was wrong. The cost was not light. He knew there was little sense of religion to be aroused, and that any remonstrance would be received with taunts and laughter. The temptation of human respect was strong, but grace triumphed. A brief struggle, an earnest prayer, and then he rose: "Gentlemen," he said, "this conversation is neither fit for you to hold, nor for me to hear. I wish you good evening." And he bowed and left the room. The noisy mirth that had been checked for an instant broke forth again before he reached the door, and many a contemptuous word was flung after him. But the reward followed speedily. Next morning, as he was alone in his room, there was a knock at the door. A young Protestant nobleman, who had kept aloof from the conversation of the night before, had come to express his admiration of the courage which all had witnessed, "I have often," he said, "noticed you on Friday keeping the laws of your Church, in spite of difficulties on every hand. But your conduct last night was beyond all praise. I am convinced it could only be inspired by a strong sense of religion, and I feel bound to inquire without further delay into the doctrines of the Catholic Church." The inquiry thus started brought the young man into the true Fold. On the day of his reception he sent his Catholic friend a magnificent Missal enriched with precious stones.

"A splendid proof of the force of example," some may be inclined to say, "but we cannot all bring peers into the Church by standing up for our faith and conscience." No, but we can all do our duty; the consequences are in God's hands. He bids us let our light shine before men. The result of the shining depends not on us, but on Him. The light may be a very quiet one and do its work quietly.

A clergyman visiting in a Protestant family was struck by the modest, retiring manner of the girl who waited at table. So much so that he made inquiries about her, and learned that she was a Roman Catholic, a convert, who had been instructed at the nunnery close by. The more he saw of her behaviour, the more it pleased him. Wishing to make her a little present before leaving, he wrote to the convent asking for the name of a suitable book. *Fabiola* was proposed, and at the same time it was suggested that he should look into the religion of the young convert who had impressed him so favourably. He took the advice, and for several years read indefatigably and prayed still more. At last the grace of Faith was given him and he was received into the Church.

One more story, and about a very small individual this time. Our Lord says: "Woe to those who scandalize the little ones that believe in Him." For the most part the little ones take the scandal in silence, but now and then they speak out:

"Dadda, I sood be samed to be eating dat on Fiday," lisped a little mite of four, as she pointed with her spoon to the muttonchop on her father's plate. Week after week she had watched with astonishment the dish of meat before him, and at last her amazement was beyond her powers of control. To all appearance the dadda *was* ashamed, for his head dropped awkwardly over his plate, and there was no attempt at self-defence. Whether the rebuke made any difference in his Friday dinners from that day forward, I never heard, but if it made no difference in the dinners, it must at least have made a difference in the comfort with which he took them.

"Cannot I do what these and those have done?" said St. Augustine to himself, as he thought of the lowly and the little ones, who had done great things for God. And I—cannot I do what a poor girl and a baby of four have done—show myself God's faithful servant at all times and everywhere? Why should He be so well served by others and so badly served by me? How is it that their light shines before men, whilst I scarcely do good to any one?

My God, it will never do for me to go on so. I am coming to the turning-point of my life, my First Communion. I must be different now. If I have been careless, I must be so no longer. Make me more fervent in Your service. Make me more in earnest about saving my soul; more careful to keep myself from sin and the occasions of sin. I know that it is no use to expect to keep good if I waste my time with foolish companions or books, or throw it away in idleness. I see now how much harm may come to me in these ways, and how I must be on my guard. It is not fair to expect my Guardian Angel to guard me, if I do not guard myself. Help me always to watch and pray, and then I shall be safe—*to watch*, by keeping myself as far as I can out of harm's way; and when, notwithstanding, temptation comes—*to pray*, which is the sure means to overcome.

# XXI
## Our Enemy at Home

"What an extraordinary thing, auntie, to use ants instead of stitches for closing up wounds!" said Selina, looking up from her work.

"Not extraordinary at all, my love," replied Aunt Tryphosa, "quite ordinary as far as I can learn, *but exceedingly wonderful.*"

You, too, may say, "What an extraordinary thing to have *enemies at home!* We thought they were only in battles."

"Not extraordinary at all," as Aunt Tryphosa said, "quite ordinary, *but exceedingly unpleasant.*"

We have a most decided enemy at home, and it is our business to-day to deal with him. It can be no use whatever to get rid of enemies abroad, if there is one lurking about at home, doing no end of mischief because undetected. Let us pull off his disguises and find out all about him.

It would be the greatest mistake possible to suppose that preparation for First Communion means saying prayers and learning words of Catechism only. It means hard work; tracking our enemies and fighting them.

"But what enemies?" you say. Ah, that is just what we have to find out. You have not heard much as yet about grown up people's troubles. The time has not yet come for that. But about one of their troubles, even you children may have heard something, for it finds its way into the nursery and the school-room. You may have heard it said, with a sigh, "Ah, servants nowadays are not what they used to be, hard-working, respectful, contented. Formerly they *were* servants and knew their place—times are sadly changed."

Few of us know enough of servants in general to be able to judge how far these complaints are just. But we all know one servant that deserves plenty of blame, and yet, strange to say, rarely gets any. Lazy, stubborn, stupid, more troublesome than any other servant, we ever heard of, it is nevertheless such a general favourite, that it not only escapes without rebuke, but gets a vast amount of attention and consideration. People as a rule never dream of being put out by its provoking ways, or astonished at its outrageous demands. On the contrary, they give it all it wants quite as a matter of course. This servant *does not know its place.* It did once, but that was a long time ago. Suppose we go back a long way, and try to learn something of its history. We shall thus come to understand it better and learn better how to deal with it.

I wonder if you have guessed who this servant is? What if it should turn out to be that *enemy at home* of whom a word was said in passing yesterday? Its history will tell us.

God created the Angels pure spirits, not to be united with bodies. They are a very wonderful creation. But man, composed of spirit and matter, is in some respects a more wonderful creation still. There is the soul, able to know, love, and will. This is his noblest part. And there is the helpmate and servant of the soul, which it has to rule and keep in order, and whose salvation it has to work out as well as its own. The body cannot save itself. If it is to be saved, the soul must do it, and the soul can only do it by remaining what God meant it to be—master.

In Paradise it *was* master. The body was its submissive servant and helped it with all its might. Look at Adam and Eve in prayer. Everything in them prayed—the knees, the hands, the eyes, the lips, the tongue, the brain—all helped the soul to rise to its Creator. All worked together in order and harmony. Those happy creatures could truly say, "Bless the Lord, O *my soul*, and let *all that is within me* bless His Holy Name."

Oh, how different it is with us now! Our whole nature is so changed and spoilt, that the body, instead of serving the soul, expects to be served by it. Almost the first question in our Catechism is: "Of which must you take most care, of your body, or of your soul?" What have we come to, that we should be asked such a question as that? What should we think of the state of the palace, if the question could be asked, "Who gets more honour there, the Queen or the scullion?"

The body, then, is the *enemy at home.* It is a very dangerous and treacherous enemy, and unfortunately we cannot keep it out of the palace, like the *enemies abroad.* Nay, we are obliged to have it there as a servant, to feed it and take care of it, although we know what a dangerous servant it is.

What does a king do with a servant he is bound to keep about him and employ, if he knows he is inclined to be a traitor? He does not trust him; he keeps his eye upon him; he does not let him do as he likes; and if this servant shows any signs of revolt, he puts him into prison at once.

History has many sad stories of Kings and Queens who fell into misfortune and misery by giving themselves into the power of unworthy favourites—servants really, who ought to have been kept in their place, but who changed places with their sovereigns and ruled those whom they should have served. It is hard to say whether those who thus degraded themselves, and by so doing, not unfrequently lost both crown and life, deserve more pity or contempt.

There was once a Queen who had a servant of this kind. A nice life that servant led her royal mistress; well, *mistress* we

## Abel's Sacrifice

"Abel also offered of the firstlings of his flock...and the Lord had respect to Abel and to his offerings." (Genesis 4:4)

must not call the Queen. She was no mistress at all. Every one knew who ruled the palace, and whose will was law there.

In palaces, you know, even servants have grand names—gentlemen-ushers, ladies-in-waiting, and the like. This servant, the Duchess of Marlborough, was "Mistress of the Robes." And she was mistress of most other things besides.

It did not matter in the least what the Queen wanted; what was good for Her Majesty; what the honour of royalty required. But what this upstart servant required, this was everything. Oh, the airs she gave herself! Oh, the attentions she expected, and the spite she showed when thwarted! Who was there that dared to thwart her! The Duke of Marlborough, who never quailed before the enemy's guns, did not care to face his Duchess in one of her tantrums. The Queen stood trembling in her presence. She would have given anything to free herself from this tyrant, and a word would have done it. A word would have put Sarah Jennings into her place. But that word the poor weak Queen could not bring herself to say. You see, she had begun by making a friend of this servant; she had treated her with a familiarity unbecoming in a queen; and the consequence was the servant turned upon her and treated her with contempt.

The Duchess had the keys of the palace and she used things just as she liked, not for the service of the Queen, to whom they belonged, but just for her own selfish pleasures.

Now I am sure you are all hoping that this insolent servant got her deserts at last, and that the Queen summoned up pluck enough to free herself from this miserable bondage. Yes, happily, she did. Things came to such a pass that she felt she *must* show herself to be ruler in the palace. The royal word went forth, and the proud Duchess was ordered to give up her keys. It was the Duke himself who demanded them in the Queen's name, and who received them in a way which even to him was a little surprising—for they were flung at his head.

To see royalty brought so low is sad indeed. But how often something happens sadder still. How often do souls destined to reign in Heaven, lose their life here and their crown hereafter through making a favourite of a servant. What must we do to prevent anything so dreadful happening to ourselves? Our soul must remember its dignity, and be master always. The moment it lets the body get the upper hand, the moment it makes a favourite of this servant, that moment the work of the salvation of both begins to go badly. What a shame it is for the body to try to upset the order established by God, and to drag down to Hell the soul which has to save it!

By reason of its evil inclinations, the body has become our most dreaded enemy, with whom we can have neither peace nor truce. Does this seem hard? What sin brings about is always hard. But there it is—the harm has been done, we have to face the consequences now, and to face them bravely.

No one, surely, will be so foolish as to deny that there is this struggle within us. Why, we feel it every hour. What are curiosity, idleness, gluttony, and other evil inclinations, but the body crying out for what it must not have? Is the soul to give in to it? No. There is nothing for it, then, but to fight for its freedom—in other words, to practise mortification.

This mortification we all need. St. Luke notices that our Lord said *to all*, "If any man will come after Me, let him deny himself and take up his cross daily and follow Me." Denying ourselves, the Catechism tells us, is "giving up our own will and going against our own humours, inclinations, and passions." And it goes on to say that "we are bound to deny ourselves because our natural inclinations are prone to evil from our very childhood, and if not corrected by self-denial, will certainly carry us to Hell." How sin has spoilt God's work! In the beginning it was not so. The natural inclinations of our first parents lifted them up to heavenly things. Body and soul lived together in harmony, the body knowing its place as a servant and keeping it. Now all is changed. From the day the eye was attracted by that fair apple in Paradise, and the body for the first time wanted what would hurt the soul, and gained its first victory, the harmony was at an end. Then began the struggle which Adam and Eve had to keep up for nine hundred years, which all their poor children have to keep up until death, their Immaculate Daughter, Mary, alone excepted.

The Saints surprise and frighten us by the holy hatred they show to the body. It comes from their thoroughly realizing that it is our greatest enemy, an enemy which, for a moment's pleasure, would often inflict eternal death on the soul.

In hurting the soul, the body hurts itself. It cannot plunge the soul into Hell without falling itself into those flames. And yet it is willing to do this for a pleasure that will be over in a moment. What wonder, then, that those who truly love their souls should hate their bodies! If we hate the devil on account of the harm he is always trying to do us, how much more ought we to hate the enemy at home, without whose help the devil could not hurt us. The Saints see this plainly. Hence the spirit of mortification and penance, which we find in all of them without exception—those who have always been good and holy, as well as those who had once been sinners. We have no better word than hatred to express what the Saints feel for the treacherous enemy we have within us. But it is not quite the right word, for hatred means wishing evil. And the Saints are so far from wishing evil to the body, that they try by every means in their power to correct its bad inclinations, and thus fit it to be the soul's companion in Heaven for all eternity.

Look down into Hell after the Last Day, when bodies and souls will be there together, and see if those truly loved their bodies, who for the sake of sparing them a little pain here, have condemned them to those awful torments for ever. On the other hand, look at St. Peter of Alcantara, the confessor and friend of St. Teresa, and one of the most mortified of the Saints. Appearing to her all glorious after death, he exclaimed in a transport of joy, "O happy penance which has merited for me such exceeding reward!"

Are we, then, all bound to do penance like St. Peter of Alcantara in order to get to Heaven? No. But we are most certainly bound to do what is necessary to get there. And the very least we can do is to use for the good of the soul the common sense which we are using every day for the good of the body. Two persons are ill. One eats and drinks whatever he fancies, will take no medicine and suffer no pain in order to get well. The other restricts himself to what the doctor allows him, takes his medicine, however disagreeable, and submits to whatever the doctor thinks will do him good. Which of the two really cares most for his body? Now we are all of us sick persons, and often want what will hurt us, just as sick people do. Are we going to be like the first man, who killed himself because he would have his own way? Or are we going to bear a little passing pain for the sake of our soul's health?

Of course I am. Of course I must take more care of my soul than of my body. Think of the Catechism having to tell me *that!* It looks quite plain now, when I am thinking it over quietly. But do my actions all day long show it is plain to me always? Does the body never get what hurts the soul? If one or other is my favourite, my spoilt child; which is it? The spoilt child always gets its way, no matter how unfair or unreasonable its way is. When these two have a quarrel and come to me to decide it, which has to give way? Oh, how readily I hear the pleading of the body—it is so hungry, or so thirsty, or so tired. How unwillingly I listen to the poor soul asking for what it needs—asking to have its rights, showing me how unjust and unreasonable I am to expect it to save the body which never gets rebuked nor thwarted. St. Francis of Assisi treated his body so severely, that just before his death, when he could afford to make peace with it, he asked its pardon for the hard life he had led it. When *I* come to die, will it be my body or my soul whose pardon I shall have to ask?

My dear Angel Guardian, guardian of my soul and body, how hard I make your work for you by thinking so much of my body and so little of my soul. You must envy the Guardian Angels of the Saints. Pray for me that I may be more like them, more in earnest about the work of my salvation; that I may have the courage to say "No" to myself when I ought to say it, and to bear patiently the pain that comes of saying it. The pain will grow less as I grow more expert in battle, so that what seems hard now will come to be easy. Besides, a soldier of Christ must not mind a little pain. The pain will pass, but the reward in Heaven and the joy of having given glory to God will not pass. Stand by me, dear Angel, in all my battles, and when the last struggle is over, present me to my King. Your reward as well as mine will be to see His smile and hear Him say, "Well done."

## XXII
## More About the Enemy at Home

Some of us think, perhaps, that mortification, which is to be looked for of course in great Saints and great sinners, is unnecessary for those happily placed between the two. But what does our Lord say? St. Luke tells us that His words were, "If *any one* will come after Me, let him deny himself," and that He said this *to all*. We all, then, stand in need of self-denial, not only those who have bad inclinations, but those also who have very good ones. Let us see now in what things we have to practise it.

First, we must mortify ourselves in whatever prevents us from following Christ our Lord; that is, from keeping His Commandments. All sin, mortal and venial, and all negligence in God's service springs from a want of mortification. We sin only to avoid some pain or trouble, or not to lose some pleasure. If, at our examination of conscience to-night, we look for the cause of the faults we have committed to-day, we shall find they all come from this fear of pain, or love of pleasure, and most of them, perhaps, from indulgence of the body. I could not bring myself to face the cold this morning when I was called, so I stayed ten minutes longer in bed. I could not deny myself the pleasure of indulging curiosity by untying that string and peeping into that parcel. And then I told a story about it. We must see what evil inclination occasions the greater number of our daily faults, and mortify ourselves in that first.

Holy Scripture says, "If you give yourself up to your desires, you will become a laughing-stock to your enemies." Nothing pleases the devil more than to see us giving way to our passions, to any passion whatsoever. Like an unruly horse, any one of them will carry us towards a precipice, unless we keep a strong hand upon it, and make it go our way and not its own. When any evil inclination begins to torment us, the devil makes out we shall have peace only by yielding to it. If we believe him, we shall find, to our cost, how we have been deceived. It is not by yielding, but by resisting, that we get peace. And the quicker and more vigorously we resist, the easier the work will be. Our bad inclinations are like weeds—easily plucked up when they are young, but very hard to pull up when they have taken deep root.

The next practice of mortification is to take up our cross daily as our Lord teaches us; that is, to submit patiently—better still, cheerfully and gladly—to all that crosses our inclinations in our daily life, and—which belongs specially to our present purpose—to all that causes bodily suffering or inconvenience. We are hungry or thirsty, too hot or too cold; we have a headache or a toothache, or we get a bruise or a cut; the dinner is not to our liking, or a wet day puts a stop to our drive. But, you will say, we cannot help ourselves when these things come to try us, so there can be no merit in bearing them. There may be very great merit, even though we cannot help them. We can always make a virtue of necessity. To see God's will in whatever comes, and embrace it heartily, shows solid virtue, and if we have the habit of doing this, we are a long way on the road of self-denial. Still we can go further. Besides taking up their cross daily and *being crucified*, they that are Christ's, *crucify themselves*, as St. Paul says, and this brings us to the third way of denying ourselves by voluntary mortification.

We can restrain our inclinations, not only when this is necessary to avoid sin, not only when there is no way out of a trouble, but also in things lawful for us either to do or omit. These voluntary mortifications are very useful, and very meritorious and pleasing to God. They are useful, because by overcoming our inclinations in things which do not come under the law of God, we accustom ourselves to obey readily whenever the soul gives the word of command, and to submit easily in things that are of obligation. And they are meritorious, because, as Thomas à Kempis says: "Nothing, how little soever, that is suffered for God's sake, can pass without merit in the sight of God."

The ways in which we may practise little secret acts of self-denial are innumerable. It is said that a Saint found eight opportunities of mortification in eating an egg. Without being so ingenious, we can find plenty every day. There is no need to peep into every room we pass; *always* to take what we like best at table; to seek the most comfortable posture when praying or reading. We may deny ourselves sometimes in occasions like these, without overtaxing our strength, or ruining our health!

There was a novice who resolved to train his senses in the practice of mortification, by exercising them in turn on the different days of the week. On Monday he restrained his eyes by not looking at what attracted his curiosity. On Tuesday, Wednesday, and Thursday, the senses of hearing, smell, and taste had their turn. On Friday they were all to contribute an act of self-denial, so to share in the sufferings of our Blessed Lord in His Passion. Saturday brought the turn for the sense of touch. Our novice would not make himself too comfortable to-day. He would avoid, rather than seek, what felt soft and pleasant. And he would not *stroke the cat*. What was left for Sunday, or which of the senses got an extra turn that day, I never heard. It may be he gave them all a holiday. But this is not likely, for he would have had them roving all over the place, and found it hard to get them all into school again on Monday. He was a fervent novice and died young. It is possible we do not like his plan of mortification. Well, we need not like it. There is no obligation. We are quite at liberty to prefer our own. *But what is it?* If we are inclined to laugh at his very babyish act of self denial on Saturday, it is probably because we do not happen to care for cats ourselves. He did happen to care for them, and to pass puss on the stairs without a friendly stroke was a real act of mortification *to him*. He looked out for things that he really felt, and made them an offering to our Lord. In this at least we can imitate him. Which of us could not, on a Friday, make some little sacrifice in honour of the Passion, deny ourselves a fruit, a sweet, anything, however small? It is not the importance of what we do, but the love with which we do it, that gives it its worth before God. "He looks," says Thomas à Kempis, "not at the gift of the lover, but at the love of the giver." Now we can all love Him, and bring Him our little gifts, as well as novices. The Curé d'Ars was speaking not to novices, but to a great crowd of people of all ranks, ages, and conditions, men, women, and children, when he said: "Oh, how I love those little mortifications, which are seen by no one, as not to warm oneself, not to drive away a fly, and the like."

And as mortification may be practised in such little easy ways, there is not one of us who can find a reasonable excuse for shirking it. The only thing is the pain. But is that a reasonable excuse? And it is the *fear* of the pain much more than the pain itself that frightens us so. The holy Curé used to say, "The fear of crosses is our greatest cross." You have seen children screaming with fright on the steps of a bathing-machine, when the morning happened to be fresher than usual, and the great green waves came splashing up. They are so afraid lest those precious little feet of theirs should find the water colder than they fancy. We laugh at their tears. The Saints would laugh at ours, only they are too charitable and too humble. They tell us that a little mortification hurts more than a great deal. It is quite certain our tiny acts cost us more than their big ones cost them. And all because *we are so afraid.*

Some of us are saying by this time. "I see quite well that self-denial is absolutely necessary, and I am ashamed of being so afraid of it. But in spite of all, I cannot help thinking of the pain. It does seem so hard that the body and soul, which have to be companions till death, must be always at war with one another."

It *is* hard, so let us see if we can find any thoughts to encourage us.

The first thought that will help us is the necessity of securing our eternal salvation at any cost. Oh, if we could only realize the worth of our immortal souls as the Saints realized it, even the very young ones! They all saw that there is really but one thing necessary; that it will profit us nothing to gain the whole world, if we lose our souls; and that whatever endangers our salvation must be got rid of, were it an eye or a hand, as our Lord says. The Saints took His words as said specially *for them,* specially *to them.* Why do not we do so too? They were said specially *for us,* specially *to us.* He had us in His mind as well as His Saints when He said them, and He has ready for us the same grace which strengthened them. He does not leave us alone in this struggle. To all of us He says, as to St. Paul, "My grace is sufficient for thee." And we can all of us say with this great Apostle, "I can do all things in Him Who strengtheneth me."

It will help us, too, to think of all it cost the Sacred Body of our Lord to save us: all the cruel pain in that Divine Head, in those Blessed Hands and Feet, all the torture of the Scourging, all the slow agony of the Crucifixion. "It would be a shame," says St. Bernard, "to be delicate members under a thorn-crowned

Head." Our Lord said of His Passion, "Ought not Christ to have suffered these things, and so to enter into His Glory?" If *He* ought, surely *we* ought. And can we begrudge a little pain for our own salvation, when He gave for it the sorrows of the Three-and-Thirty Years?

And then think of the reward. If the Saints consider they have bought Heaven for nothing, at the price of all their labours and sufferings, shall we think God asks too much of us when He says: Deny yourself for a little while and I will be your reward exceeding great?

St. Paul tells us that those who raced and wrestled in the Grecian games, "refrained themselves from all things," that is, submitted to all kinds of self-denial, often for years, in order to fit themselves for the contest, and to have a chance of the prize. "And they," he says, "that they may receive a corruptible crown"—it was a garland of fading leaves—"but we an incorruptible one." Is it not worth striving for? A few years, and all the pain and struggle will be over—*and then!*

Fra Angelico, a holy Dominican artist of the fifteenth century, has a beautiful picture of the Resurrection, which furnishes as many thoughts for meditation as it has figures. I wish you could see it. The Last Trumpet has sounded. The earth is giving up its dead. And there, beside the graves of the elect, are the Guardian Angels embracing them as they rise to their new and eternal life. What an embrace that will be! But before it there will have been another, closer still and tenderer, when the souls of the blessed, speeding to earth from Heaven or from Purgatory, unite themselves once more and for ever with the faithful companions of their pilgrimage.

We can scarcely bring ourselves to think of those other graves, by which no eager Guardian Angels will wait. "We shall all indeed rise again, but we shall not all be changed," says St. Paul. Oh, what will be the anguish of the souls that rise from Hell, only to go in search of the miserable bodies they have to reanimate; and their horror when they see the hideous, loathsome forms into which they must enter, there to dwell for ever! What curses those companions in misery will pour forth against each other; the body against the soul, because it did not force it to mortify itself whilst there was yet time; the soul against the body, whose corrupt inclinations have dragged it down to Hell. And to think that this will be the lot of so many! That it may never be our own, let us learn now, and learn well the lesson it should teach us—we can never learn it too well.

And then, turning once more to the Saints rising in glory, let us learn the same lesson from them. Oh, with what joy those souls and bodies will meet again! How they will thank each other for the help each has given in the working out of their common salvation! Glorious as it is in its own spiritual beauty, the soul will be filled with admiration for its beautiful companion, the same as in the old days of their journeying together, and yet how different! No more to be feared and suspected, no more to be an instrument of sin, or a cause of suffering; but to enjoy with fullest freedom all the delights of the blessed eternity on which they are both entering. The soul will invite it to Heaven saying: "Arise, my beautiful one, and come. For winter is now past, the rain is over and gone."

The thought of this joyful resurrection has encouraged the Saints from the beginning. Job in his troubles said, "I know that my Redeemer liveth; and in the Last Day I shall rise out of the earth. And I shall be clothed again with my skin, and in my flesh I shall see my God; Whom I myself shall see, and my eyes shall behold, and not another: this my hope is laid up in my bosom."

All the Saints have looked to the Resurrection when the body was tempted to complain at its life of penance here. They were flesh and blood as we are, and they had their moments of weariness and dejection as we have. St. Paul encouraged his converts in Rome and Corinth, by telling them "that the sufferings of this present time are not worthy to be compared with the glory to come that shall be revealed in us. For our present tribulation, which is momentary and light, worketh for us above measure exceedingly an eternal weight of glory." And St. John said, as he saw in spirit the coming Resurrection of the Saints, "God shall wipe away all tears from their eyes; and death shall be no more, nor mourning, nor crying, nor sorrow shall be any more: for the former things are passed away."

Have pity, my God, on a poor little weak child. I know all this is true. I know how much I need mortification to keep down and overcome my evil inclinations, and prevent them from leading me where they have led so many—and still I hesitate—and still I am afraid. I want to overcome myself bravely like the Saints, and when the least little pain has to be suffered, the least little effort made, I shrink back like a coward. Is it that I have a weaker nature than the Saints, or is it that they overcame the weakness of their nature by prayer, and went to You for the strength they had not in themselves? If it was this that made them so strong—and I know it *was* this—I can become strong too, by going to You and asking for the strength You gave to them. My God, I do ask it with all the earnestness of my soul. I ask it because I feel my need, because I feel so weak. I ask it because You are so good and so ready to give. I ask it through Your merits, O my Saviour, and through that tender love which made You shrink in the Garden of Olives from pain and shame, so to encourage me. Strengthen Your little frail disciple. Give me *courage* to deny myself, whenever this is necessary to keep your laws and those of Your Church. And give me *love* to deny myself sometimes, even in things that are not necessary, that so I may prove my love to You, and make my salvation more secure.

# XXIII
# How We Must Meet Our Enemies

So much for the means of preventing temptation. But as, in spite of all we can do, we cannot escape it altogether, let us now see how to meet it and come off conquerors in the fight,

Our Lord teaches us in two words how to escape unhurt from temptation. "Watch," He says, "and pray." "Watch"—that is, do what you can to avoid dangerous occasions and being taken by surprise. This is before temptation comes. "And pray." This is when temptation is upon us. Some people are too frightened to do anything. They are like a general who loses his presence of mind at the beginning of a battle and so can give no orders. Now, in temptation we must be cool and calm, or we shall give our enemy an advantage over us. God is with us, ready to help us, and He is stronger than all our enemies, who cannot hurt us unless we want to be hurt. So there is nothing to be frightened about.

Look at that baby tripping along between father and mother. The little feet scarcely touch the ground. It is all but carried forward as it goes dancing on its way.

Now the road has to be crossed. Not a cart in sight—not a sound of wheels to be heard—yet, see! Father's head turns one way and mother's the other, lest any danger to their darling should be near. If a big dog comes up and dares to look at the child, mother calls out, and father shows him his stick. If a drove of cattle pass this way and the great horns frighten baby, father must take it up in his arms till they are out of sight.

Oh, what a silly baby it would be to be afraid of anything whilst those strong arms are round it! Of course, it may run on in front if it likes and put itself into the big dog's way, or it may go and sit down in the road in front of a bull. Then no one will answer for the consequences. But if it keeps close to father and mother, what in the world has it to be afraid of?

And what have *we* to be afraid of? We can run into danger, of course. But the devil cannot bite us, or toss us about for his amusement, *unless we like*. If we like, we may always be safe—with our mother's eye upon us, and round us the strong arms of our Heavenly Father.

The best way to get rid of the devil is to take no notice of him and to treat him with contempt. He is proud and cannot bear to be despised. What do you do when you get one of those tiny summer flies upon your hand? Blow it off, do you not? Blow off in the same way this insignificant tormentor, a whiff will do it. Urban said of him, "He is a big bully, *but such a coward.*" A sign of the Cross, a drop of holy water, and he takes to flight.

But contempt does not mean we are to do nothing. God helps those who help themselves.. Watching and praying includes fighting. We must be prompt in turning away from the temptation the moment we perceive it. We must shake it off as we shake a spark off our hand—instinctively, without a moment's hesitation. It is a spark from hell-fire and must be put out at once. If we act promptly and courageously, the devil is frightened; if we are negligent or cowardly, he grows bolder. "Resist the devil and he will fly from you," says St. James. But some of us seem to be made of such poor stuff that at the least breath of temptation we give way, as the Curé d'Ars says, "*like a piece of wet paper.*"

We must turn to our Lord at once and make an act of love. An act of love is better than an act of the virtue contrary to the temptation. The names of Jesus and Mary are an act of love, and they have great power to put the devil to flight. Then we should turn our mind to something else—anything that will occupy it in another direction—the multiplication table, or a hymn with a good jingling rhyme in it, or a game, or a storybook. We cannot be thinking of two things at the same time, and one thought will be thrust out by another. If we cannot get rid of the thought that teases us, we should renew our act of love. The devil will soon find this a losing game for him and will give it up.

When the temptation has left us, we should not go back upon it, either in our examination of conscience at night, or in our preparation for Confession, saying, "What was it I was thinking about? Did I consent?" But we should say, "Did I make my act of love?" If not, then there has been negligence. If I did, then I thank God for it and go on. We must not revive temptations. The devil will let us know fast enough if we were conquered and we have no need of examination.

Do not hide your temptations from your confessor. Troubles that are shut up are double troubles. And besides, we often need advice about our temptations. The devil knows this, and so he persuades us to keep them to ourselves. He knows we are ignorant and inexperienced and that if we try to fight him single-handed he will have a great advantage over us; whereas if we get our confessor to help us, his chances are far less. So he does all he can to get us to say nothing about our temptations. In hot countries serpents are often found hiding under stones; they like the darkness and the concealment.

Take away the stone and they make off with themselves. So does the old serpent.

It is a great thing to keep up our heart in time of temptation. We have plenty of motives for keeping it up and none whatever for letting it be cast down. We are always to remember that it is not wrong to be tempted. How can it be, when temptation is the devil's work, not ours. "If," says St. Ignatius, "I shall not be rewarded for the good works of the good angels, neither shall I be punished for the evil works of the evil angels."

Our temptations depend a good deal upon our natural dispositions, but this does not make them sinful. Some have a temper which is hard to overcome: others are naturally inclined to sloth, gluttony, and other evil passions. There is no sin, nor even imperfection, in feeling these inclinations, nor in bad thoughts of any kind whatsoever, but only in giving way to them.

It is not wrong to be tempted, and it is not surprising either. It would be very surprising were it otherwise. Anyone marching straight on to Heaven, and especially to a high place in Heaven, without being molested by the devil, ought to be caught and put under a glass case as a curiosity. It is just those who want to be good whom the devil tempts, and if he sees they want to be very good he tempts them more. Does not this look as if temptation were a good sign; as if we ought to be *set up* by it instead of being cast down?

All the Saints have been tried by temptation and have overcome. St. John saw the great multitude which no man could number, of all nations, and tribes, and peoples, and tongues, standing before the Throne *with palms in their hands.* Our Lord Himself, the Saint of Saints, speaks of Himself as a Conqueror and invites us to fight and conquer with Him. And what a reward He promises—"To him that shall overcome, I will give to sit with Me in My Throne: as I also have overcome, and am set down with My Father in His Throne." "Happy the souls that are tempted," says the holy Curé d'Ars; "it is when the devil sees that a soul is drawing near to God that he redoubles his rage." "Temptation," he says, again, "is the time of spiritual harvest, when we store up for Heaven. We have to work hard as in harvest-time, but we must not complain, for we are laying up stores."

Our enemies, as we have seen, cannot harm us against our will. With what light hearts our troops would go to battle, if they knew for certain they would not be killed or even wounded, *unless they wished it*. Now our Lord's soldiers have this assurance. They know He has been through it all before them. He has met the devil in His own temptations and conquered him there for us. To beat a beaten foe is not hard surely—what are we confirmed for, but to be our Lord's soldiers and to fight His battles! "As a good soldier does not fear the fight," the Cure d'Ars used to say, "so a good Christian ought not to fear temptation. All soldiers seem good in garrison; it is on the battlefield that the difference between the brave and the cowards is seen."

The devil has no chance with the fervent, so he waits for their fervour to cool. He gets them to be careless about prayer, the Sacraments, little faults. And then he comes with a strong temptation. Carelessness about small faults is often more dangerous than about greater ones. The harm that comes of great faults is plain and seen at once. They startle us and we right ourselves quickly. Because the damage done by lesser faults is not so apparent, we are apt to think lightly of them. They do not kill the soul, it is true, but they weaken it and prepare it for some serious fall. This is why we should fear them so much. It often happens that when a person's strength is run down, a sudden illness comes and carries him off. So when the devil sees a soul weakened by carelessness in little things, he comes with a strong temptation to mortal sin—and it is overthrown.

How we have to be on our guard! In how many ways our crafty enemy tries to lead us into sin! How much we stand in need of our Lord's injunction, "Watch and pray!" If we had to depend on ourselves only, we might well despair. But God is on our side. We must depend not on ourselves, but on Him. "I can do all things in Him who strengtheneth me." St. Ignatius tells us that God defends most vigorously what the devil attacks most violently. He strengthens what the devil tries to upset, and rewards most abundantly the generous efforts that cost us most.

So much good can be got out of temptation, that Almighty God will not tie the devil's hands altogether. But he is not allowed to tempt us just as he chooses and beyond our strength. For the very least temptation of the least little child, he must get God's leave, Who knows exactly how much it can bear and what grace He will give. What a mortification for this proud spirit to be beaten again and again by little bits of children—to see all his malice turned to their good—to see that instead of hurting them, he has put the palm-branches into their hands.

But suppose we fall in the temptation, what are we to do then? Why, get up to be sure—what else should we do? What else does a traveller do who has stumbled upon a big stone or been tripped up by a little one? Of course we must be sorry, because God has been offended; but sorrow is not discouragement.

Discouragement is one of the very worst of temptations, because it is the most frequent, leads to so many others, hinders us from trying again, and takes away all our strength. If our Lord would have nothing more to do with us after our falls, there might be some reason for being discouraged. But when He is so compassionate, so forgiving, when He bids us come back to Him after every fall with fresh confidence, and promises us fresh grace—what excuse have we for our sulkiness? Discouragement after a fall does us more harm than the fall itself. Often and often, it is not the fall the devil wants, so much as our discouragement afterwards. How can we be so stupid as to give him a double satisfaction?

Some people make such a bad use of their victories by turning them into matter for pride, that they lose more than they have gained. And some make such good use of their defeats, that the devil bitterly regrets having meddled with them. We can *always* get good out of evil and turn our faults to account. St. Augustine tells us to cast them under our feet and make them a ladder by which to climb up to God.

Sadness and vexation when we have committed a fault are signs not of sorrow, but of self-love and of pride. We are so surprised that *we* should break our resolutions. The Saints, who had not so high an opinion of themselves, were not surprised when they fell into a fault. "Behold, O Lord, the fruits of my garden," St. Aloysius said, simply. And after a loving act of sorrow, he went on as before. So all the Saints did; so we must do—not being cast down—not trusting our Lord one bit the less, rather trusting Him more. And if we fall seventy times a day, or seventy times seven, coming back to Him always with the same confidence and the same determination to try again.

"Is that you, Pet?" asked a lady, as the sound of small feet was heard passing the open door of the room where she was writing. "No, mother," said a sad little voice, "it's not Pet, it's *only me*." So we may say after our falls: "See, dear Lord, I have fallen again, but don't be angry—it's not St. Aloysius—it's not St. Agnes—*it's only me*."

I wish the story I am going to tell you were less sad, but I cannot alter facts, and you must have it as it happened, only a few years ago.

In consequence of his extravagant habits, a young man had contracted debts which he was unable to meet. The fear of being brought to trial by his creditors, and the disgrace of having to go to prison, so preyed upon his mind, that he fell into a deep melancholy, from which no efforts of his friends could rouse him. The devil took advantage of his state of mind to tempt him to despair. He painted the critical condition of his affairs in the blackest colours, representing to him that he could never bear the pain and shame that was coming, and that the only way to escape from his misfortunes, was to put an end to his life by suicide.

Had he prayed for help when this most awful of temptations assailed him, the poor young man would have had strength to resist it. God *always* hears prayer. He has promised to help us in every trouble, even in such as come through our own fault, provided we pray. And as nothing is impossible to Him or difficult, He has innumerable ways of helping us. But see what happened. Instead of praying, the young man gave himself up to his gloomy thoughts. Day by day the temptation increased in violence, till at length the moment came, when seeing no other way out of his difficulties, he yielded to it and put an end to his own life.

And all the while God was ready at hand with the help he needed. A fortnight later, one of his relations, an officer in the army, was killed by a fall from his horse. He had just come into a considerable fortune, £6,000 a year having been bequeathed to him by a stranger in Australia, on account of the name which they bore in common. By his death, the money thus swiftly passing from hand to hand, fell to the nearest relative—and this would have been the young man, who had perished by his own hand only a few days before. Had he resisted the temptation and put his trust in God, what a reward there would have been for him even in this life!

What chance has a little weak child against an enemy so fierce, so crafty, and so strong? But *God* and a little weak child are more than a match for all the hosts of Hell.

I have seen a child riding in front of its father and trying to control a powerful horse. The little hands *touch* the reins, but the father's *hold* them, and the horse knows it.

My Heavenly Father, make the devil feel that You are always behind me in my temptations, that Your Hand curbs and governs him and directs all for my good. I shall not be afraid if You are there. You know I am not strong, and You will never let me be tempted beyond what I am able to bear. To You I trust all my temptations. Keep away such as would overthrow me, and suffer those only to touch me which You know I shall overcome by the help of Your grace. Above all check the power of the tempter at my last hour, when he will come to me in great wrath, "knowing that he has but a short time." Everything depends upon my overcoming him then. If I conquer him and pass safely through his snares then, I shall be safe for ever. I must practise overcoming him now, that I may come off victorious in that awful struggle which will decide my lot for eternity. Much, very much, depends on the way I meet my temptations now. Help me, my God, to resist them promptly and generously. Teach me to run to You as the child runs to its father in every danger. If this be my habit throughout life, You will take care of my death. You will shield me from the last temptations, strengthen me to persevere to the end, and bring me safely through this life of warfare on earth to the rest and security of the life to come. Amen.

Lead us not into temptation, but deliver us from evil.

Holy Mary, Mother of God, pray for us sinners *now* and *at the hour of our death.* Amen.

# XXIV
## The Pet Passion

We all know what a pet is—the airs it gives itself, the attitudes it assumes, the attentions it expects. In an animal these things are not so bad; indeed, they amuse us by their absurdity. But a petted child is a very different thing. To pet a child is almost always to spoil it. And a spoilt child—why, we take fright at the very thought of it. If you are in a house where there is such a thing, get out of that house as fast as you can. That little tyrant is ruler there, and right or wrong, it must have its way. No matter who or what you are, you must bow down before it; if you attempt to cross it, the whole place will be upset.

Supposing we have not got a petty monster like this in our own house, we know plenty of houses where there is one, and we shun them carefully. Stop a bit. Are these pets such monsters after all, and are we quite sure we have not got one at home? We are fortunate exceptions to the rule if we have not.

If we make our examination of conscience at night at all carefully, we shall find that the same old faults come over and over again. Now what is the reason of this? Some of us never take the trouble to ask, and so we go on fighting feebly and making little or no way, till at last perhaps we get thoroughly discouraged and give up the struggle. If, instead of trying to put all things straight at once, we had hunted for the *cause* of our faults, we should have found that in nine cases out of ten, they came from a pet passion.

"A pet passion"—what do we mean by these words? "Pet" is clear enough, but "passion" we use in more senses than one. The word really means *something suffered*, and so we speak of the Passion of our Lord. But we may suffer from ourselves as well as from others, and nothing, as we shall see presently, causes us more suffering than our disorderly passions, so we must try to understand what they are and how they act.

The passions are strong, natural inclinations, which we must watch over and guard against. The strongest of these in each person will be his *predominant*, as it is generally called—that is, his chief or ruling passion. When we give way to these inclinations, they grow stronger, while steady resistance to them, when the voice of our reason and of our conscience warns us against them, makes resistance easier.

A predominant passion unchecked becomes the cause of countless faults. It is this that makes all the mischief and disturbance in the house. It is our spoilt child, and does more harm than any spoilt child, which is saying a good deal.

*Why* was I so cross yesterday? *Why* did I pout and toss my head and answer saucily instead of obeying at once? How was it that I idled away my time so? Why were my prayers so badly said, and why did I go to bed so tired and discontented? Because I was put out in the morning, and did not get right all day. Yes, but *what was it* that put me out? It was that little word somebody said, which I might have forgotten in a moment if I had tried. But it hurt my pride, and instead of driving it out of my mind, I let it rankle there. Oh, what a little thing to do so much harm—to spoil a day that ought to have been spent for God! All the crossness and the sauciness and the laziness, all the distracted prayers and the discontent came from this wounded pride. And as it was yesterday, so it will be to-morrow. So it was last year and will be next if I do not take care. Does it not look as if *pride* were my pet passion, and should I not do wisely and overcome my other faults more easily, if I were to turn all my attention *to that?*

It is not pride, however, with all of us, and at our night examination, conscience may have another tale to tell. I took something that was not mine, and told a story to escape being found out, and then a bigger story to hide the first. And at last I threw the blame on another. See what a number of venial sins! A theft to begin with, then two stories, and at last a calumny—venial in this case, because the harm done to another was slight only. But how many sins? And what was the cause? I did not steal or tell stories, or injure my neighbour for the pleasure of doing these things. For what then? It was that box of candied fruits which made my mouth water, and this must be the sixth or seventh time I have taken things of that sort. The first time I was very unhappy about it. The next time and the next, though, I took more—there was less fear of offending God; the only fear was lest I should be found out. It is getting harder and harder to resist the sight of what is good to eat. I am always thinking about food too, and at table always want the best of everything. Is not a habit forming, and forming fast? And will not my pet passion be *greediness* in a very short time, unless I set to work at once to conquer it?

Supposing I am not particularly greedy; there are other quarters still from which the reproaches of conscience may come. It may remind me that because I did not get up this morning when I was called—I never do now—my morning prayers were put off till after breakfast and never got said at all. My lessons were not known, because it was too much trouble to learn them last night. Somehow everything seems to be too much trouble. I cannot give my mind to anything. I am never in time. I cannot find my things, and they get spoilt or lost because it is too much trouble to put them away in their proper places. Worst of all, that preparation for confession this afternoon was not carefully and honestly made. I did not take pains enough to examine my conscience, and I took less pains about what is more important still, my contrition. It has been so hard to examine my conscience before confession since I gave up examining it carefully at night. But why did I give it up? What is the matter with me? Is *sloth*, then, coming to be my predominant passion? It looks very like it. Why, it is getting too much trouble to join in the games.

If all this comes of slothfulness, I must set to work and conquer it before things get worse. I have no time to lose, for they say there is scarcely anything more dangerous or more difficult to shake off when it gets a strong hold. It is like the numbness that creeps over the traveller lost in the snow, making him want to lie down and go to sleep. If he does, it is all over with him, for that sleep is death. He must rouse himself and force himself on. And so must I. I must bestir myself, exert myself, *make* myself take pains in prayer, in study, in play, in all I have to do. Thus, by one habit driving out another, I shall make myself free of this sluggishness which is taking all the strength out of my soul.

We have looked now at three examples of the ruling passion. If our own is not among them, we can find it by searching for the cause of our chief faults.

These examples show us that a pet passion is not troublesome only and mischievous; it is often very dangerous. It gathers round it all our other passions, as in olden times a king gathered his vassals and made them fight for him. Its restless cravings are never satisfied, and the more we yield, the more it asks. If we want to have any peace then, the only way is to prepare for war.

Some years ago the peace of Egypt was disturbed by a native officer named Arabi. England and France interfered to restore order, and Sir Garnet Wolseley, now Lord Wolseley, was sent out by our Government to lead the British troops. His determination from the first was to strike a decisive blow and so bring the war to an end as soon as possible. He was not going to waste time and strength in attacking petty foes. He would meet Arabi himself and force him to fight or flee. From what he knew of the enemy, he could guess his plans pretty well, and he made his own accordingly; providing like a skilful general for every need and taking all necessary precautions.

One day, before he left England, he was seen poring for a long time over the map of Egypt making his calculations and maturing his plans. At last he rose from the table, and laying his finger on a place called Tel-el Kebir, exclaimed: "There I shall beat Arabi!"

And there he did beat him. One by one the strong forts seized by the enemy were recovered, and at last Arabi was led to the place where Sir Garnet had resolved to give him battle. The battle was a victory for the English arms, and the war was at an end.

We too—most of us at least—have an Arabi disturbing the peace of the land—some passion or evil inclination, which lords it over the rest, and makes them all fight for it and do its bidding. With some it is pride, with others selfishness, with others anger, with others sloth. It is a great matter to know our enemy, for then we can lay our plans. Only we must not rely on these, or even on our strong determination, for success, but only on God's help which is given to prayer.

And we must not expect *our* war to be ended by one victory. There will be many and many a defeat, especially if we trust much to ourselves, and many a sore wound. But after each discouraging overthrow God will be at hand to put us all right again. We have to go back to Him with the same trust as if we had never been beaten. "Try, try, try again!" He says to us.

We do not fight alone; He and all His Heavenly Court are watching us and helping us. The Saints look down upon us with an intense interest. They have fought their fight and won, and they do so want us to be brave and give glory to God as they have done by conquering the devil, who only hates us so much because we are God's servants and soldiers. They know from their own experience how important it is to overcome Arabi, the chief among our foes, for that after his defeat all the rest will be easy.

Although we must trust in God and not in ourselves, we are not on that account to be careless or slothful. We are to *pray* as if all depended on God, and *act* as if all depended on ourselves. And so it is very useful to lay our plans beforehand and be prepared for the enemy's attack. In the morning to say: *There* and *there* during the day I shall have to overcome pride, or wilfulness, or sloth, or dislike. I shall be inclined to show my airs; or to struggle for my own way; to shirk a disagreeable duty; or to fire up when So-and-so comes with that trying face, and those ways that tease me so. These are *my* Tel-el-Kebirs—I will not be afraid of them—I will go forward humbly and trustfully, armed with watchfulness and prayer to the place where the enemy awaits me—there I shall meet Arabi—and there, by God's grace, I shall beat him.

Yes, by Your grace, my God. You know what a miserable little soldier I am—how often I am defeated and lose the battle, with You and Your Saints looking on. If I could remember to call You to my help—to say, "Lord, save me, I perish," I should not be so often or so easily overcome. But I forget till it is too late. Tell my good Angel to remind me. And when I fall, help me to rise at once without being discouraged. Even if I fall seventy times a day, give me grace to make a hearty, loving act of sorrow each time, and then humbly and perseveringly *to try again*.

# XXV
## The Wedding Garment

The King is very near now. The hour is come for us to look carefully into ourselves to see if we are ready to go out to meet Him.

"Rejoice greatly, O daughter of Sion, behold thy King cometh to thee meek." Yes, He is meek and lovable, so winning and so sweet, so anxious to have us as His guests, that His one thought seems to be how He may take away all fear from our hearts as we draw near to Him. His words are words of the tenderest invitation. By the mouth of His Prophet He had said: "My delight is to be with the children of men...If any one is a little one, let him come to Me." And by His own mouth He says: "Come to Me all you that labour and are burdened, and I will refresh you. Suffer the little children to come unto Me, and forbid them not." The hard things that have to be said He leaves St. Paul to say, keeping all the sweet things for Himself.

Yet He does say startling things at times, and we have heard Him give very solemn warning, even to First Communicants. As our Master and Teacher, He must not keep from us anything that we are bound to know when we are drawing near to these tremendous Mysteries. And therefore we must lay up in our hearts what He is going to say to us now. At this stage of our preparation He has a stern lesson for us, a sterner never came from His Lips. He gives it with all the authority that belongs to Him as God, and as He is accustomed to do, in the form of a parable.

A King gave a feast for the marriage of his son. To this feast were invited "the poor and the feeble and the blind and the lame." His servants were sent out into the streets and lanes to make them all come in and sit down at his table where they were to be treated as dear and honoured guests.

When all were seated, the King went in to see the guests, to bid them welcome, to help them himself to all the good things set before them, and to send them home laden with the rich presents he had provided. As he looked round graciously upon the white-robed throng, his eye fell upon one who had not on the wedding garment. Instantly his countenance changed, and its terrible wrath made all around him tremble. He sent for this man and asked him: "Friend, how camest thou in hither not having on a wedding garment?" But he was silent. Then the King said: "Bind his hands and feet and cast him into the exterior darkness: there shall be weeping and gnashing of teeth."

Here was an awful ending to that marriage-feast. Instead of the King's smile and favour which he might have had, and which those enjoyed who had come prepared, instead of the rich presents that had been provided for him—to be hurried out of the banquet-hall, and bound hand and foot, to be cast away for ever from the presence of the King, into a place of darkness and of torment.

It was to strike fear into our hearts—that holy fear which is the beginning of wisdom—that our Lord told us this story. He wants us to see what punishment those deserve who dare to come to His holy Table without that wedding garment He so strictly requires—the white robe of sanctifying grace.

But you say, "Perhaps the man did not know what the King required, and he was poor, perhaps he could not afford to buy the robe, and so could not help going to the feast as he did." He knew perfectly well. He could help it. It was his own fault entirely. They no more dreamed in the East of going to a marriage-feast without the wedding garment, than an Englishman would dream of presenting himself at the royal table with his hat on. And that the poverty of the invited might be no excuse, white robes were provided for all guests and kept in a room adjoining the banquet-hall, where all could have them for the asking.

There was no excuse, then, for this man. The King gave him the opportunity of making his excuse, if he had any: "Why camest thou in hither not having on a wedding garment?" But he was silent. Only his own carelessness and laziness had brought him before the King unprepared. Ornaments the King did not require, but only the pure wedding garment which he had neglected to bring. And he was justly punished. He ought to have prepared himself. He ought to have taken trouble. Just what St. Paul tells us we are bound to do before we come to our Lord's Table. He says we must "*prove*," that is, examine ourselves, "*and so*," after proper preparation, "eat of this Bread,...for he that eateth unworthily eateth...judgment to himself." Because he has not "discerned the Body of the Lord," he deserves to be cast into the outer darkness, into the fearful place, "where there is weeping and gnashing of teeth."

What we have to do now then is to *prove* ourselves by a good confession. We all know that ante-chamber near the Banquet-hall, where the white robe is kept. We know the white robe is there waiting for us, to be had for the asking, and that it is impossible to ask for it as we should, and not to get it.

We can say "perhaps" about many things. "My father is kind, but perhaps just to-day he may not give me the half-crown I am going to ask for." But about the Sacraments there is no "perhaps" at all. They *must* give us grace. It is what they were made for. And so we do not *hope* we may get the white robe. We *know for a certainty* we shall get it, *if we do our little part*. That, of course, we must do—God will not work without our co-operation. But if you know your father will give you what you ask, provided you ask properly, have you any fear for the result?

So we come with great confidence to the Feet of our Heavenly Father, asking Him to do His part and promising we will do ours, which, as we know, consists of four things:

1. We must heartily pray for grace to make a good confession.

2. We must carefully examine our conscience.

3. We must take time and care to make a good act of contrition.

4. We must resolve by the grace of God, to renounce our sins and to begin a new life for the future.

We will take these four things in order.

1. *We must heartily pray for grace to make a good confession.*—See how we want God's grace from the very first. We want His light. When you are going to look for a thing in a dark room, the first thing you do is to turn up the gas. So we beg for light to see into our hearts. They are dingy little places, and it is hard for us to see the harm that is in them, though to God and His holy Angels it is so plain, nay, staring us right in the face. To ask God's light we may say one of the hymns to the Holy Ghost, or any prayer we like: "My God, I do so want to make a good confession. You know I want it, and You want it too, so it is safe. Give me Your light that I may see my sins clearly as You want me to see them—that I may be truly sorry for them, and resolve with your grace to begin a new life for the future."

2. *We must carefully examine our conscience.*—There are several ways of doing this. We may use the examination of conscience we find in our prayer-book—asking ourselves

the questions and giving ourselves time to think whether we have done any of these things, and if so, how many times, and whether by ourselves, or with others. Or we may take our Catechism and go over the sins forbidden by the Ten Commandments, and see in the same way if we have done any of them. Or, again, we may think of our three-fold duty: (1) to God, (2) to our neighbour, and (3) to ourselves. Some people find this examination the simplest and the easiest.

Most of us fail not in *many* things, but many times in a *few* things. This is because our lives are much the same week after week, and the same duties bring the occasions of the same faults. There is no need, then, if we go to confession often, to go over many points. A short examination of conscience may be enough for us. If we have committed any sin that is not a usual one with us, our conscience will have noted it in our daily examination, and we shall remember it when we go to confession.

Anything that makes our religious duties easy to us is a gain. God meant them—above all meant the Sacraments—to be our chief happiness, as well as our chief helps. He never meant us to turn them into torture. Now what makes some of us dread confession—dread it so much that we stay away, or go very seldom—is that we find it such a tedious business to get through. It is well for us, therefore, to follow some simple examination of conscience, such as the following, which may bring our chief faults quickly to mind and do all that is necessary without tiring us.

## Examination of Conscience

(1) *Duty to God.*
- Confession. (Did I do the four things by way of preparation? Did I say my penance carefully?)
- Communion. (Did I make the usual acts before and after? And how?)
- Mass. (Have I been attentive and said my prayers?)
- Benediction.
- Behaviour in Church.
- Speaking of God and holy things.
- Sermons.
- Catechism.
- Morning and night prayers.
- Examination of conscience.
- Grace at meals.

(2) *Duty to our Neighbour.*
- Parents, masters, mistresses. (Disobedience, disrespect in word or manner. Stubbornness or sulkiness when corrected).
- Brothers and sisters, companions. (Quarrelling, teasing, bad example, lies, calumny—that is, saying what is injurious and not true; detraction—that is, saying what is injurious but true).

(3) *Duty to ourselves.*
- The holy virtue of purity. (Anything wilfully contrary thereto, in thought, word, deed)
- Employment of time at studies, play, free time.
- Meals. (What about greediness?)
- My predominant passion. (What is it—pride or anger, or sloth, or what? Am I striving against it?)

Some method of this kind we may have made for ourselves. Whatever we do for ourselves in such matters is likely to suit us better than what others do for us. No one can tell as I can whether the glove I have on fits or not.

Here is our examination for confession. But before we begin our preparation at all, we know of course what kind of confession we are going to make. Most children are advised to make a general confession before First Communion, that is, a confession going back upon all their life so far. For some cases this is necessary; in others it is only useful and advisable. It is necessary whenever there is question of bad confessions in the past.

A bad confession is one which was known to be bad at the time it was made, either because a mortal sin was wilfully concealed, or because the person *knew* he had no true sorrow for past grievous sin, or purpose of avoiding it in future; he had taken no pains to ask for it or to make use of the considerations which lead to it, and he had no determination to avoid such or such a mortal sin, or the immediate occasions which led him to commit it.

If such a confession as this has not been set right afterwards by a good confession, in which the mortal sin was told and the hiding told, and in which there was true sorrow and purpose of amendment, then a general confession is necessary to put all right again, and that general confession must go back to the last good confession. Mind, the person must have *known at the time* that the confession was bad. Fears afterwards do not make it bad. Unless then there has been a bad confession, a general confession before First Communion is not *necessary*.

But it may be very *useful*, and this for several reasons. Now that we are preparing for our First Communion, we are supposed to be quite at our best. When should we be fervent and in earnest, if not now that we are preparing for the greatest act of our lives? At this time, when we are thinking of all God has done and is going to do for us, it is well to call to mind all we have done against Him, that putting one by the side of the other, as we put black beside white, we may be moved to make a thoroughly good act of contrition, and so secure forgiveness for all our sins in the past, and prepare ourselves to receive great helps for the future, in the confession we are going to make.

Another fruit of such a general confession is that it makes our souls peaceful and happy. We come to receive our Lord with greater joy and confidence. And if, in the future, doubts and troubles should arise in our minds, we shall be able to say, "Well, I know at any rate in the confession before my First Communion I made all right. I need never look behind that." Still, as we are not to be our own judges in matters of importance concerning our souls, we must ask our confessor what kind of confession we are to make, and do as he tells us.

If we make, as most do, a general confession from the time when we were quite little, that is, as far back as we can remember, it will help our memory in the examination of conscience to think of the places where we have lived—the churches there; the different houses and the rooms in them; the people we have lived with or played with; the way we spent our time there, whether at lessons or at play. This will bring to our minds the way in which we have offended God in thoughts or words or deeds or omissions. As to the number of times we have fallen into such or such a sin, we can tell whether it was once or often, whether we had a habit of it or not.

The care we are to give to this examination of conscience is to be a *reasonable* care, the care we should give to a matter of importance. The Catechism says we are carefully to examine our conscience. It does not say we are to fidget over it. You do a drawing carefully that is to be sent up to South Kensington, but you do not fidget over it. It would be silly to do this. And it is silly to worry ourselves about our examination of conscience. See why:

Those who care at all about serving God and saving their souls, cannot commit a mortal sin without knowing it, for there must be three things to make a mortal sin: (1) grave matter, (2) full knowledge, (3) full consent; that is, the sin must be a grievous sin—known to be grievous or mortal at the time it is committed—and there must be full consent to commit the mortal sin.

Do you think there can be all that without our remembering it afterwards? Do you suppose I could get into a train going to Edinburgh, knowing the train was going to Edinburgh, and settle myself down with my bag and umbrella, without remembering afterwards I had done this? Of course I could not. Neither do we commit mortal sins without remembering. Now, mortal sins are the only sins God requires us to confess. It is good to confess our venial sins, but we are not obliged. Where is the sense, then, of worrying ourselves to see whether we have left out mortal sins in our examination of conscience, when we should know them even before we examine—*if they were there.*

Persons going to confession often, could not forget a mortal sin, and it is silly to torment themselves about it. "But I have all my past life to think over, and perhaps there may have been mortal sins that I have never confessed properly and now I have forgotten them." Your past life has not been so very long. You can remember if ever you went to confession *knowing* you were hiding a mortal sin, or knowing you did not want to be sorry for it, and were not going to try to avoid it for the future. If you ever did this and have never put it right since by a good confession, you must, as we have seen, put it right now, by confessing that sin and that you have hidden it all this time, and confessing any mortal sin of that or any other kind which you may have committed since—confessing them now with true sorrow and purpose of amendment.

But if, please God, there has been nothing of this, and you are only afraid you have forgotten some mortal sin in your confession, you see there is nothing to be troubled about, because you could not have forgotten it if you were at all in earnest. And even supposing you had forgotten it, it would be forgiven with the rest of your sins in the first good confession you made. The only thing you would have to do would be to confess it if it ever came to your mind afterwards and you knew it was a mortal sin, and you had never confessed it. You would have to do this because of God's law, that every mortal sin must be confessed once. But it was forgiven before you confessed it.

"But suppose I had committed mortal sins and confessed them without knowing I had not true sorrow for them—what has become of them?" They were forgiven in the next confession you made in which there was sorrow, just as forgotten mortal sins are forgiven, because in every good confession we make, our sorrow extends to every mortal sin of which we have been guilty.

All this about the confession of mortal sin, and of past mortal sin. There is no harm in making it all clear, lest any one should have troubles at a time when our Lord wants our souls to be all peace and happiness. It helps, too, to show us that God's law about confession, and therefore our duty of examination, strictly speaking, concerns mortal sins only. So that when we have examined our conscience as to that, we have nothing more to do in the way of examination *that is strictly necessary.*

It is well in our general confession to tell all the chief sins we can call to mind after a reasonable examination, in order to make our souls as fit as possible to receive the Divine Guest Who is coming. He Himself showed this in the washing of the feet. But it is important to remember that we are *not obliged* to confess our venial sins, so that if we do leave out any, or forget any, it is no sin—God's precept is that *all known mortal sins discovered after reasonable care must be confessed once*. If, after reasonable care, a mortal sin should be forgotten in the examination of conscience and in the confession, it is forgiven with the rest. Only, if we remember it afterwards, and know it was not confessed, we are bound to confess it next time we go to confession.

There are two faults we have to be on our guard against in examining our conscience—doing it in a hurried and careless way, not giving time enough—and doing it in a fidgety way, giving too much time so that none is left for the more important part of the preparation. If you *hurriers* are so quick over it because you want to have more time for the more important parts, you might be excused. But the probability is, you will be quicker still over these. And if you *fidgets*, who are so careful about the examination of your conscience, were equally careful about your contrition, nobody would blame you either. But both of you are apt to neglect that part of the preparation which is all-important—*contrition*.

The right way, then, is to get through our examination of conscience briskly, in a business-like manner, not dawdling over it, not wool-gathering. We should have a method of arranging what we have to say, so that our sins easily fall into classes in our memory. If you like to take in order, duties to God, to our neighbour, and to ourselves, as suggested above, you will be able to leave your sins quietly when you have made your examination and turn to your next point. If you have no order in your arrangement, this examination becomes very difficult and wearisome, and even when it is finished you will be running after your sins instead of thinking how to get rid of them.

What makes preparation for the Sacrament of Penance a very simple and very easy process is: (1) to go frequently, so that we have not much time to go over from one confession to another; and (2) to have the habit of examining our conscience well every night and of making a good act of contrition. We thus come to our preparation for confession with our work half done. Then, when we get into church, we should begin our preparation at once—no looking about and wasting time in distractions before we can pull ourselves together to begin, but beginning at once with the first of the four points.

Some boys were in church preparing for confession. Among them was a big fellow who had evidently finished his preparation, for he was lolling over the bench with his eyes everywhere and his head nowhere. The master went up to him, and said, "The priest is there, go first." "I am not ready, sir." "Not ready? How long have you been here?" "I am not sure, sir." "Well, how long will you be getting ready?" "I can't tell, sir." "Whereabouts are you in your preparation?" "I don't know, sir." "There is not much business being done here," said the master to himself, and he went to a small lad whose finger was keeping his place in a dirty little book that proved to be his Catechism. "Are you ready for confession? "Not quite, sir." "How long will you be?" "Five minutes, I have just started the last point." Which of those two do you suppose found it easiest to prepare for confession? And which, to all appearance, would profit most?

3. *We must take time and care to make a good act of contrition.*—Here we have the chief part of our preparation and the part which almost all of us think least about. There are some who will spend half an hour over examination of conscience and barely two minutes over their contrition. This is like a housemaid sweeping all the dust into the middle of

the room, and instead of taking it away, leaving it there to be blown back into the corners where it came from. Whatever is the good of that? The main thing in the preparation is to secure our contrition, not to heap together our sins. The chief thing we have to bring to the Sacrament is not our sins, but our sorrow for them. God will forgive sin without confession when confession is not possible. He never has and never will forgive it without contrition.

Contrition is part of the matter of the Sacrament—there can be no Sacrament without it. A priest goes to the church for a Baptism. The baby is there and the sponsors, everything ready except the water—"Except the water! Why, that is the chief thing—how can there be Baptism without water?" Just as easily as there can be the Sacrament of Penance and forgiveness of sins without contrition.

God cares so much for contrition that He will forgive sin, mortal sin even, as soon as He sees an act of perfect contrition in the soul—before confession therefore—provided there is the desire for the Sacrament and the intention to confess the sin. But without contrition, neither self-accusation nor the priest's absolution will help us one bit. We may have confessed every sin we ever committed—not forgotten one—and the priest may have given us absolution, and all the while there has been no Sacrament, because the matter was not there—there was no contrition. God has not made His forgiveness depend on our good *memory*, but He has made it depend on our good *will*—on our contrition. Bring Him contrition, and He will forgive any sin and any number of sins; He never has, He never will, He *cannot* reject a contrite and humble heart.

There have been periods in history when the Courts of Justice were shamefully unjust, indeed they were rather courts of injustice. People accused of smaller offences against the laws could escape the consequences by means of a bribe which we may call "hush-money." On payment of this bribe, proceedings against them were stopped, the affair was hushed up and nothing more was heard of it. The custom was an evil one, and it was unfair either to take or to give "hush-money." Happily, it is a thing of the past.

No, not quite. There is a tribunal now where something of the kind takes place every day—where a Judge sits and takes "hush-money," not for smaller offences only, but for the greatest crimes. And nothing more is heard of the guilt, for He has "cast it all," He says, "behind His back." O goodness of our Lord, which to encourage us makes Him do what we should never have thought He could do—liken Himself to an unjust Judge! O holy contrition, O blessed "hush-money," which can make us safe in the terrible Day of Judgment.

The Judge before Whom we must appear twice—once as soon as our soul has left the body, and again at the Last Great Day—is the same Who sits in the confessional now. The sentence He gives now, He will never change. What He forgives now, He will forgive always. Neither when we stand alone face to face with Him at the Particular Judgment, or with the whole world to hear our sentence at the General Judgment, will He change the sentence He pronounced again and again in the confessional. Our trial is going on now. We can bribe our Judge now. He holds out His Hand now for our "hush-money." Oh, how can we be so foolish as to think any trouble too great to satisfy Him now—to get Him on our side—to make Him our Friend while there is yet time!

We see, then, that the great thing in our confession is to make sure of our contrition. Nothing can be done without it. The absolution has nowhere to go to if there is no contrition for it to fall on.

You have seen a bee on a bright summer day flying from flower to flower. Some of the bright blossoms it passes by altogether; on some it alights for an instant, but flies off again directly—it cannot find there what it has come to seek. But let there be a bed of thyme or mignonette about anywhere and the bee goes to it straight. There it settles, there it collects the sweet juice which it will transform for us into honey. Just so does the absolution come in search of our contrition. If this is not there, it can do nothing. If it finds contrition, it does its blessed work—the work that is so sweet to us and to our Heavenly Father.

We must have contrition then—how are we to get it? The Catechism tells us "we must earnestly beg it of God." Yes, for we can get it from Him alone. He must provide the "hush-money" with which we are to bribe Him. He only wants to be asked. But we *must* ask and ask *earnestly*. Not in a careless, off-hand way, but with our whole heart. "My God, give me true sorrow for having offended You. I must come to You for it, I cannot give it to myself. But I know You wish to give it to me more than I want to have it. You have told me to ask and I shall receive, to seek and I shall find, to knock and it shall be opened to me. For *every one* that asks receives, and *every one* that seeks shall find."

God is ready to give it, but, as usual, He will not do all. Not only must we earnestly beg Him to give us contrition, "but we must make use of such considerations as may move us to it." You know, of course, that the sorrow which is contrition is sorrow from a supernatural motive, that is, a motive which is put before us by faith. To be sorry because our sin has brought upon us some temporal trouble or punishment—a scolding, or the like, is not contrition. No amount of such sorrow is of any use for the forgiveness of sins in the Sacrament of Penance. But an imperfect sorrow, or *attrition*, will do for the Sacrament.

The chief motives for this sorrow are—that by mortal sin we have lost Heaven and deserved Hell—crucified our loving

Saviour Jesus Christ—and offended God Who is infinitely good in Himself. You see these motives rise like steps in a ladder: we begin with the lowest, and so climb to the highest. We ought not to pass over the lower motives, but use them sometimes at least.

A child preparing for First Confession was asked if the motive of having lost Heaven and deserved Hell was sufficient for the Sacrament of Penance. "Certainly not," was the answer, "because you are only sorry for yourself." However, our good God is so compassionate that He says it *is* sufficient. But we should try to be sorry for the other motives too.

A gentleman turning a street corner came upon a baby crying pitifully. He stooped down to ask, "What is the matter, little one? Have you lost your father?" No answer. "Are you crying for your father?" "Na-a-a." "What are you crying for then?" "I'm crying for myself."

And an excellent thing it is to cry for oneself; there is only one thing better—to cry for having grieved, perhaps for having lost, our Father Who is in Heaven.

"Making use of such considerations as may move us to contrition," means thinking of those things which will make us sorry—how, if I have ever committed mortal sin, my name over a beautiful throne in Heaven was taken down and put over a dark terrible place in the dungeons of Hell. St. Peter said that when Judas died he went "to his own place." Every one who commits a mortal sin has a place of *his own* in Hell.

I can think that by venial sin I have made the dreadful possibility of mortal sin and of Hell greater; I have deserved the grievous pains of Purgatory; and have lost many degrees of glory in Heaven.

Then I can think of some part of the Passion—of those sufferings of our Blessed Lord that move me most. I can kneel before Him at the Scourging or at the Crowning with thorns, or under the Cross, and there looking up at Him, make my act of contrition. I can think how good God has always been to me; how much He has done for me already; how much He wants to do. And so gratitude will lead me to sorrow for having offended Him Who must be infinitely good in Himself to be so good to me.

And here I have reached perfect contrition. Gratitude brings perfect contrition after it as the needle draws the thread. I, to whom God has been so good, so forgiving—I have let this sin, this bad passion, come between Him and me. I have disappointed and grieved Him Who loved me from all eternity, Who is always thinking of me and planning everything for my good, to make me happy here and happy with Himself for ever.

Let us see how one who loved our Lord dearly made use of Calvary as a consideration to move him to sorrow for his sins:

"I go to the foot of the Cross and look up. I look at Him Who hangs there, and see how from the sole of His Foot to the crown of His Head there is no sound spot in Him. And all this *for me*. I look at that Head with Its cruel crown, bowed down in pain and shame, because mine has been held up in pride. I look at His Eyes, blind with blood and tears for my sins, for which I have never wept—for sins of sight. I see His Lips bruised with the blows from the soldier's fist, because my lips have said so many hard and bitter things. I see His Tongue parched with thirst and tormented with wine and gall to atone for my greediness—His Face covered with spittle to atone for my vanity—His Hands pierced through with nails to atone for the evil deeds my hands have done—His Feet throbbing with fiercest pain, because my feet have wandered away from God to follow my own will—His whole Body torn with scourges, pulled out of joint, cold, trembling, racked with pain in every limb, because I have thought only of indulging my body, of giving it all it asked, of seeking my comfort in everything.

### The Brazen Serpent

"As Moses lifted up the serpent in the desert,
so must the Son of Man be lifted up." (John 3:14)

"He loved *me* and delivered Himself *for me*...All this *for me*. All this Blood to wash away my sins. What have I done for Him? What am I going to do now? Am I going to sin again?"

> My God, they nail Thy Hands and Feet,
>    They pierce Thy Sacred Side,
> The last drop of Thy Blood is shed,
>    And Thou for man hast died,
> Oh, can we wish to sin again
>    And act a traitor's part,
> To Him Who loved us with a love
>    Which broke His Sacred Heart!

We perfect ourselves in contrition, as well as in other things, by practice. So we should often make acts of contrition. No boy would dream of taking a high jump the first time he tried, but by practice he may do it in the end, and do it easily. Let us practise our acts of contrition. They will be so much easier to make when preparing for confession if we rehearse them beforehand.

Every night after the examination of conscience let us make a good act of contrition and again just before we get into bed.

And we will begin *now* to prepare for our confession by making many little acts of sorrow for our sins. They can be made anywhere—genuflecting before the Blessed Sacrament; when we take Holy Water; going up and down stairs, "My God, I *am* so sorry for having offended You, because You are so good." Each time we make an act like this we help to form a habit, and a most blessed habit it is. If, in a sudden accident, death were to surprise us before we had time to make our confession, this habit might be of the greatest possible use; we might be saved by our last act of contrition. To make your salvation sure therefore, acquire the habit of making good acts of contrition.

Contrition does not consist in tears or in feelings. It is not in our eyes, but in our will. So we need not be troubled if we do not *feel* very sorry. It is a blessed thing to feel it—a blessed thing to weep for our sins as the Saints have done. But God does not require it, and there may be a very hearty sorrow with very little feeling. If we try to say from our hearts, "I am sorry for what I have done; I wish I had not done it; with God's help I will try not to do it again," we may be happy about our contrition.

One word more before we leave this third point. When we make our act of contrition for all the sins we are going to confess, we should make a special act of contrition for a sin of our past life which we intend to mention in confession—one for which we know we have sorrow and a firm purpose of amendment. We mention it, not for the sake of getting it forgiven, for it was forgiven, please God, long ago. But because there must be contrition in our confession *for some sin we have confessed*, and we might not have contrition for our daily and smaller faults, it is very useful to accuse ourselves always of some greater sin of our past life *for the sake of contrition*. But it would be no good to get into the way of confessing such sins of the past simply by routine, without a thought of sorrow; and therefore we should do well to make a loving, heartfelt act of sorrow for it before we go into the confessional.

Make an *act* of contrition always. It is better not only to *be* sorry, but also to *say* we are sorry.

4. *We must resolve, by the grace of God, to renounce our sins and begin a new life for the future.* This resolution is not a determination never again to commit any sin whatever; but it is a determination, by God's grace, never to commit a mortal sin. This is the purpose of amendment we are *bound* to have. We should, of course, resolve to avoid venial sins, and it is well to make the resolution to avoid some particular fault between this and our next confession. Your examination of conscience will have shown you what your chief fault has been and what

therefore your purpose of amendment should be. Resolve to lessen the number of falls; to come back to God more quickly when you do fall, and without discouragement—to try again.

Do not forget the duty of Satisfaction; for example, when you have been guilty of calumny—"I shall have to restore the good name of that person whom I accused of stealing the box of sweets."

One question before we leave the subject of resolutions. Does it show that we have no real purpose of amendment if we fall into the same faults week after week? Not necessarily. Our natural character lays us open to the same temptations, and the routine of our daily life brings round the same occasions. St. Aloysius used to say that the only sins he did not commit were those to which he was not tempted, or which he had not the opportunity of committing. It is not surprising, then, that we take the old faults to confession time after time. What we have to do is to lessen the number; to rid ourselves of them by degrees; to turn occasions of sin into occasions of victory, and so, as St. Augustine says, to use them as steps by which to climb up to Heaven.

As to the confession itself, there is not much to be said. Remember you are going to confess your sins to our Blessed Saviour, Who, in the person of His minister, is there to hear you, to help you, to absolve you. This will take away any feeling of fear as to what the priest may think or say. If you have any difficulty in telling any sin, or do not know how to say it, ask the priest to help you. Do not hide anything in your conscience that makes it troubled or uncomfortable. Leave out nothing to be said at some future time—when you come to die. *Clear it all up now.* Our Lord wants to find your soul in perfect peace when He comes. If you feel it hard to speak, ask your good Angel and our Lady to help you, and think that the brave effort you make will cost only a minute's pain; that you will be rewarded instantly by a flood of peace and happiness, and that what you tell our Lord there in that tribunal He will never bring up against you hereafter.

After confessing your sins, *leave them*. Do not go back to see if you have told all; but listen to what the priest says. And then make with all your heart your act of contrition as you receive absolution. The absolution comes now, you remember, to look for the contrition on which it is to fall.

Returning to your place, thank God very heartily, very joyfully, for the Precious Blood that has been applied to your soul and has washed it from all its stains. Ask that you may keep it unstained for the future; that you may die rather than commit a mortal sin: and that by acts of contrition and good confessions you may keep your soul always pleasing in the sight of God. Say some prayer or hymn that you like by way of thanksgiving.

> Hail Jesus, hail! Who for my sake
>    Sweet blood from Mary's veins didst take,
> And shed it all for me.
>    O blessed be my Saviour's Blood,
> My life, my light, my only good,
>    To all eternity!

Say your penance, if possible, before you leave the church. *Say it*—do not merely read it; the penance should be said with the lips, though of course there is no need for others to hear it.

This question was put to a class preparing for First Confession: "What is the first thing we should do when we get back to our places after confession?"

"Be sorry, Father," said one child.

"Be glad, Father," cried another. Which was right? They were both right. We shall be sorry with a new sorrow for having ever offended Him Who has forgiven us so generously and so easily. But still more shall we be glad—glad and grateful. Gratitude is the only return we can make Him, and it is the only return He asks. He was pleased when the poor lepers He had cleansed "came back and fell at His Feet giving thanks." But He was pained that there should be only one. "Were there not ten made clean," He said sadly, "and where are the nine?"

Perhaps the thought of a poor African savage may help our gratitude and our thanksgiving.

Some years ago a Catholic missioner was making his way down a broad river in the centre of Africa. With him were twenty-six little blacks, bought from the Arab slave-dealers with the money sent for this purpose by the Catholic children of Europe, members of the Association of the Holy Childhood. On his return to the Mission House, these poor little natives would be instructed and made children of God by Holy Baptism. Their "white Father" was very different from the cruel masters they had had, and already they loved him dearly.

At a bend in the river he ordered the pirogue to be stopped. It had neared a village where traders often halted with the gangs of slaves they had captured, and the good Father hoped to find some more children he could rescue and take away with him. Here, then, he had resolved to spend the night. He had arranged his twenty-six little savages as well as he could to protect them from the cold, when a fine young fellow of thirty was brought to him for sale. The Father looked at him with pity; but in spite of his desire to buy him and set him free, he was obliged to tell his master that he could not ransom him—his money was for children.

Night came on and he had just laid himself down on his blanket, when repeated groans fell on his ear. Someone at no great distance was evidently in pain. He rose and looked about, and after a while came upon the slave he had refused to ransom, tightly bound with great pieces of bindweed. Waking his master he asked, "Why do you bind this man in so cruel a way?"

"Why?" answered the other. "Can't you see why? If I did not bind his hands and feet fast he would be sure to get away, for he is strong and active."

"Well, bind him if you must; but at least you can do it without putting him to such torture."

"What nonsense," said the trader, with a hoarse laugh. "He is a slave. If he *is* in pain, what does it matter?"

Indignant at such barbarity, and feeling sure the little children of Europe would say: "Oh, do buy that poor man with our money," the Father seized his knife and cut the bonds that held him fast. Then turning to his master, he said:

"How much do you want for your slave?"

"A hundred brass rods."

"Here they are. Now the man is free. He is yours no longer."

The poor slave looked on, dumb with astonishment. He made no attempt to rise till his deliverer said to him: "Now you are the slave of no one. To-morrow you shall go back to your village and to all you love. But first you must have something to eat. And you may sleep here to-night, unless you want to go off at once."

"I want to stay with you."

"Well, we will see about that to-morrow. Take some food now, for you must be hungry, and then go to sleep."

When the Father woke the next morning the ransomed slave was waiting by his side. He threw himself on his knees, and said with an imploring look:

"You tell me to go back to my village. White man, you are my village. You cut the bonds that hurt me so. You have saved me from a cruel master. I want to stay with you."

"I tell you, you are a free man, for I have no slaves. You may go home to your village."

"I go away? Never! I will go with you until you beat me so much that I can follow you no longer."

The Father could not turn a deaf ear to his entreaties, and the grateful fellow joyfully took his place in the pirogue, to the great astonishment of the other natives.

"White man, you are my village. You cut the bonds that hurt me so. You have set me free from a cruel master. I will stay with you. I will never leave you. I will go with you as long as I have strength to follow."

Do not the words of the grateful savage spring to our lips as we look up at the Cross, and see what it has cost our Deliverer to set us free? Shall we cast ourselves into slavery again? Shall we ever "crucify Him again," as St. Paul says, by mortal sin? Shall we go away from Him, or shall we promise to stay with Him and be His faithful followers as long as life shall last?

Some people always like to make a visit to our Lady's altar after confession, to offer their resolutions to her and put them into her keeping. And do not forget as you renew your resolutions, to ask your good Angel's help in keeping them. They interest him very much indeed.

We have stayed a long time on this subject of confession. But if you are tired it will be your own fault for going through it all at one reading, when you were advised to take it a little at a time during the days that precede your confession. If ever there was an excuse for being long, it is when we are speaking of this grand and merciful Sacrament. Our Lord shows us what *He* thinks of it by choosing the brightest of all days for its institution.

It was on the evening of the Resurrection when He was once more in the midst of the Eleven; when, breathless with joy, they gathered round Him to gaze on His glorious Wounds, that He gave them as the precious fruit of His Passion the power to forgive sins in that Sacrament which the Church calls a second plank after shipwreck, the only Sacrament left for the forgiveness of sins after Baptism. In that Supper-room before His Passion He had given us the Sacrament of Sacraments. Now in the Supper-room once more, His battle over, His victory won, He gave us that Sacrament without which even the Holy Eucharist would have availed us nothing. For how many guests would there be at the Feast He has prepared, if He had not left us the means of getting that wedding garment, without which no one may sit down at His Table?

There are two Sacraments by which, as by two feet, the children of the Church march forward on their way to Heaven. One is the Sacrament of Love, the other is the Sacrament of Mercy. We must use both in order to advance at all. But the rate at which we advance is very different. Some only creep along on the road to Heaven, because of the slovenly use they make of the helps God has provided for them. Some move along faster, some run, and the Saints seem to fly over the road. Why? Chiefly because of the use they make of the Sacraments—of the dispositions they bring to them, of their fervent preparations and thanksgivings.

We must not think of the Sacrament of Penance simply as a means of obtaining pardon of our sins. It is this, but it is much more than this. It is one of the chief means God has given for our sanctification. It gives us self-knowledge and humility. It fortifies us against temptation. It refreshes our souls continually with the blessed waters of contrition. It remits part of the temporal punishment due to our sins. It strengthens our will in good. It gives us great courage in the work of overcoming our faults, particularly our predominant passion. It helps us to persevere with earnestness in the service of God.

The measure in which we shall receive these graces will depend on the dispositions we bring to the Sacrament. If we take a large bucket to the well, we draw a great deal of water; if we take a small one, we get but little.

Our peace, our progress, our perseverance depend so much on the use we make of this Sacrament, that we should try to improve our dispositions each time we approach it. God increases in our souls those virtues, the beginnings of which we take with us to the Sacrament. If we go with a desire of perfect contrition, He will deepen our contrition more and more. If He sees in us the desire of advancing in virtue and overcoming ourselves, He will increase this desire and help us in the way of self-conquest, for the graces of the Sacraments are not given for the time only but to spread over and to sanctify our whole lives.

Remember these three things about every confession of your Life:

1. Never go in a hurry. Do not put off the preparation to the last moment, but see that you have sufficient time to prepare.

2. Never go into the confessional till your act of contrition has been properly made. If you scramble over it or make it a mere matter of routine, you will endanger the most important part of the Sacrament and prepare for yourselves great trouble of mind hereafter.

3. Whatever you may forget when you come to our Lord's Feet; whatever you risk, be sure to secure one thing—be sure of your *"hush-money."*

# XXVI
## The Lost Sheep

It was tired of being always in the fold. It was tired of following always where the Good Shepherd led. Out yonder, by the distant hills, the grass looked sweeter, and the water clearer, and the sun warmer. It was sure it could find better pasture for itself.

So one morning, when the gate was opened and the Shepherd led out the sheep, instead of following Him like the rest, it stole away by itself.

At first it was afraid He would miss it and bring it back. But the fear grows less as it wanders farther and farther from the fold, and at last when it feels quite safe, it begins to gambol about and enjoy its freedom. How nice it is to be able to do just as it likes! How much fresher the grass is here than it is at home! How silly the other sheep are not to come out here and enjoy themselves!

The sun rises higher and higher. It is far, far away now; far beyond the tinkling bells, beyond the sound of the Good Shepherd's Voice. The sky is bright, and the birds sing gaily, and the mossy banks are sweet and fresh. Down the pleasantest paths it wanders, and through the gayest meadows. When the sun is high in the heavens, it drinks at the cool brooks and lies down to rest in the shade. And then on again and on, up the purple hills and into the valley again, and through the long grass where it makes a path for itself.

The afternoon wears on and evening comes; the sun is sinking in the west. The air grows chilly, and as the shades creep up the sky, a change comes over the strayed sheep. How cold it is! How dark it is getting! How fast the night draws on! Had it not better get back to the fold? But there is no light for that now. Weary and frightened, it makes its way to a wood. There will be shelter there, and in the morning it will go home as fast as it can. If only it were there now, safe and warm! Oh, why had it come away! The far-off grass was not so sweet after all, and the Good Shepherd's stream was quite as fresh as those out here. The wood is damp and cold, but it seems safer than outside, and the poor tired sheep creeps under the long grass and tries to hide itself.

Hark! what is that sound in the distance? Often and often, when safely folded at night, the sheep has heard it, but not as it hears it now. What did they care in the fold for the bark of the prowling wolf without, when they were safe within, and the Good Shepherd with them!

Again that horrid sound! And now it is nearer. The terrified sheep bounds forward to find a safer shelter, and is caught in a thorny thicket, where the long branches hold it fast. It struggles to get free, for the wolf is very near, but the more it tries, the closer those cruel thorns press round, till panting and bleeding it falls among them, and waits for that next hungry cry.

Listen! there is another sound. Not the howl of its enemy, but a Voice calling in the distance. It is far away, but the lost sheep knows it well. Oh, has He come to seek it, and will He be in time? Has He come to look for a sheep that has wandered away from Him so far; that has not been among His most faithful ones; that has often pretended not to hear when He called, and has not followed where He led? Has the Good Shepherd left the ninety-nine and come so far for one like this? It is too weak to go out and meet Him; it must lie helpless here and die unless He finds it soon. Will He know where to seek it, will He hear its bleating cry?

The wolf has heard, and with a loud bark comes hurrying on. The poor sheep waits for it to come, and calls faintly, and more faintly still for its Shepherd. Oh, that it had never left His Side! How good He has always been to it. What care He takes of His sheep. He knows them every one, and one by one He counts them morning and evening as He lets them out of the fold and leads them back. He is ready to give His Life for His sheep. More than once a panther has cleared at a bound the stone wall of the fold, crowned though it is with clumps of thorn bushes. Or a robber has climbed up and crept in under cover of the darkness. And then the Good Shepherd has defended His flock and drawn upon Himself all the wounds to save His sheep. Oh, why has it not known Him better and loved Him more! Is it not too late now?

There is a stir in the branches! Who is this making His way through the thicket straight to His poor lost sheep? Straight through the prickly briars that press around and wound Him on every side. They pierce His Brow and wound His Hands and Feet. But He does not mind them. His Eyes are fixed on the wanderer: "It is I, fear not!" And a smile lights up His tired Face as He hears its low bleat of welcome. Now He is kneeling by it and gently pressing back the thorns.

Hark! Hark! There is a snapping of branches; a spring into the thicket, and then a howl of disappointed rage. It is the wolf at last. Oh, those dreadful eyes; how they glare at the poor sheep like lamps of fire! But it does not fear them, for *He* is here Who loves it and will keep it from harm.

Tenderly He raises it and lays it on His Shoulders, and bids it rest on Him and fear not. And so, bending beneath His burden, He gathers His robe around Him and sets forth on the journey home. The wolf cowers before Him as He passes. Just at the last moment He has robbed it of its prey. Fear and hate are in its wrathful eyes, and if it dared, it would spring up and seize that defenceless creature even now.

Out on the bleak moorland where the winds sweep past and toss His raiment and His Hair. Through the meadows where the strayed sheep wandered lazily only a few hours ago—are they the same that looked so golden in the sunlight?—past the brook where it slaked its thirst at mid-day, and the mossy banks where it rested, and up and down the slopes of the silent hills. It did not know till now how far it had wandered. Straying away was pleasant and easy work, but what toil and pain the return is costing those aching Feet! Oh, how ungrateful it has been to Him Who has loved it so! How ill it has requited all His love! And He has no reproach for it. Nay, there is a contented smile on His Face as He makes His way over the stony ground that cuts His Feet at every step. Now and again, His Eyes turn tenderly to His wounded sheep, and a silent pressure tells it how glad He is to feel it near Him, and how willingly He bears the labour of bringing it back to the fold.

It must be midnight now. But the moon is up and the trees and jutting rocks stand out almost as distinctly as in the daytime. Surely home must be nearing. Is not this the further side of the hill that shelters the fold? He climbs it wearily. Now they have reached the top. Yes, there it is, lying quietly in the moonlight, the fold that poor wanderer never thought to see again. How glad it will be to be safe within once more! He descends the slope. Now His Hand is on the gate; and now the ninety-nine that have been waiting for Him press around to welcome Him and the wilful one that has cost Him so dear.

Will it be wilful any more? Will it think it is wiser than the rest? Will it follow Him at a distance *now*? Oh, if there is one of His sheep that knows Him better than the others and loves Him more; that is seen always at His Side; that is always listening for the sound of His Voice; that loves the fold and is content—more than content—with any place He gives it there: surely it is that hundredth sheep that was once so far away.

> He took me on His shoulder
>   And tenderly He kissed me;
> He bade my love be bolder
>   And said how He had missed me.
> And I thought I heard Him say
>   As He went along His way,
> "O silly souls, come near Me
>   My sheep should never fear Me,
> I am the Shepherd true."

O Jesus, Good Shepherd, how tender You are to Your sheep! You Yourself have told us this beautiful story, that Your sheep and little lambs may not be afraid of You when they have wandered away from You. *I* have done so, many and many a time, and have grieved You by sin. I am so sorry for all my sins, and for all it has cost You to set me free from them—for those cruel wounds in Your Hands and Feet. Give me true sorrow for all I have ever done to pain You. And let me be now one of Your faithful sheep, who love You, and keep close to You, and give joy to Your Sacred Heart.

Jesus, Good Shepherd, have mercy on us!

### The Good Shepherd

"He shall feed His flock like a Shepherd:
He shall gather together the lambs With His arm,
and shall take them up in His bosom." (Isaias 40:11)

## XXVII
## Who Comes?

Let us look at two pictures of home, and see if either reminds us of the Home above where we are expected.

An Irish gentleman had a son at one of our Colleges in the north of England. As the Christmas holidays drew near, the Rector wrote to ask how the boy was to be got home—as he was a little fellow, and lived right away in the south of Ireland. The father answered that the journey would be long and costly, the holidays were short, and it was scarcely worth while to send a servant for him. He had better, therefore, stay where he was. No doubt amusements would be provided for the lads remaining at the College, and of course his mother would see that a hamper of good things was sent off in time. An excellent arrangement and excellent reasons—to the father's mind at least. He was not an unkind father, and we have no right to blame his way of dealing with his child. In many cases it is quite impossible to have the children home.

But oh, how different is our Heavenly Father's way of dealing with us. We are all His children, who have to be taken home for the never-ending holidays of Heaven. This is with Him the one thing necessary. Cost and trouble go for nothing. Whatever will help this we must have.

The father we speak of might have been able to send another answer. It was true the journey was long and costly, but of course the boy must come home. He was expected; no end of surprises were waiting for him: brothers and sisters were always asking when he was coming; his mother was counting the hours. Home would not be home to father and mother without him—if his happy face were not there and his merry laugh heard all about the place. The servants had plenty to do, but every one of them was ready to set off and fetch him. And yet, somehow, he scarcely liked to trust the child to them, trusty as they were. What if anything were to happen on the road! He had better go himself. It was very foolish of course to make all this fuss about the boy, but he was the heir—the Rector would understand.

Ah, this is more like the Home where we are expected, more like our Heavenly Father! He must come Himself for His child. Angels and Saints are employed in our service; our Mother's eye is always on us, and her prayers for us go up without ceasing. But it is not enough. He must come Himself, Father, Son, and Holy Ghost—then surely we shall be safe.

What would the boy's thoughts be, as he paced about impatiently by the side of his trunks, waiting for his father's step! What when the ring came and his father stood in the doorway? Would there not be a rush on to His neck and the cry, "O father, all this way *for me!*"

And we, too, when the meeting comes in a few days, and for the first time our heart beats close to the Sacred Heart, will not our first thought be, "O my God, my God, *all this for me!*"

"I hope it will be so," you say, "I know it ought to be so. I see how that boy would leap forward to meet his father. But how is it that we—that I at least, cannot feel as I ought towards the God Who is coming all this way from Heaven for me, to fetch me Home? I should so like to feel different, but the feelings will not come. How is it that I am so little moved? Is every one dry and hard like this, or am I the only one?"

No, you are not the only one. Many of us are but little moved by God's loving ways with us, and the reason is because we do not *think* in our meditations or spiritual reading. We flutter from one thought to another like the butterfly, without resting upon any, and then we are surprised that we are not more touched by these thoughts! The surprising thing would be if we *were* touched. We expect to feel deeply, when we will not take the trouble to consider carefully. Nothing can come of such laziness.

What is it in the painter and the poet which enables them to produce the beauties that charm us in quiet landscape or in stirring verse? It is their deep *feeling* which springs from their deep *thought*. So it is with the Saints. What we skip lightly over, they ponder on again and again, going back upon it, examining it, applying it to themselves, making their meditations upon it— and this quietly, day after day, till they are *soaked* with spiritual things and *feel* them as we feel things that affect us most.

"But do you mean to say we should all be Saints if we thought about these things as the Saints did?" And why not? Taking for granted, of course, that we used our graces as the Saints used theirs. Almighty God does not make two sets of people and say: "Now these are to be Saints, whether they like it or not; and these shall not be Saints, however much they try." But He wants us all to be Saints. "This is the Will of God— your sanctification." St. Paul wrote at times to his converts as if he took it for granted that the early Christians were all Saints. To the Corinthians he says, "All the Saints salute you." To the Colossians, "Salute ye every Saint in Christ Jesus. All the Saints salute you, especially they that are of Caesar's household." And to the Hebrews, "Salute all your prelates and all the Saints."

We have seen again and again, and we cannot make it too clear to ourselves, that it is possible to serve God truly with very little feeling. Dryness, which often comes through our own fault, as we saw in our meditation on the "Loss of the Child Jesus," is not our fault always. At the same time, it is quite certain that if we want to "taste and see" with the Saints "that the Lord is sweet," we must do as the Saints did: we must quicken our faith. We shall *feel* with the Saints when we have the *faith* of the Saints. What is wanted is a strong faith. The Apostles knew this when they said to our Lord, not "Lord increase our *feelings*," but "Lord, increase our *faith*."

Now, faith is increased in two ways: by consideration or careful thinking, and by exercise. Something in this way: You find yourself watching a game of tennis. The dexterity, animation, and keen enjoyment of the players strike you, and you think, "I should like to be able to play like that." You watch the game another day, and say, "I wish I could play like that." You come again and again to the same place, and at the same hour, to watch the players, and each time with increasing interest. At last your reflections take a practical turn. It is no longer, "I should like—I wish I could play like that," but "*I will* play like that." You learn the rules of the game, and you take your place in the tennis-court. At first your efforts are awkward enough, and you are tempted to throw them up. But you persevere, and after a while, become quite a crack player.

Now, it is the same with the acquirement and increase of faith and every virtue. Consideration must come first and do its work, and then exercise must follow. All the watching in the world would not have made you a tennis-player unless you had used the rackets yourself. Neither does faith produce its wonderful effects without effort on our part. And just as the running and the striking develop and strengthen the muscles of your body, so does exercise increase and give vigour to your faith. Every reverent genuflection increases it; every thoughtful spiritual reading increases it. It is increased whenever you make a hearty act of faith—"Blessed be Jesus in the Most Holy

Sacrament of the Altar." "O Sacrament most holy, O Sacrament Divine, all praise and all thanksgiving be every moment Thine."

"But why are we staying so long upon faith," you say. "We must have it of course, but we want other virtues as well; we want humility, and love, and hope, and contrition, and desire to prepare us for our Lord's coming." Certainly you do, and you are quite right to be anxious about them. And it is just because you want them all that you must secure your faith. Faith includes them all; they all depend on her; she is a queen and brings them all in her train. When our Lord wanted the Supper-room prepared for His coming, He sent the two Apostles who were most remarkable for their faith. The cry of one was, "Thou art Christ, the Son of the Living God! and the cry of the other was, "It is the Lord!" They loved our Lord dearly. They felt His love in their hearts. It was their faith that made them love as they did.

Look at this little tree; it is one mass of blossoms. Each blossom is borne on a separate branch, but we can trace all the branches to the parent stem, and this springs from the root. It is the root on which all those fair blossoms depend. Cut them from the root, or let the root have no depth of earth, or be exposed to the blasts, or be eaten by insects—what will happen? All the flowers will die.

So it is with faith—neglect it, expose it, let it be on the surface only, and all the fair virtues that depend on it will die. Shall we see how they depend on it and how naturally they grow out of it?

I begin to think Who He is that is coming to me in a few days. Oh, how little we know Who He is! We have been trying all this time to understand something of our Blessed Lord. We have seen Him in type and in prophecy before He came. We have tried to study Him at Bethlehem and at Nazareth, in the Temple, on the Lake, by the sea-shore. Yet when we have put together all we have learned about Him, we have scarcely begun to know Him; we are as far as ever from being able to answer that question, "Who comes?" To His own Blessed Mother, who held Him in her arms, who lived with Him thirty years, He was always—He is still—the Wonderful, the Incomprehensible God. What then can *I* know of Him! All I can do is to bow myself down in the dust before Him, and own that He is far above all my little mind can understand.

But I can get to learn more and more about Him. I can think of Him in His Majesty and glory, or in His humility and sweetness. I remember that He is King of kings and Lord of Lords, and that on His Head are many diadems. "Thousands of thousands minister unto Him, and ten thousand times a hundred thousand stand before Him." I remember what the Disciple, who leant on His Breast at Supper, tells us of His exceeding glory: "And when I had seen Him, I fell at His Feet as dead."

As I ponder quietly these thoughts which my faith presents to me, a great reverence comes over my soul. I, too, fall on my face before Him, and adore Him, "very God of very God." I feel how little I am—how I am nothing in His sight—how worse than nothing by reason of my sins—and how good He is to bear with me in spite of my unworthiness, and to desire to come to me. Shall I not love Him for it and desire to be with Him! And since He is so great, so powerful, will He not do great things for me when He comes? Come then, O Lord Jesus.

Now just see what has sprung from that root of faith. Faith led me to adoration, and adoration led to humility, and that again to love and hope and desire. And it all came quite naturally—I did not notice how one act was passing into another, and how all sprang from faith.

Faith will produce the same acts if, instead of thinking of our Lord's Majesty, I think of His humility and His sweetness.

I may ask Him with St. Paul, "Who art Thou, Lord?" And because He does not want to frighten me, He answers, "I am Jesus of Nazareth." Oh, that does not frighten me. I think of the little Child at Mary's knee, or the Boy in Joseph's shop, or the Carpenter taking His work home—and my whole heart goes out to Him in love, and in wonder and in thanksgiving—

> Art Thou, weak Babe, my very God,
> Oh, I must love Thee then,
> Love Thee and yearn to spread Thy Love
> Among forgetful men.

Here are acts of adoration and love and zeal all flowing fast from faith.

Do you see now why we are laying such stress upon faith—why instead of trying to arouse our *feelings* we should try to arouse our *faith?* Our feelings depend on our faith, much in the same way as our shadows depend on the sun. Strong sunshine, strong shadow; faint sunshine, faint shadow.

Yet this is not the case always, for you know at the equator, where the sun is just overhead, he casts very little shadow, and on some days in the year none at all. So there may be strong faith with very little or no feeling. This is as God wills, Who knows what is best for us. One of His greatest Saints bids us say: "Give me Thy love and Thy grace, and this is enough for me."

Still, if we cannot have feelings of devotion when we like, we can unfortunately hinder through our own fault what God intended for us. Venial sins of habit, shabbiness with God, carelessness in our duties, wilful distractions in prayer—all these things are hindrances. We cannot hope to have the sweet experience of the Saints, if we will not follow the way of the Saints. If we want to go by train from London to Southampton, we must get on to the right line. Any line will not do, and if we insist on going by the Great Northern we shall never get there.

So we will take care not to deprive ourselves by our own

fault of these feelings of devotion. And then we will leave it to God to give them or not as He sees best, not disturbing ourselves if we feel cold or dry, but doing our best, in spite of difficulties, with the hope that He means to keep the whole of our reward for the next life.

It is important to have sensible views on this matter—and now especially when the Great Day is close at hand—lest if our First Communion should find us without the feeling of joy to which we look forward; sadness and discouragement, perhaps even fears and troubles, should overcloud our souls.

"But," you say, "suppose I feel that I really have been careless sometimes during my time of preparation, and so it is my own fault I am so cold and dry. What must I do then?" Tell our Lord now that you are sorry for it all—sorry for anything you have ever done to displease Him, to grieve Him, to keep you away from Him, and that if He does not now see good to give you what you would like to have, you will take it as a little penance and kiss His Hand as He gives it. But you will not think it means He is angry with you, and you will not come to Him with one bit of confidence less, because you know He is always ready to forgive us as soon as ever we ask Him as we ought.

Once for all, then, we are going to remember that feelings are not necessary, but faith is. And now that we want many flowers for our Lord's Presence-Chamber—Humility, and Hope, and Love, and Contrition, and Desire—what can we do better than strengthen the root from which they all spring? *Lord, increase our faith!*

If you want to see faith producing all manner of beautiful acts, just those we want before Communion, read slowly and thoughtfully a page or so of the Fourth Book of the *Imitation of Christ*. You will nowhere find better acts than those in that golden book. Do you know it? If not, make acquaintance with it now. Next to the Holy Scriptures there is no book like it. It will be a friend to you all your life through if you get to love it when you are young. And you could not do better than begin your acquaintance with it by reading a little from the Fourth Book, both before and after First Communion, by way of preparation and thanksgiving. It will teach you how to make the acts for yourself. Of course you need not do this; you may content yourself with using those you find in your prayer-book. But those which spring from your own heart are sure to have more in them and to be sweeter—to our Lord's taste at least—than those which you find ready made. Mind, He does not want grand prayers with long words in them, but He wants just what comes into your own head and into your own heart to say to Him.

Urban said at this part of His preparation, "I will tell you how I made an act of hope: 'O my God, I hope that when You come to me You will help me against the devil—he is very strong and I am very weak—but I hope when *You* come to me, he will find I am stronger.' " And he added, using one of the long words in his vocabulary, "I feel embarrassed making acts here, but I am not embarrassed in church." He thought it very foolish not to prepare plenty of petitions to take to our Lord, "because, you see, He begs us so to ask. He worries us that we may worry Him, isn't that it? I tell our Lord that, as He is so gracious as to come to me, He might as well do a little more, and give me grace to receive Him worthily."

Multiply *now* the acts before Communion. If you are making a daily visit to the Blessed Sacrament, you can make these acts in church, in our Lord's Presence. But up and down the day, at all times, let loving aspirations rise like sweet incense before Him.

And practise other acts of virtue too—acts of kindness to the poor and to those among whom you live; acts of cheerful obedience, of patience, of mortification. Every one will help to prepare you for our Lord's coming. He will count each one and remember each when He comes. Each will help to form the habit of some particular virtue in your soul. And whatever you bring to Him in the way of virtue, He will multiply, just as He multiplied the loaves of bread which the little lad took to Him in the desert. If the boy had had nothing to take to Him, there would have been no multiplication.

Have a method always in your preparation for Holy Communion. The acts before are: Faith, Hope, Charity, Humility, Contrition, Desire. These you will find in your prayer-book. But if you like to make your own, have an order in making them, and keep to it. If you get distracted, you will thus know what to go to when you come back from your distraction. Some people remember these acts by the letters with which each begins—F, H, C, H, C, D.

My God, will You teach me how to speak to You—how to adore and praise You, how to ask You for what I want, how to make my acts before Holy Communion. I see how necessary it is for me to have a strong and lively faith. And so I say to You, with all the earnestness of my heart, "Lord, increase my faith." If faith is what it ought to be in my soul, all other virtues I need will be there too. "Increase my faith," and that You may hear my prayer, help me to do my part by often remembering that You are present and see all I do and all I think; by being reverent always when I am in church, when I genuflect before the tabernacle, and when I speak to You in prayer.

# XXVIII
## To Whom Does He Come?

If yesterday's question—"Who comes?" was hard to answer, to-day's is hard too: "To whom does He come?"

"Oh, I do not see that at all," you say. "Of course I do not know Who God is—I mean I do not know properly—nobody does. But I know quite well who *I* am. I am a child, seven[1] years old. I have a good father and mother, brothers and sisters, and a happy home. I have got some talents, I think. My masters say I have a good head and a capital memory, and I have lots of certificates and prizes and—"

Stop a moment, please. No one asked what you *have*, but what you *are*. What you *have* has been given to you, or rather, it is lent, and you will have to give an account of it. But now about *yourself*. What is there of your own—your very own—that has not been given to you? "Nothing, of course." Well then, of yourself you must be nothing. Now it is not easy to understand what nothing is when the nothing happens to be oneself. Most people, at least, find it anything but easy.

So it is not easy to answer the question, "To whom does He come? "If we are clever or, what is much better, good—truthful, obedient, industrious, kind—all this makes no difference, for it

---

[1] The original text here said "ten;" however, in 1910, 14 years after this book's original publication, the age for reception of First Communion was lowered to seven.

is still God Who gives us all that we have or are. "But," you will say, "what if we have made ourselves clever by studying hard, and good by fighting against our faults? Is not this our own? Does not this come from us?"

To answer this, a little explanation is needed, so we will just think it over together.

Suppose you want to buy a violin that will cost £15. You have only threepence towards it, but your father wants you to have it, and he says, "Well, you have not much, certainly, but I don't mind helping you; we will do it between us. There is my share: £14 19s. 9d., now put down yours and go off and get it." Will you show off your violin as a treasure *you* have bought, or will you be almost ashamed to say anything about it; because of your tiny share in the buying?

Something like this happens with our good works. They are God's and they are ours, but they are God's much more than ours. We both contribute, but He gives the larger share. Let us see if this is so. Before we can do the least little good work deserving an eternal reward, God must put the thought of doing it into our minds. Next, He must draw us and help us by His grace to do it, just as the sun gives warmth to plants, as well as light to make them grow and flower. If the work is at all difficult, His help must be strong. If very difficult, it must be very strong. Sometimes we pretend not to hear His knock at the door of our hearts, or to know what He wants—then He has to knock louder. Sometimes we send Him away and He has to come again. He has to coax us by promises, He has to put up with our delays, and when at last we give in and consent to accept His grace, He rewards us. He gives us a new degree of merit here, which means a new degree of nearness to Him and of happiness for all eternity. This is His share. Now, what has ours been? Just our consent to accept His grace, perhaps after a great deal of pressing. This is our poor little threepenny-bit in the £15. Is it anything to be proud of? We may be thankful for it indeed, but proud—surely not.

God will not work without our co-operating—that is—working with Him. Our will, then, has a real share in the work, but He does expect us to understand the difference between His share and ours.

Look at this pretty picture. It is a fishing-smack out at sea. The fisherman has taken his boy of four with him, and they are bringing the boat home. We must say *they*, for the name of the picture is, "Father and me." The haul has been good, and the fish with their silvery scales line the bottom of the boat. A breeze is getting up and freshening the boy's cheek and blowing the curls across his forehead. Look at those two—the rough weather-beaten man and the fair-haired child. The strong arm is plying the oar and doing all the work, and close by, tied on to the plank, lest a sudden lurch should throw him overboard, sits the baby-boatman, shouting with delight as he lays his little hands on the oar: "See, see, father and me!"

"Father and me," indeed, you little rascal, how can you have the face to say it? And how have we the face to crow over a good work done? Are we going to be like that baby? "We are not like that baby," you say, "for we really do help, we have a share in the good works we do, you said so just now." Perfectly true, so it really is "Father and me." Our share is a real one. All I say is, are we going to be proud of it? Oh, no, let us be fair; let us give to our Father what is His always—all the praise, all the thanks; and He will give us—surely it is enough—all the usefulness and all the reward.

The reason why God hates pride is because it is unfair. He is always fair with us. He says to us in every good work, "We will work together and share the results together. The honour and glory is to be Mine, all the reward shall be yours." How unfair it is of us to want what is His and what we have no manner of right to want. We, too, like what is fair, it is one of the beautiful points in which is seen our likeness to our Father in Heaven. We like fairness everywhere, we like it and we will have it in our studies and in our games. In every nursery, in every playground we hear the words, "It isn't fair and I won't play." And if there is any sign of cheating in examinations, we are up directly. Yet we can cheat God without any remorse. We cheat Him out of His glory and steal it whenever we take to ourselves the praise and honour of our good works. It is not our share and it is unfair to take it.

God loves humility so much, because it is fair, because it is true. The humble give to God what is His, and keep for themselves what is theirs. They know their place and stay there. Some of us think that humility is very low and contemptible. They think it is smart and plucky to be proud, and very affected and ridiculous to be humble. Now the truth is just the other way. It is pride that is affected, pretending to be what it is not.

"But how," you say, "can the Saints really believe themselves to be such sinners when they know quite well how God loves them and how much they love God." This seems to you hard? Well, it is hard, because we are so much in the dark, because we live in a fog. It is not hard to the Saints, because they live in the light and see what we do not see. They see short-comings in themselves where we see nothing but holiness, just as when the sunbeams come in between the shutters we see the air thick with specks of dust floating about. They were there before, but we had no light to see them. The Saints see, too, how much there is yet to be done. A great musician was found weeping one day because, as he said, he knew so little of music and there was so much yet to learn. But the child who, with a dozen false notes, has got through its first scale, must have the whole house come to hear it.

The highest of all the Saints, the Queen of Saints, was the most humble of God's creatures and had no difficulty about it at all. "He has looked down," she says, "on the lowliness," that is, the littleness, "of His handmaid." So, in Heaven, the Saints cast their crowns before the Throne, and never think in their overflowing joy of taking any glory to themselves. They give it all to God. The light of Heaven makes it so clear to them that all they have comes from Him, that they cannot help seeing it plainly. Happy those on earth who see it plainly too! Some of the Saints have said they could not take pride in a good work if they tried. We do not see clearly like this, so we can manage to feel proud.

We are nothing, then, of ourselves. But we are something worse than this. See what we have done with God's gifts over and over again. We have not only wasted them, we have turned them against Him whenever we have used our eyes, or ears, or tongue—any of the senses of our body or the powers of our soul—to sin. And this I have done many, oh, how many times! The confession I have made or am going to make will help me here, and show me how much I have to be ashamed of and to be sorry for.

What should I think of a soldier who took the weapons put into his hands to defend his King and turned them against the King? Should I think such a traitor had anything to be proud of? And I have nothing to be proud of either. At last I have found something of my own, my very own—*my sins*. In everything else God has a share—and the greater share. But here, He has no share at all.

My sins—all the marks of my ingratitude to Him, Who has been so good to me. Oh, can *I* be proud! Yet thoughts of pride come to us and are sometimes hard to put away. A good means to get rid of them is to thank God at once for any good we have done. *Deo Gratias* is a splendid little aspiration to have often on our lips. Another way is to offer to God beforehand what we are going to do, and renew our offering when thoughts of vanity come in. "My God, for Thee!"

And now there is one thing we must make quite clear to ourselves. The thought of our sins and of our weakness, and that we are nothing of ourselves, is not meant to make us glumpy in the very least. God does not want that. All He wants is what every father wants—that his children should be truthful. He wants us to be glad and happy. Even though we are weak and full of faults, we are not to be discouraged or unhappy. Our Lord does not mind coming to us just as we are. He does not measure the distance and the difference between Himself and us. He longs to come to us:

> Out beyond the shining
> Of the furthest star,
> Thou art ever stretching
> Infinitely far.
>
> Yet the hearts of children
> Hold what worlds cannot,
> And the God of wonders
> Loves the lowly spot.

Pride takes many shapes. If we are discontented, touchy, quarrelsome, selfish, impertinent, or sulky when found fault with, we must blame pride for it all. "The mother of seventeen daughters"—so the Saints speak of pride and her ugly family.

And to be proud of being proud, as some children are! Reproach them with other faults and they resent it, but call them proud and they are rather flattered!

Pride is a mean sin, as we have seen. It is dangerous, too, because it removes God from us. Holy Scripture says that He loves to be with the humble, but the "proud He sees afar off." He keeps away from them. He leaves them to themselves, and we know what that means. Is there any harm that may not come to us, any sin we may not commit, if He leaves us to ourselves?

When our Blessed Saviour was on earth, He was called the Friend of sinners; even the worst were not afraid of Him—He was so gentle, so ready to forgive. It was only the proud

Pharisees for whom He had no kind word. They thought themselves better than any one else; they expected every one to show them respect, to make way for them and to praise them. And so our Lord's words to them were words of anger and condemnation.

Humility, then, we must have if we are to get to Heaven. There is no room for pride there; all must stoop who go in at its low door. And as we are all naturally proud, we have to learn humility. But how? We must find out in what shape pride chiefly attacks us. This we do by noticing our chief and most ordinary faults. Then we must set to work to fight it in that shape by prayer and our Blessed Saviour's example. We must come back to God very humbly and very trustfully after a fall—come at once, saying with St. Aloysius, "My God, I *am* so sorry—behold the fruits of my garden!"

"Oh, there is nothing difficult in that."

You think not? Just try.

"But if our Lord dislikes the proud and turns away from them, what is to become of us, as we are all proud?"

He turns away from those who like to be proud, who mean to go on being proud. But not from those who are sorry for their pride and want to get rid of it, and ask Him to help them. These he loves very much and pities with all the pitying tenderness of His Sacred Heart, because He knows how hard a struggle they have. He will not leave them alone in the struggle. He will come to them in Holy Communion and make them strong. He will encourage them and show them how to fight. Our best way—our only way—is to look at Him, to learn of Him.

Oh, how wonderful His example is! He—the Lord of Heaven and earth—to be what we have seen Him to be, so meek and humble of heart; to bear so patiently to be passed over; to be thought little of; to be blamed and scolded and punished for what He had never done, nay, even for the good which He had done. Can we not try to be like Him? "It will be a little hard at first," He says to us, "but I will stand by and help you. Try not to be upset and surprised if you are found fault with, but think, 'Well, I dare say I did it, and I am sorry, and I will be more careful another time.' And when little things are said that pain you—things that nobody meant to hurt but that did hurt—think how such things were said of Me."

"Oh, but they *were* meant."

"And the blow on My Face was meant to hurt Me. Will you ever have to bear that? Will you ever hear those cruel words, 'Away with Him, crucify Him'?"

"Ah, Lord, but You were God."

"Yes, child, but I was Man too, and I felt in My Heart all the shrinking you feel in yours. And I will help you to stop the hot words on your lips, and to still the angry feelings in your heart—help you to become like Me. It will not come all at once. You will fail again and again, but come back to Me each time and try again."

"My God, help me, I will try."

# XXIX
## Why Does He Come?

He comes to satisfy His need and ours, His desire and ours. He comes to join together two things most unlike, yet admirably fitted for each other—His greatness and our littleness, His strength and our weakness, His riches and our poverty, and He says, "Behold, I come quickly!" Yes, the day after to-morrow. In a very little while we shall meet our God. He too is counting the hours, and oh, wonderful thought! He is looking forward to the meeting with an intense desire.

"Behold, I come." So our Blessed Lord said on the first Christmas night when He came into the world. And now again He is saying to Himself, to our Lady, to our Good Angel, to all who love us—and in Heaven they all love us—"Behold, I come."

There have been many prayers going up to Him from those who know better than we do how much we need Him. In Heaven they see our dangers: dangers from without, dangers from within. They see our cruel enemy, the devil, going round about us like a roaring lion sometimes, and sometimes like a cunning serpent. They see perhaps bad example, or bad companions, or bad books, or amusements that will hurt us grievously if we are not upon our guard. And worse than all that is *without*, they see growing *within* the bad passions that the devil is watching so anxiously. They are small now, like little seeds, but he will try to make them grow into great poisonous plants that will kill the soul.

During a morning walk in the country, we must often have noticed the poisonous fungi lying thick under our feet in places where there was no trace of them the night before. They spring up as if by magic, yet so strong is this rapid growth that some species have been known to raise paving-stones to the height of several feet.

We must never think light faults do not matter. In every soul the devil has won, the beginnings of evil were small and little noticed, and because they were little noticed they grew bigger. Little carelessnesses in God's service, little lies or thefts, acts of disobedience, acts of unkindness, detraction, revenge, pride or vanity, anger, gluttony, or sloth, bad thoughts not checked at once, rash judgments or dislikes consented to—these things grew and grew and became habits. There was venial sin first, and then came mortal sin—mortal sin unrepented of, and death, and the soul was his at last.

Oh, how the devil watches the beginnings of evil in our hearts! *He* watches and we are unconcerned. Our Guardian Angel watches, and our Patron Saint, our Blessed Mother above all. And they are frightened, for they see we are weak and foolish, and our enemy is wily and strong. They turn to our Lord and say, "How long, O Lord, how long?" And His answer is, "Behold, I come." The devil hears those words and trembles. With us by ourselves he has every chance. With our Lord on our side, fighting for us, backing us up always, he has no chance at all, if we do our part. No wonder he fears those words, "Behold, I come."

St. Paul, writing to some of his converts at Corinth who were not behaving themselves as they ought, gave some directions which were to be carried out at once by way of preparation for his visit. He winds up his instructions with the words, "And the rest I will set in order when I come." So our Lord says to us now: "Do what you know I want you to do to prepare yourself for Me; try to correct what has been pointed out to you, what I have told you secretly in your heart I expect of you, and then fear nothing; the rest I will set in order when I come."

St. Ambrose says, "We have all things in Christ, and Christ is all things to us. If you want to cure a wound, He is the physician; if you are laden with sins, He is holiness itself; if you want health, He is power and strength; if you fear death, He is life; if you desire Heaven, He is the way; if you fly from darkness, He is the light; if you seek food, He is nourishment."

Our soul has two chief needs: the curing of what is evil in it or the preventing of such evil, and the strengthening of what is good. We will see how the Holy Eucharist supplies both these needs, and first, how It remedies the evil.

When we are obliged to go to a place where fever is raging, we take something beforehand to prevent the air we are going to breathe from poisoning us or even from making us ill. What we take is called an antidote, or a medicine given against poison. The Holy Eucharist is called by the Council of Trent an antidote "whereby we are freed from daily faults and are preserved from mortal sin." It keeps us from the deadly disease of mortal sin which would kill the soul, and it also hinders venial sin, which, though it is not deadly, is dangerous, and if neglected may lead to mortal sin, just as slight ailments not attended to have often serious consequences.

Some of us can remember that at one time our health caused a good deal of anxiety to those about us. We saw father and mother talking gravely together as they looked at us, and we caught the words, "London" and "specialist," "long journey and high fee—must be managed somehow—expense and trouble not to be weighed in such a case."

And one fine morning we found ourselves whirling away in the London train, then mounting the high staircase of an hotel, and a few days later seated between father and mother in a big room of a strange house, talking to an old gentleman who always looked over his spectacles when he wanted to see anything. We had been told beforehand we were going to a doctor, a very great man indeed, who was kind to children that told the truth, but very cross to those that did not. So we must not be silly or say there was nothing the matter with us, but tell him just what we told mother. This frightened us a good deal, so we got ready all our information, and at the doctor's first question said it off pat like a lesson—where the pain was, and what it was like, and what brought it on; we were not hungry, but hot and thirsty, and sometimes chilly and shivering; and we felt very weak and tired after study and even after play.

The doctor listened, and asked us a few questions. He said it was a good thing we had come to him in time, there was not very much the matter now, but—and then He said something we did not understand, about "evil unchecked inducing serious consequences." We were to lie a good deal on our back, and not to do things that hurt us; to take his medicine, to have good food, and to come and see him again.

A long expensive journey, nasty medicine that cost a great deal, tiresome remedies, giving up things we like, all this for the sake of the body! It only shows what we must be ready to do for the soul, which is to have still greater care.

Its diseases, like those of the body, are often hidden as well as dangerous, and need very skilful treatment. How glad we ought to be to have such a Physician as our Blessed Lord. He knows everything, for He is God, and He is most willing to care for us and cure us, for He is our Father and our Friend. He knows everything. But He means us to ask Him all the same. If we do not tell Him things, He acts as if He did not know them.

We are not obliged to go a long way to consult Him, nor have we to get His help at great cost. He is ready to come to us whenever we want Him, and to come again and again. So we call in the Divine Physician, and He takes His place beside us to hear all about our sick soul. "Dear Lord, I have a bad pain in my heart when I see others praised, or succeeding better than I do, or getting nicer things than I get. I have many and many a tumble, and I feel bruised and sore for a long time after. I have no appetite for the things the Saints relished so much: for being near You in the Tabernacle, for talking to You in prayer, for learning about my religion, and how to love and please You. I have no relish for these things. I am hot and restless and discontented when any one contradicts me or I cannot have what I like; I am chilly in my ways when I have to talk to people I do not care for. And when I try to overcome the faults into which I fall oftenest, I feel so weak—too lazy and too cross to try."

Our Lord listens and says He will send us a Medicine that will cure any and all of these diseases and make us well and strong. *Send* it—no, *bring* it—for He will come Himself, He will be our Medicine as well as our Physician. To what lengths our God can go in His unspeakable love for us! O wonderful Physician, shall we not hope to get well now!

Another thing we look for in our doctor is kindness. He may be skilful and experienced, but oh, if he is rough, how we feel it!

At the beginning of last century there was a surgeon of such repute in London that his consulting-room was full from morning till night. Yet every one went in quaking. It was not that he was a hard-hearted man, but the hastiness of his words and manner frightened people.

Our Lord is not like this. He is very gentle with us. He said

## The Divine Physician

"It is I, fear not."
(Luke 24:36.)

to one of His Saints: "My child, I love so tenderly all who are Mine, that if I could get them to Heaven without giving them any pain or trouble, I would do it. But as this cannot be, I take care not to hurt them more than I can help." When He laid His hand on the hideous sores of the lepers, it was very tenderly. The gentle touch did not hurt before it healed. He need not have touched their sores at all, but He wanted to show us He would never be disgusted at any wounds of our poor souls, but would pity them and lay His healing hand upon them.

Among the things we noticed at our visit to the London doctor were the funny little remarks he kept making to himself:

"Let us see—summer in Wales—put up at out-of-the-way places, eh? Ah, I thought as much, damp sheets again. Stop a bit, there was that fall. Hurt you much at the time, that tumble off the pony?"

"What tumble? Did he mean when Brownie shied at the bicycle? We had almost forgotten it. Can a little thing like that do any harm, and so long after too?"

Indeed it can. Little things may have very serious consequences. Damp sheets and a tumble off a horse have often ended in disease and death. And carelessness about venial sin may often lead to disease and death too. See, then, how much we need our Physician. How we ought to welcome Him when He comes.

The London doctor said particularly that we were to go back to him soon. And this our Lord says to us. He does not expect even His Medicine to cure us all at once. He does not say when we go again: "You are no better, and you ought to be well after what I have done for you." But He says tenderly, as He sits down beside us and takes our hand in His, "Well, child, how are you getting on? Not so well as you expected? A little weaker even than usual? Well, never mind; the sick must have their ups and downs. You are really better and stronger, though you do not know it, and if only you do as I tell you, take your medicine regularly, and keep away from the things that harm you, you will get well in time."

This we must do. It is our Lady's advice: "Whatsoever He shall say to you, do ye." Nurses are so careful to carry out the doctors' prescriptions that they put them down in writing—when the patient may get up and for how long, what he may eat and what he must not eat.

So our Lord leaves His directions with us. "You must keep quiet there, child, though it will cost you something. And there you must exert yourself, though you feel inclined to be lazy. You must not read those books, they are bad food and will end by making you very ill indeed."

It is said that the late Queen used to see her physician every morning. Physicians are summoned to kings and queens for very trifling ailments, and to the royal children too. This is because the heath of the royal family is considered of great importance by the nation. But it is not half so important as is the health of every soul, the soul of every little child, in the eyes of the God Who made it. We are all royal children, children of the King of Kings, children of God. So every care must be taken of us; we must have a Divine Physician, ready at any moment to come to us, and He must bring with Him a Divine Medicine to do good to our souls.

The Holy Eucharist, then, is our medicine, remedying what is evil in us. But Its chief grace is a nourishing grace; It is before all things the *Food* of our souls, as necessary to their life as material food is to the life of our bodies.

We cannot help noticing how our Lord, speaking of the Blessed Sacrament, constantly connects It with *life*. "Except you eat the Flesh of the Son of Man and drink His Blood, you shall not have life in you." What is this life of which He speaks? Let us look at it in its beginning. He says, "Unless a man be born again of water and the Holy Ghost, he cannot enter into the Kingdom of God." Unless we are born again by Holy Baptism, we cannot go to Heaven. Baptism gives us a new life, the life of the soul, which is sanctifying grace. It makes us children of God and heirs of Heaven, and gives us a right to the Kingdom of our Heavenly Father.

But this life given in Baptism will not last unless it is nourished. Our souls, like our bodies, must be fed, or they will die. Our Lord Himself tells us this: "Except you eat the Flesh of the Son of Man...you shall not have life in you." What will happen to a traveller making his way through a sandy desert, if he has no food? He will never reach the country on the other side; he must die and leave his bones in that dreary waste. So our Lord tells us it is with those who do not eat this Heavenly Food.

How many there are—how many in this country—who know nothing of the Bread of Heaven which they need to keep their souls alive. We might have been like them, but for God's goodness to us. Let us thank Him for putting this Food within our reach, and take care never to grow careless or indifferent to It. If we do, we shall fall into mortal sin—our souls will die.

A teacher stood in front of a bright little class, explaining the mysteries of long division, with the help of the black-board. The children watched her with interest and answered briskly, but were in such a hurry to start on their own account that she had some difficulty in keeping them quiet till her explanations were finished. At last they were set free. The signal was given, and down came the pencils on the slates like a small hail-storm. The hum of many voices was heard; many fingers were seen busy at work above the desks, and many busier still doing the counting underneath. Looking round to see if help was needed in any quarter, she noticed a child sitting dull and spiritless in the midst of that eager set. Her eyes wandered wearily round the room, and ended by fixing themselves on a little parcel near her, carefully wrapped up in newspaper.

"Are you poorly this morning, Peggy?"

"No."

"Can you do the sum?"

"Yes."

"Well, set to work then like the others, and show it to me when it is done." The head bent over the slate; the lips moved; Peggy was at work, and the teacher went round to see how things were going on elsewhere. Presently her eye fell again on Peggy. The brain had stopped working; again there was that weary, listless look; the hands were lying still.

"Come, you are lazy to-day. Set to work like a good child, or you know you will have to finish that sum when the rest go home. What is the matter with you? Are you hungry?" she added, suddenly, as a thought flashed upon her. The child's eyes had turned again to the parcel which contained the lunch of the little fatty sitting next her on the bench.

"Have you had your breakfast?"

"We haven't any breakfast in our house."

"Poor child! Had you any supper last night?"

"We never have supper."

"What had you for dinner yesterday?"

"Mother gave me two crusts; she said she must save the others for to-day."

This poor child was not ill; she was not lazy; she did not want medicine; she did not want scolding; what she wanted was *food*—food to make the eyes bright and the limbs active, and the whole frame eager to be at work—to make work a pleasure, to make it a success.

It was *food* the exhausted child sought. And it is food, a Divine Food our souls must seek if they are to have life in them.

"If you seek food," says St. Ambrose, "He is Nourishment." Yes, we seek food. Our soul, like our body, needs to be refreshed—built up, kept from death, kept in health, strengthened to do its work—by means of food. But on what food can the soul feed? What food has He provided for it Who made it and Who knows all its needs? *Himself.* He will be the food of the soul. It is not enough to give grace—He must give Himself.

*Divine Food*—Food that is God Himself! The more we think about it, the more wonderful it is. That He should be true Man, "the Son of Man," as He loved to call Himself—our Companion, our Friend, our Brother—all this is wonderful. But *our Food*—who could have believed this to be possible if we had not His own word for it? Food is something beneath us—and that God should be our Food—what a marvel of love!

If you look at Brittany in the map of France, you will see it is a corner to the north-west. This perhaps accounts for its inhabitants being, in some respects, a people quite by themselves. Amidst the changes going on around them, they have kept much of the spirit of olden times. New doctrines, new fashions, new ways of doing things find little favour with them. They like the old ways best, and cling fondly to the religion, the customs, and the simple habits of their forefathers. One of their beautiful characteristics is their love of home. To a Breton, separation from home is a very keen pain indeed, and home sickness has been known to bring them to the verge of the grave.

Far away from his dear Brittany, a young soldier lay dying. A comrade who watched beside him and caught some of the words that escaped his lips in the weakness of delirium, guessed the root of the evil, and wrote to his parents begging that some of his friends would come to see him. The old father set out at once. After a long journey he arrived at the barracks and knelt at his son's bedside. Those who stood by and saw the meeting said they would never forget it—the smile that lit up the boy's face; the tenderness with which he took the white head into his thin, trembling hands, and covered it with kisses; the strength with which he held the rough hands clasped within his own, as if he could never let them go any more—it was a touching sight indeed.

The tears ran slowly down his cheeks as he listened to the news from home, and when asked if there was anything that would do him good, he answered, eagerly, "Oh, if I could have a piece of home-made bread!" The old man had taken a loaf of coarse brown bread as provision for his journey, and he had a piece left. Dry and hard, it was strange food for one lying on his death-bed. But it was *bread from home*. The boy took it— looked at it with delight—began to eat. From that moment his friends dated his recovery.

Can you think of a Bread from Home that is to be brought to us in our sickness? What if our Good Angel and our friends in Heaven should date our recovery from the day we receive It for the first time? It cures our sickness, and yet, strange to say, there is a sickness which it does not cure, but increases. Oh, blessed Home-sickness of the Saints, which the Bread of Angels fosters for ever in their hearts! St. Paul felt it when he cried out, "I desire to be dissolved and to be with Christ!" St. Ignatius felt it when, looking up into the starry skies, he said, "How dull this earth appears to me when I look up to Heaven!" And our dear English Martyrs felt it when the cry went up from their prison:

> Jerusalem, my happy Home
> When shall I come to thee?
> When shall my sorrows have an end,
> Thy joys when shall I see?

This Home-sickness is a great grace from God. Those who are smitten by it, "pass through the good things of this world so as not to lose those that are eternal," and are strong and brave amid its troubles, "knowing that we have not here a lasting city, but seek one that is to come."

You have heard of the Blessed Imelda, that happy child who longed so earnestly to receive our Lord, that He had to give Himself to her when she was quite a little thing. The story of the gentle girl-saint every one knows. But you have not heard, perhaps, the story of a young savage whose last act was a longing desire to receive Jesus into his heart.

Come away to the far West to a place called Lake Qu'appelle, in the province of Manitoba, Canada. You see that miserable hut. There, on a winter's morning in 1894, a missionary was going to say Mass. The hut belonged to an Indian, Oskaïssis, or "Little Calf." He was still a pagan but very good to Father Campeau. He had seen "the Black Robe" pour the "water of life" on the head of his son "that he might be able to look upon the Great Spirit in Heaven," and he often said to him, "Father, speak to my boy of the beautiful things of the other life, for I know he will soon go."

Yes, he was going fast, this boy of fourteen, and he was ready to go. He bore his sufferings with an admirable patience and resignation. He was willing to leave his father and all who were dear to him. Yet there was a grace he asked and asked earnestly to have before he died. He had made his First Communion, and his one desire was to receive Jesus once again into his heart.

On the eve of his death, when his dear "Black Robe" wished him good-night, he said, "Father, do you think I shall still be alive to-morrow? I should be so glad if I might again receive God made Man into my heart!"

"Yes, dear child," the priest answered; "God will preserve you until to-morrow; and then, I promise you, you shall hold in your heart Jesus our God, Who became Man and died for you upon the Cross."

"Thank you, Father, thank you!"

Very early in the morning Father Campeau arranged his altar, and all was soon ready for Mass.

What a strange chapel it was—what an altar on which the King of Heaven was to descend—what a congregation to welcome Him! The hut was small, low, and very dirty; at one side of the altar and near the fire, which gave out a suffocating heat, lay the dying boy upon the ground. Oskaïssis, his wives, and the other members of his family, all pagans, knelt around in an attitude that would have befitted Christians.

Just as the priest was beginning, *In nomine Patris*, he was seen to stagger. The bad smell of the small, confined space, added to the dirt and the fearful heat, made him feel terribly sick. He hesitated to begin Mass. But He had promised the sick boy to give Holy Communion. He determined to try. Scarcely, however, had he finished the Gospel, when a great faintness came over him. A cold perspiration streamed down his forehead. Everything seemed to be turning round. Nevertheless, he succeeded in getting as far as the *Sanctus*. Then, feeling he was going to faint, he threw himself, vested as he was, on the bed that had been prepared for him the day before.

Oskaïssis and his people never stirred, but knelt watching him with the greatest attention. The sick boy looked from time to time towards the altar, and repeated again and again, "Jesus, I love Thee; come and do good to my soul."

Wishing at any cost to procure for him the happiness of receiving his God, the priest arose and returned to the altar, but his strength failed him, and when he reached the "Canon," he was again obliged to lie down on his bed. This time he rested longer, hoping to regain strength enough to continue. Oskaïssis and his people remained kneeling, straight as arrows and motionless.

The sick boy seemed to be sleeping, but the agony was at hand. Believing he was stronger than he really was, Father Campeau resumed the Mass for the third time. He was able to say all the prayers up to the "Consecration;" then the giddiness came on again. He waited a little, resting against the altar. At last, gathering up all his strength, he took the host into his hands to pronounce the words of Consecration. But it was no use—a violent trembling seized him.

Oskaïssis, who had observed all, at last said to him, "But, Father, you take a long time to say your great prayer; the other Father that speaks the Crees' tongue does not lie down as you do, to offer his great prayer."

The poor priest was suffering from burning thirst. He drank a little wine and water, took a few mouthfuls of food; then he slept for a few minutes. They came to wake him.

"Father," said Oskaïssis, "my boy is dying, speak to him."

He hastened to the dying boy. He gave him the last blessing and absolution, and said aloud the words: "Jesus, Mary, Joseph." They were the last sounds from this world. With the Father's crucifix in his hand, the child breathed forth his soul without a struggle, and went to gaze upon Him Whom he had so ardently desired to receive for a last time on earth.

"Jesus, I love You, come and do good to my soul!" I think it would be hard to find a nicer prayer than that, dear Lord, when I invite You to come to me. Faith, and hope, and charity, and desire are all there in a few words that I can remember easily. When I think of that dying boy, I feel ashamed of myself. How much he did with so few opportunities of learning to know and love You! How little I do with so many! I may well take a lesson from him. Perhaps if I were to say his prayer often, I should come to love You and to long for You as he did. I could say it in church, or in the streets. I could say it when I wake in the night; when I am tempted to do wrong; when I go up and down stairs; and now and then during my study and my play. "Jesus, I love You, come and do good to my soul." Remind me, my Good Angel, or I shall forget all about it. "Jesus, I love You; I love You, come and do good to my soul."

## XXX
## Come Lord Jesus!

We looked up into the starry skies on the first Christmas night and thought how the Creator of all those glorious worlds was coming to seek a home on this earth of ours. He is coming tomorrow to seek a smaller home than the stable at Bethlehem. Oh, how small it is for the Immense, the Infinite God!

> Out beyond the shining
> Of the furthest star
> Thou art ever stretching
> Infinitely far.
>
> Yet the hearts of children
> Hold what worlds cannot,
> And the God of wonders
> Loves the lowly spot.

There is the secret of our happiness—that He loves the lowly spot. What should we do if He did not love it? His coming would crush us back into the nothing from which we came. But He comes in love and in gentleness and with a great desire to be with us. So we take courage and look once more to the dispositions of our hearts on which so much depends. The maidens who were to appear but once before King Assuerus prepared themselves for a whole year beforehand, anointing themselves with oil of myrrh, and with perfumes and sweet spices. The myrrh of contrition, then the sweet perfumes and

## The Magi

"And entering into the house, they found the Child with Mary, His Mother, and falling down they adored Him." (Matthew 2:11)

spices of other virtues—these will make us pleasing to the King.

Perhaps you have your confession still to make. If so, read over again what was said the other day about contrition and its motives. Or perhaps you made your confession some days ago, and are going again to-day, that the Precious Blood may wash away anything by which you have stained your white robe since then. There may be little faults only. All the more reason to remember that sin of your past life which you mention *in order to secure contrition*, the matter of the Sacrament.

When you have received your white robe, the wedding garment in which you are to appear before the King, take care not to soil it. If you happen to commit a fault, get rid of it at once by a hearty, loving act of contrition.

Now about the sweet perfumes. Soul and body have to be prepared. We must look to the dispositions of each—the soul of course first.

1. The dispositions of the soul may be either (1) sufficient or good, (2) very good, or (3) perfect.

(1) Sufficient dispositions are such as are absolutely necessary, without which our Communion would be bad or sacrilegious. The Catechism tells us we must be in a state of grace—that is—we must be free from mortal sin. We must not, like Judas, pretend to welcome our Lord with a kiss when we are betraying Him to His enemies. The punishment of the man who came without the wedding robe to the marriage-feast shows us how fearfully the wrath of God falls on those who dare to come to His Table without sufficient preparation. If the state of grace has been lost by mortal sin, it must be regained by the Sacrament of Penance; an act of perfect contrition is not sufficient.

(2) Very good dispositions are such as more befit the dignity of this Sacrament. God is coming into our souls, the Saint of Saints, the Holy of Holies, Purity and Holiness itself. Should we not do our best to be free from all sin, venial as well

as mortal! He hates venial sin. He will not have us with Him in Heaven whilst there is a single venial sin of any kind upon our souls. Is it fit, then, that we should force Him to come into them when they are stained with venial sins? For our own sakes, too, we should do our best to be free from every sin. We have seen how dangerous venial sin is. It leads to mortal sin. It risks the loss, or delays the gaining, of Heaven. It holds back the blessing our Lord has ready for us, tying His hands so that He cannot give what He comes on purpose to give. If we love our own souls we shall spare no pains to free ourselves from all sin. God gives us so many means of doing this—confession, contrition, almsdeeds, the devout use of holy water, the sign of the Cross, &c.

(3) Perfect dispositions are those which our Lord looks for in order to bless us most abundantly—Faith, Hope, Love and Gratitude, Humility, Contrition, and Desire. These are the dispositions we must aim at. Surely it is not enough to come to Him without having anything hateful to Him about us. We want to be pleasing in His sight by many graces and virtues. Let us ask Him for them, and ask earnestly, for the time is short. "Ask and you shall receive." Let us make our acts of these virtues fervently—they are strengthened by exercise—and slowly, a few words at a time, that so they may sink into our hearts.

*Faith.*—I believe, my God, that You are really present in the Sacred Host I am going to receive—the same Jesus Christ, God and Man, Who was promised in Paradise—and was adored in Bethlehem by the shepherds and the Kings—Who lay in Mary's lap, and worked in Joseph's shop—Who went about doing good—and blessed the little children—Who taught from Peter's boat—and calmed the storm on the Lake—and prayed on the hill-tops for me—Who gave the Twelve their First Communion at the Last Supper—Who died upon the Cross—

and rose again—and ascended into Heaven—Who will come again to judge the living and the dead—and Who has come to us meantime in the Blessed Sacrament to prepare our souls for that coming at the Last Day.

"I believe that Thou art Christ, the Son of the Living God."

"Lord, increase my faith."

*Hope.*—What can You refuse me, O my Friend and my Brother, when You give me Your very Self? You *cannot* say that anything is impossible or difficult to You. You *will* not say You have no desire to cure what is evil in my soul—and to strengthen what is good—to give me grace to keep free all my life from mortal sin—to persevere to the end—to come safely to Your Feet in Heaven. All these things, and all the blessings that You see will be good for me to have in this life—I ask You now—and believe with a firm trust that You will give me. You invite me now to come to You—You *tell* me to come to You—surely I may hope for great things from Your visit.

*Love.*—I do not know half as much about You, dear Lord, as I shall do some day. But surely I know enough even now to love You with all my heart. I know You are infinitely beautiful and good—tender and gentle and loving—generous and forgiving—and I know that besides being so good in Yourself—You have been wonderfully good and kind to me. In return You ask only my love: "My child, give Me thy heart." Take it, Lord. I give it to You—to be Yours always. Let me love You with all my heart—with all my soul—with all my mind—with all my strength. And help me to love as myself all these whom You invite to share with me this Gift of Your love.

*Gratitude.*—My God, how good You have been to me. How many things You have given me. How much more You have done for me than for millions and millions of other children who are in the world to-day. I have a good father and mother and a happy home. You have made me a child of

Your Holy Catholic Church when I might have been one of the little Protestants I see all around me, who do not know how to get their sins forgiven, who have never heard of Your Real Presence, or of a First Communion Day. Why have You been so very good *to me?* Why have You loved me so? I cannot think why, for I am sure I have not loved You very much. What can I give You in return? David cried out in the fulness of his heart: "What shall I render to the Lord for all He has given unto me?" Yet David had not so much to thank You for as I have. What would David have said had he known what You are going to give *to me?* Many kings and prophets have desired to see the things I see and have not seen them, and to hear the things I hear and have not heard them. Wait till to-morrow, Lord, and I will pay You all. Yes, tomorrow I will give you as much as you have ever given me—more than any favours You have ever bestowed upon me—more than the Heaven You are getting ready for me—I will give You Yourself.

*Humility.*—I think it ought to be very easy for me to be humble—for, first, I have nothing to be proud of—and next, I have plenty to be ashamed of. My God, all that I have of good You have given me. I have nothing of my own, but my sins. And how many sins there have been. I have been so naughty, so careless, so ungrateful. St. Elizabeth was surprised that our Lady should come to see her. St. Peter cried out: "Depart from me, for I am a sinful man, O Lord." The pagan centurion said, "Lord, I am not worthy." And I too wonder that the God of Heaven and earth should come to me. I will not say, "Depart from me," but I do say with all my heart: "Lord, I am not worthy that Thou shouldst come under my roof." "O God, be merciful to me a sinner."

*Contrition.*—My sins have made me most unworthy. But I am sorry for them—very sorry for them. I am sorry, because of all the harm they have done to my soul—more still because they have cost You so much, dear Lord—because they hurt You so much in Your Passion—they tortured Your Heart in the Garden of Olives—they stung You in the scourges—they pricked You in the thorns—they drove the nails into Your Hands and Feet. I am sorry for my sins, because they crucified You, my Saviour. And most of all I am sorry, because they have offended You, Who are so good in Yourself, so infinitely good. My God, I think perhaps You might be good to others without being infinitely good, but You must be infinitely good to be good *to me*. And so I am sorry with all my heart for having displeased You.

*Desire.*—Our Lord loves to be desired. In this He is like us. Which of us cares to make a visit where we are not wanted? Desire is the chief part of *His* preparation for coming to us. It is His main disposition—a desire of six thousand years! To those who desire Him in return He comes willingly and joyfully.

In the days of our Lord's preaching in Judea, there was a man in Jerusalem whose name was Zacheus. He was the chief of the publicans, and like the rest of his profession, was hated and despised by the Jews. This man had a great desire to see the young Prophet of Galilee, of Whom every one was talking. And hearing He was passing along a certain road, he determined to wait for Him among the crowd. But Zacheus was a little man, and he soon found that, in the dense throng that pressed around our Lord, his chances of seeing Him were very small indeed. So he ran on in front and climbed up into a sycamore-tree, where he could have a good view. The moving mass of people drew nearer and nearer. Zacheus strained his eyes to get a first sight of Him.

There He is. Oh, He is worth waiting for. He comes nearer and nearer. Now He is nearly under the tree. And see, He stops, and the whole multitude stops. He stops as if He had come to the tree by appointment, expecting some one. He looks up and Zacheus' heart beats fast. "Zacheus, make haste and come down, for this day I must abide in thy house." Nothing ready, no preparation—only that loving desire. But it was enough for Jesus. "And Zacheus made haste and came down and received Him with joy."

I am poor and weak and unworthy to come to You, dear Lord—and yet I do so want to come. Do not think the desire is all on Your side—for I do indeed love and long for You. You know all things. You know, Lord, that I love You. David said: "As the hart panteth after the water-brooks, so panteth my soul after Thee, O God." I wish I could long for You like that. Your loving words and ways make me desire You. And You like to come to those who desire You. Because Zacheus wanted so much to see You, You gave him more than He hoped for—not only one glance at Your beautiful Face as You passed him under the sycamore-tree, but the sound of Your voice, and Your Blessed Presence in his house, with all the change in him that Presence wrought.

And how You liked to go to Bethany, to the two sisters there, who were always looking forward to Your coming. I wish I could receive You and make You welcome as they did. Martha spared no trouble in getting ready for You. She made the house clean and tidy, and bright with flowers, and prepared all she could think of to show You honour. Help me to be like her—not cold now, nor careless—but loving and diligent. And Mary sat at Your Feet and heard Your words. So let me listen to You when You come to me to-morrow—and in all the Communions of my life. You will speak to my heart, if only I will listen: "Speak, Lord, for Thy servant heareth."

These acts are only examples of those we should make before Holy Communion. They may help you to make acts for yourself.

2. The dispositions of the body are (1) fasting; (2) reverence.

(1) Fasting.—The Catechism says we must be fasting from midnight. This means from twelve o'clock the night before our Communion we must not eat or drink anything. We must not take anything, however little, *in the way of food*. The law of fasting before Communion was made by the Church to teach us respect for the Body of our Lord. The Church dispenses with this law when we are in danger of death. But except in this case it would be a mortal sin to go to Communion after breaking our fast. So that, if by mistake, we happened to swallow anything—for example, to take some medicine—we could not go to Communion that day. But notice the words, *in the way of food*. If we were to swallow anything that is not used for food, as bits of pencil, or thread, or finger-nail, this would not break the fast, for such things are not food, they cannot feed us. Again, if we were to swallow a drop of rain, it would not break our fast, for this is not taken by drinking—in the way of food.

Remember, too, that to break the fast, something in the way of food must be taken into the mouth after midnight. So that to swallow anything that was in the mouth before midnight does not break the fast.

We must not be over anxious or fidgety about breaking our fast. Unless we *know* that we have broken it, we may take it for granted that we have not.

Out of respect for the Blessed Sacrament, nothing should be taken till the Sacred Species are consumed, which is about a quarter of an hour after Communion.

It was the feast of Corpus Christi, and the First Communicants were passing through the corridor of an old French convent on their way to the church. One of them saw a chocolate on the ground before her, and without thinking picked it up and put it into her mouth. No sooner had she swallowed it than the heedless act and its consequences rushed upon her mind. At once there was a storm of trouble where all had been so peaceful a moment before. What was she to do?

Her Guardian Angel whispered: "Take off your veil; say you have broken your fast by mistake, and that you must put off your Communion till to-morrow."

The devil whispered: "What will people say? How disappointed your father and mother will be who have come so far on purpose to be present today. They cannot stay till to-morrow. Everybody will think how thoughtless it was of you. How ashamed you will be to have to stay in your place when all the others go up to the rails."

What did the child do? There was a short struggle between the good and the evil spirit, and then she made her choice. She could not bear the thought of what every one would think and say. She would go to Communion as if nothing had happened, and she would confess the sin afterwards. All through the Mass her Angel tried to frighten her by the thought of the sacrilege she was going to commit, but she would not listen, because—"What would people say?" At the *Domine non sum dignus* she went up to the rails with the rest, went up in her white dress, her white veil, and her wreath—*but without the wedding garment*—her soul dead in that whited sepulchre, and so she received her God and made her First Communion *in mortal sin*.

Think what she felt when she returned to her place and knelt in the midst of the joyous and the innocent who were making their thanksgiving. Think what she felt when she came to confess her sin; what she felt when she saw First Communicants go up to the altar-rails all her life through; what no bitter tears of contrition could ever undo: "*I made my First Communion in mortal sin.*"

Now, what would have happened if she had taken off her veil and told bravely what she had done by mistake? There would have been the disappointment, of course, to herself and others. That could not be helped. But what of that! Every one would have pitied her and tried to console her by saying she would only have to wait one day more. And supposing her father and mother could not have stayed, well, what of that either? Supposing even that any one had reproached her for being careless—what would all this have mattered, so long as our Lord was not offended, so long as He was ready to welcome her the next day and make up to her for all she had suffered in order to come to Him with her robe unstained by sin! Oh, how many sins are committed by listening to the devil's whisper, "What will people say?" Whenever he whispers that in your ear, answer: "And what will *God* say?—*that* is all I care about—all the rest does not matter one bit."

Another First Communion story brings us back to our own land. It was not Maundy Thursday this time, but Holy Saturday. A number of little fellows had been to confession that day, for they were to make their First Communion on Easter Sunday. And now it was night, and they were going to bed. One of them stayed behind to speak to the master. His miserable face was pitiful to see and showed signs of a sharp struggle. He said he was very unhappy. Since his confession that morning he had committed a mortal sin and he could not go to Holy Communion till he had been to confession again. Might he go to-night? The master was very kind. He said it was not possible to go before morning, but he would see to it the first thing. Meanwhile, there must be a good act of contrition to-night before going to sleep. Sleep! Poor boy, he was afraid to close his eyes. How many acts of perfect contrition he tried to make with all his heart.

He had had a hard struggle with human respect. The devil whispered: What would his master think of his wanting to go to confession again? What would the boys think when they saw him going the next morning? The church would be full, every one would notice him. What remarks So-and-so would make afterwards.

And his good Angel had whispered: "Courage, child; never mind what others think and say. Mind your contrition and take anything that hurts as a penance, and one far less than you deserve."

He had made His choice. Yes, he would care only for what God thought, care only for God's forgiveness, care only for having grieved the Sacred Heart.

Quite early he was in the confessional. As it happened, nobody was about, and when, an hour later, he took his place among his companions, no one knew where he had been or had noticed his absence. His preparation during Mass was a humbler one than it would have been, had he been one of the ninety-nine who need not penance; humbler and less joyous perhaps than that of many kneeling round about him. But his heart was in peace. He had offered his "hush-money" to the Judge, and when our Lord had come and gone, and the thanksgivings were over, and the church was empty, there were tears in that poor boy's place such as many an innocent heart might have envied, tears that were gathered up by his good Angel and laid before the throne of God.

Now we must go back to the second disposition of the body—reverence.

2. Reverence requires that the body, which is to be our Lord's tabernacle, should be suitably prepared for Him. Our dress should be clean and tidy, the best we have, but not showy, and we go up to the altar-rails without gloves. Our minds are

full of the holy action we are going to do, so our manner is reverent and recollected. We have our immediate preparation to make and we use our prayer-books or say what little prayers we know. At the *Domine non sum dignus* we go up to the rails, with our hands joined and our eyes cast down.

And now about our petitions. We must have them ready for our Lord when He comes. Those who are to have an audience with the Holy Father do not wait till they find themselves at his feet to think what they are going to ask. Everything must be ready beforehand, for the time of audience is so short. But some of us are not quite clear as to what we should ask. It takes a little trouble to get it clear. Think what you would ask our Lord to do for you if you were going to see Him as He was during His earthly Life, when He lay in Mary's lap, or blessed little children, or walked by the Lake. Think what is the greatest trouble your soul has, what fault you find it hardest to overcome, what you take oftenest to confession. Perhaps you have forgotten about Arabi and the pet passion? Have you an Arabi, a leader of revolt in your heart? Take him to our Lord if you have and ask to be freed from him.

If you still cannot think of anything to ask, you might beg the assistance of your parents, your masters or mistresses, your brothers and sisters and companions! "Do, please, give me a little help, all of you. Can you see anything that wants mending? Does it strike you that there is any virtue I have not got?"

A bright ring of children stood round their master one September morning to begin their reading-lesson. It was the 24th, the Feast of Our Lady of Mercy. As he took his seat, he reminded them of the feast, and advised them to ask our Lady for some special favour on a day when she would feel herself bound to be more than usually kind and compassionate. A little fellow near him remarked, dolefully, that he had "nowt to ask."

"Oh, if that is all," said the master, "perhaps I could help you. I know a lad," he said, looking up to the ceiling, "who never by any chance gets his home-lessons done. He was helping father, or going errands for mother, or minding baby—doing every mortal thing except his lessons. That lad might ask to have his laziness cured." The little face beside him brightened up. "Please, sir, I know what to ask."

With this encouragement there was another venture. "And please, sir, *I* don't know what to ask."

"There is another boy," the master went on, "so particular about getting his own 'spot' when we stand here for reading, that he shoves out of the way any poor little fellow who happens to get it. Suppose, now, that boy were to ask for a little more good-nature and a little less selfishness." A pair of merry black eyes twinkled with satisfaction. "I know what to ask, sir," said their owner.

And so the *Confiteor* went round, one after the other coming forward, as the cap fitted, with a complacent smile at his good luck.

Perhaps our eyes do not twinkle with satisfaction when our short-comings are brought home to us. Well, at any rate we may often get useful hints from those about us who know us pretty well—know us at our prayers, at our lessons, and at our play; and thus we shall be saved from the misfortune of having "nothing to ask" when we go to pray.

Ask that you may keep free all your life from mortal sin. Ask that you may be a true child of Holy Church. Ask for the greatest of all graces—perseverance to the end.

Ask for those you love, for your parents, and brothers and sisters, and for your friends. Ask for any conversion you want very much—for those who have asked you to pray for them. Urban thought carefully over his petitions on the Great Eve:

"I shall pray in general for every one," he said, "and in detail for some. I shall not pray in detail for *all* who have asked me to pray for them, but only for four. *Of course* I shall make the conversion of England *a special subject*—and Ireland, that it may never lose its faith."

Thinking of all our Lord would do for him next day, he said, "Oh, what a lot of grace I shall get! Do you know, I think that when our Lord goes away, He must leave our souls almost, but not quite—*dissolved in grace.*"

Always have the intention of gaining all the Indulgences you can, when you go to Holy Communion. The usual conditions for gaining a Plenary Indulgence are Confession and Communion and some prayer for the Pope's intentions. If you go to Confession every week, your usual Confession will suffice for all the Indulgences you can gain that week, and one Communion will suffice for all the Indulgences you can gain that day. If you belong to the Apostleship of Prayer, or to any Confraternity, you will often be entitled to many Indulgences on the same Feast.

You will do well always to say after Communion the prayer, "Behold, O kind and sweet Jesus," before a crucifix. A Plenary Indulgence is attached to the recitation of this prayer each time you go to Holy Communion, if you say some prayer for the Pope's intentions; five *Paters* and *Aves* will suffice for this.

You cannot gain more than one Plenary Indulgence for yourself at each Communion. But there are the holy Prisoners in Purgatory always holding out their hands for our alms. Never forget them in your thanksgiving after Communion. Many people make over to them all the Indulgences they gain, and a blessed act of charity it is. Some prayer for the Pope's intention should be said for each Indulgence you propose to gain. But not to tire yourself, say five *Paters* and *Aves* before you leave the church, and offer for this intention any other prayers you may say during the day.

As you go to bed to-night your heart will be full of one thought—"*To-morrow!*" If you wake in the night, say with David, "My soul hath desired Thee in the night. Come, Lord Jesus, come!"

And so the time has come at last. My God, I can scarcely believe that by this time to-morrow I shall have You in my heart. How welcome You will be! I shall have so much to say to You. Of course I shall not begin to ask You for things at once. I shall first welcome You—adore and praise and love and thank You—but I shall ask You for plenty of things before You go. And I know You will give me all I ask, that is good for me to have. Assuerus said to Esther, "What is thy petition, Esther, that it may be granted thee? What wilt thou have done?" And You, the King of Kings, will ask me to-morrow what I want. And, like Solomon, You will give me besides, out of Your royal bounty, things I do not ask, which You know will be good for me to have. I want many things, and yet, after all, I seem to want but one. Give me, O Lord, Your love and Your grace, for this is enough for me.

My good Angel, pray for me.

My Patron Saints, pray for me.

And you, dear Mother Mary, see that my wedding garment is ready for your Son—not spotless only, but bright with the jewels of many virtues, or at least with that beautiful quiet gem which He loves best of all—humility. You must be close by when He comes, to make up by your adoration, thanksgiving, and love, for all that is wanting to me. Your prayers made such a difference at the marriage-feast at Cana. Let there be a change too in me—because you will have stood by me and prayed for me—because "the Mother of Jesus was there."

# Part the Third:

# "Thanks be to God for His Unspeakable Gift!"

# XXXI

## Our First Communion

"Zacheus, make haste and come down, for this day I must abide in thy house. And he made haste and came down and received Him with joy."

If there is one day in our life when it is easy to do as the Catechism bids us as to rising in the morning, surely it is to-day. "What should you do when you wake in the morning?" "I should make the sign of the Cross, and offer my heart and soul to God. I should rise diligently, dress myself modestly, and entertain myself with good thoughts."

The sign of the Cross comes first, surmounting our Lord's new Tabernacle, and then the offering to Him of that heart and soul which are to be honoured so unspeakably by His Presence—body and soul are to be honoured, and both must be consecrated to Him and treated with all reverence. Think, as you are dressing, of the wedding garment with which your soul should be adorned, rather than of the adorning of the body. We are so easily distracted, that the very things we are obliged to do for God's service often carry our thoughts away from Him. So may it be in this matter of dress. In some places it is the custom to give a watch as a First Communion present, and it is worn to-day for the first time. What a pity it would be if a smart frock or a silver chain were to take up much of our thoughts on such a day as this!

Begin to-day the practice of always arriving in church soon

enough to have at least a quarter of an hour before Communion for preparing your soul. The best preparation is to hear Mass with this intention. Whilst waiting for Mass to begin, you can make the acts before Communion we made yesterday; or read what follows about the acts after Communion; they may help you to make your own after receiving our Lord.

But remember that what was said to you at the beginning of the book about the prayers you find in it, applies most of all to those of your First Communion Day.[1] If they help you, use them: if you can pray better by yourself, pray by yourself—our own prayers are what our Lord likes. But some of us come to the end of our own prayers rather quickly.

A little mite of three had been praying that father might have a good night. He was very ill, but the doctor said if he could get some sleep he would be better. He *had* a good night and plenty of sleep, and he was better. We must always thank God when our prayers are heard, mother said, so Winnie was to go with her to church in the afternoon, and make a visit to the Blessed Sacrament. Mother wanted to thank God, too.

It was the first answer to prayer that Winnie could remember, and she was very full of it. While nurse was getting her ready, she told her what a lot of prayers she had had to say to get father well, and that God was making him well because He always did what little children asked Him. She tripped along by mother's side, and prattled away till they reached the steep flight of steps leading to the church porch. These she climbed expeditiously, and, too full of her thanksgiving to wait to be lifted up to the holy-water stoup, made her way to the door. A curtain hung across the entrance; Winnie drew it aside, and genuflecting on one knee, called out in a loud voice, "Thank You, God." The curtain dropped, and before the few

---

[1] A little book has been printed with prayers for the "Mass before First Communion." See Preface, p. xv.

worshippers had time to look round, Winnie was on her feet again, hurrying back to mother, who reached the spot just in time to see the beginning and end of the thanksgiving.

Some of us are like little Winnie—our devotions, however fervent, are apt to be short.

After Holy Communion we should make acts of (1) **Adoration,** (2) **Thanksgiving,** (3) **Love,** (4) **Contrition,** (5) **Petition.** Let us go over these acts together. If you know how to make them, you will not want a book for some little time after Communion. Your own heart will tell you what to say to our Lord, and how to welcome Him. The holy Curé d'Ars used to say, "I do not like people to begin to read as soon as they come from the Holy Table. Oh, no! why use the words of men when God is speaking?"

Our first act after receiving our Lord is (1) **Adoration.** You may offer Him first your own act, bowing down your soul at His Feet as you would have bowed down before Him in Bethlehem and on Calvary. As truly as He was present in the Manger and on the Cross, so is He present with you now: "Profoundly I adore Thee, O hidden God."

Then, because your act is so poor, so unworthy of Him, you may offer Him the adoration of your good Angel prostrate at your side; the adoration of all those thousands and thousands of blessed spirits of whom we have thought so often as His Court in Heaven. Not more truly do they adore Him there on the Throne of His Glory, than on the little humble throne to which His love for you has brought Him.

Your holy Patrons, too—invite them to help you. They see what you cannot see. Be glad that they can adore so profoundly because they see so clearly. Be glad, too, that whilst waiting to see Him with them, you have the blessing our Lord promised to those who have not seen but have believed.

Then His Blessed Mother's adoration—offer Him that. She adores Him in your heart no less than when as a little Child He lay in her lap, or was folded in her arms and pressed to her heart, or when she received him into her own pure heart in Holy Communion. Rejoice that you have such deep adoration as hers to offer Him, and ask Him to accept it as if it were your own.

Yet Mary's adoration is not enough. She is a creature, and she cannot understand what is due to the great Creator. Only God knows what His Majesty deserves. Oh, how far beyond your reach it is to give Him that! Yes, at all other times, but not now. *Now* you can give Him adoration as deep as He deserves, for the Sacred Heart is adoring Him perfectly. And Its adoration is your very own, because this Sacred Heart is your very own. How glad you will be and how grateful that you can offer It to the Three Divine Persons to fully pay what you owe Them.

(2) **Thanksgiving.**—In the same way you may offer Him first your own act of thanksgiving. God has given you now the greatest Gift He can give you in this life. Not till He receives you into Heaven and shows you His Unveiled Face, can He give you anything greater than He gives you now. What can you give Him back? Give yourself to Him as He gives Himself to you without reserve. Give Him your heart in return for His. Give Him your love, for He loves you dearly. Give Him all that you have and are, now that He has given you all that He has and is.

When you open your eyes in the next world, the moment after death, you will see clearly that the state of every soul in Eternity depends on one thing only—whether it possesses God or not. The souls in Hell do not possess God, and never will possess Him, and so they will be eternally miserable. The poor Souls in Purgatory do not possess God yet, and their one cry is to get to Him, to have Him, to be united with Him. The souls of the Blessed in Heaven possess God and are perfectly happy;

### The Holy Foster Father

"Art Thou, weak Babe, my very God?  Oh, I must love Thee, then."
-*Faber.*

they have all they want, for in Him they have all things. "My God and My All!" is their happy cry to all eternity.

And this God Whom *every* soul in the next life so intensely desires to have, *you have now*. He is all yours. Oh, hold Him fast, and Heaven is yours, for "he that eateth this Bread *hath* everlasting life." "My God and my All!" "I have found Him Whom my soul loveth, I hold Him and will not let Him go."

> Oh, how can we thank Thee
> For a Gift like this?
> Gift that truly maketh
> Heaven's eternal bliss.

Call upon the Angels again. Call upon your good Angel, your Patron Saint, and our Lady. Call upon those, who know so well what the infinite God is, to thank Him for you, to thank Him with you, for giving Himself to you thus before the time. He tells us not to look for our reward in this life, "I *will be* thy Reward exceeding great." And see! Whilst we with our cold love are content to wait, our Reward Himself cannot wait. He must come to us before the time: "Behold, I am with you all days."

We know what the thanksgivings in Heaven are like. We know how proud they are of their God. We know the shouts of praise that go up for ever before His throne: "Salvation to our God Who sitteth upon the Throne, and to the Lamb... Benediction, and glory, and wisdom, and thanksgiving, honour, and power, and strength to our God for ever and ever, Amen... Amen, Alleluia. Give praise to our God, all ye His servants, and you that fear Him, little and great." Here is my place—here I come in among the little ones. I will call upon all these great and blessed ones to come round me now, and adore their King on His little new throne, the tiny throne of my heart. I will listen to them singing round me, "Salvation to our God Who sitteth upon the Throne."

Here is a grand thanksgiving, and yet you have a grander still to offer. Far, far above all the praise His Heavenly Court can give Him, is the thanksgiving going up to God from the Sacred Heart really present within you. Like sweet incense from a thurible, the thanksgiving of the Sacred Heart is going up from your heart before the Throne of God. You can offer It to God as your very own, for the Sacred Heart of Jesus is yours. You can do with It what you will. Oh, make use of It whilst you have It!

(3) **Love.**—Will this be hard? How can we help loving Him Who has loved us like this? Whom shall we love if we do not love Jesus! Surely we can say now with St. Paul, "Who shall separate us from the love of Christ? If any man love not our Lord Jesus Christ, let him be anathema."

"I have found Him Whom my soul loveth. I hold Him and will not let Him go." Yes, hold Him fast—He does not stay long. Hold Him fast, He is your Father, your Brother, your Master, your Companion, the Friend and Lover of your soul. Hold Him fast: you will not find any one so faithful and constant as He is—no one who will ever love and care for you, feel for you, provide for you, make allowances for you, comfort and support you as He does:

> Then why, O Lover of my soul,
>    Should I not love Thee well,
> Not for the sake of winning Heaven,
>    Or of escaping Hell.
> Not for the sake of gaining aught.
>    Not seeking a reward,
> But as Thou first hast loved me,
>    O ever loving Lord!

Love Him, not only for what He gives, not only because He loves you so dearly, but for what He is in Himself—Infinitely Holy and Beautiful and Lovable—the God of Infinite Perfection. "We praise Thee. We bless Thee. We glorify Thee. *We give Thee thanks for Thy great glory*, O only-begotten Son of God."

You may offer Him the love of all His Saints, and especially of His Blessed Mother, to make up for the poverty of your love. And then offer the Love of the Sacred Heart to the Three Divine Persons as Love enough *even for Them*, as a Present from yourself *worthy of Them*, most acceptable *even to Them*.

(4) **Contrition.**—Does contrition seem a sad thing to come back to? Does it seem out of place to-day? It is never out of place. We can never be too sorry for our sins, never renew our sorrow too often. And this glad day is just the opportunity we want for telling our Lord how sorry we are for having ever offended Him. When shall we tell Him this better than when we have Him with us! When shall we make our act of contrition better than when we have the Sacred Heart to help us! Surely our contrition will be perfect, at least in our thanksgiving after Communion to-day!

To think that I have offended Him after being so many times forgiven! To think that I have offended *Him* Whom after all *I do love!* My God, I *am* so sorry for all my sins: give me a tender, loving, and hearty contrition for them, because they have offended You Who are so good, and a firm purpose not to offend You any more.

(5) **Petition.**—Now the time has come for asking all you want. Your petitions will have been prepared beforehand. This precious quarter of an hour must not be spent in thinking what you have to ask, but in asking.

"What is thy desire, Esther, and what wilt thou have done?" "What wilt thou that I do for thee?" said our Lord, kindly, to the blind man. Tell Him what you want Him to do for you. Tell him of the needs and troubles of your soul; where you find it hardest to be good, to overcome yourself. Tell Him what virtue you want most. Ask Him for more faith, more trust in Him, above all, for more love, "Give me Thy love and Thy grace, and it is enough for me." Ask Him with great confidence: His Hands are full of gifts. He knows what you want; He has got it ready beforehand and brought it with Him. But He means you to ask for it.

Oh, how many gifts we might have for the asking! How many our Lord brings with Him—just the very things we want, and we do not ask. The time goes; we are distracted; we do not care enough about our souls to find out and ask for what they want. And so, when the time comes for our Lord to leave us, He has to gather His treasures up sadly and take them away. There were presents He had made ready for us; there were graces He had purchased for us and was looking forward to giving us. But we did not care to ask, and He has to take them away with Him or give them perhaps to the one kneeling next to us, who is holding out both hands to Him and getting so rich. Oh, what a pity!

Ask for others as well as for yourself, and never forget the Holy Souls in Purgatory, particularly any of your relations and friends who may be there. For these and for all others, say with your eyes upon the crucifix, the prayer, "Behold, O kind and most sweet Jesus," with five Our Fathers and five Hail Marys for the Pope's intentions.

But before you end your thanksgiving, make an offering to our Lord of all you have to give. In the East, no one appears in the presence of a King without some costly gift. So the Magi took offerings for the new born Child. So Holy Scripture says, "Take with thee presents and go to meet Him. There shall not appear before the Lord any empty. But every one shall offer according to what he hath."

Do not say you have nothing. You have your soul stamped as a precious coin with the image of God Himself. It is more His than yours, It is His by creation, His by redemption, for "you are not your own, you are bought with a great price." Give, then, to God the things that are God's. Give Him this soul which has His image and superscription upon it, with its three powers: memory, and understanding, and will. Give Him your heart with all its affections, and your body with all its senses, that He may freely dispose of you and yours in all things for time and eternity. Give Him your resolutions too, and ask Him to bless them, to bless you now that He is going, and to keep you carefully as something belonging to Himself, so that when He comes to you again He may rejoice to find in you the fruits of His Presence. "I will not let Thee go until Thou bless me."

As you leave the Church, take away with you the counsel of the holy Curé d'Ars: "If you have a vessel full of some precious perfume, you close it well. In this way you keep its sweetness as long as you like. So if you guard your heart after Holy Communion, you will keep our Lord with you, and the sweet fragrance of His Presence will make you love all that is good and hate all that is bad." Of course, you may be bright and happy—when should you be happy if not to-day? But this does not mean that you are to be rough and boisterous, or so taken up with the duties and amusements to which you are returning as to forget what you have been doing and what you now are, the tabernacle of God. We like to see the Tabernacle look bright and festive. But we always remember Who has His dwelling there. We touch it reverently; we guard it carefully.

Do not lose sight of our Lord. Bring your heart back to Him every now and then during the morning by some short, tender acts of love. "Jesus, dear Jesus, never let me be separated from You." "Lord, what would You like me to do here?"

*If you can get to church again, pay our Lord a little visit in the afternoon. You can, if you like, say the prayers you will find in your little Mass book and renew your resolutions.*

# COMMUNION BEADS

*On the cross*, the Prayer of St. Ignatius:

### ANIMA CHRISTI

Soul of Christ, sanctify me;
Body of Christ, save me;
Blood of Christ, inebriate me;
Water out of the Side of Christ, wash me;
Passion of Christ, strengthen me.
O good Jesus, hear me,
Within Thy Wounds hide me;
Never let me be separated from Thee.
From the malignant enemy defend me.
At the hour of my death call me
And bid me to come to Thee,
That with Thy Saints I may praise Thee
For all eternity.            (300 days' Indulgence).

*On the large beads*, Our Father.

*On the small beads*, Hail Mary, full of grace, the Lord be with thee, blessed art thou amongst women, and blessed is the fruit of thy womb, Jesus, Whom thou didst receive so worthily. Holy Mary, Mother of God, pray for us sinners that we may receive Him worthily, now and at the hour of our death. Amen.

*Three decades.*

### *Let us pray:*

O God, Who in this wonderful Sacrament hast left us a memorial of Thy Passion, grant us, we beseech Thee, so to reverence the Sacred Mysteries of Thy Body and Blood, that we may find in ourselves the fruit of Thy Redemption. Who livest, &c.

## XXXII

## "Stay with us, Lord!"

It had been a day of cloudless light and beauty. Surely there had never been a brighter even in that bright land. Not a speck in the deep blue overhead, for the sun had put forth all his strength and flooded earth and sky, as if to make up to them for his loss three days before, when he had been blotted out of the heavens at noon. He had seemed determined to find his way into every nook of the wide earth, and to make everything glad with him.

Yes, there was sunshine all around. Yet none had made its way into the hearts of the two travellers who walked sadly side by side on the white dusty road leading to Emmaus. The darkness at noon on Calvary was on their hearts still, and, unable to bear the sights and sounds of the festive city, they had left Jerusalem behind them and were making their way to the little village which was a two hours' walk to the northwest. One thought filled their minds; one Name was in their mouths—the memory and the Name of the Master they had lost. The Shepherd had been struck and the sheep scattered.

The Twelve—no, it was the Eleven now—had hidden themselves away on the day of His shame, and when in the evening they met again under the cover of the darkness in the Upper-room on Mount Sion, how sadly all was changed! His place was empty. His Voice was silent. He had gone away and left them orphans, and there was none to comfort them.

One by one, our Lord's other disciples gathered round them there. All was over; all their hopes were crushed; and bitter disappointment weighed down the hearts of all. It was no use going back upon the past. And yet the past was all they lived for now. They wanted to hear, from the lips of those who had spent the last evening with Him, all that had passed in the Supper-room—where He sat, and how He looked, and what He had done. Over and over again, first one and then another of the Apostles had to go over the story, one supplying where the memory of another failed. Again and again had they to tell of the washing of the feet, of His tender words, and, oftenest of all, of that wonderful Gift He gave them when supper was over. How He took bread and blessed, and broke, and gave to them saying, "Take and eat, this is My Body." How He took wine and said, "Drink ye all of this, for this is My Blood." And how, as He spoke, the promise at Capharnaum came back to them, and they ate and drank, discerning in that bread and in that wine the Body and the Blood of the Lord.

This was what those two disciples were talking about that sunny afternoon. It was sad to speak of Him, and yet they could not help it—the thought of Him was all that was left to them now. This day only a week ago, Jerusalem had turned out to meet Him, and amid waving palms and *Hosannas*, He had made His way to the Temple. They thought that now at last His hour, the hour of which He had so often spoken, had come. And all had ended in this bitter disappointment. The three years they had spent with Him, following Him about from place to place—those blessed years of teaching and of miracles—were gone. He was gone—they would never see Him again.

So they talked sadly together, till they were suddenly surprised and silenced by finding that they were not alone.

A Traveller had come quietly up and joined them, and was walking by their side. He asked what they were talking about, and why they looked so unhappy. One of them, whose name was Cleophas, inquired in surprise if He were a stranger in Jerusalem, and had not heard of the things that had just been done in the city.

"What things?" asked the Stranger.

Here was the outlet their burdened hearts needed, and they poured out all their troubles to Him—how Jesus of Nazareth, a mighty Prophet, had done great things in the land—how their chief priests had condemned Him to death and crucified Him—how bitterly all His disciples were bewailing His Death, for they had hoped He was the Messiah promised for the redemption of Israel. And it was three days ago since these things had happened. All was over with Him and with them too. Even His Body had been taken away from them. Before they left the city, a strange story was going about, that some women of their company, who were at the Sepulchre before it was light, had found His Body gone, and had seen a vision of Angels who said He was alive. So even the consolation of having Him in the tomb was gone; well might they look sad.

The Traveller listened without interrupting them. He let them tell all their story—and then He spoke. His words were not of comfort, but of reproof. He called them "foolish and slow of heart to believe in all the things which the prophets had spoken." "Ought not Christ," He said, "to have suffered these things and so to enter into His glory?" And beginning at Moses, He went through the types and prophecies with them, giving them a Scripture History lesson, and showing how He had been foreshadowed, and how if they had been less dull, and had had truer notions of the Messiah, they would have seen in His sufferings and death the very signs by which He was to be known.

What we have to notice here is that our Lord, Who had come to visit these poor disciples of His in order to cheer them and bring them back into the right path, began by words of reproof. It was His way with them; it is His way with us. In His visits to you after Holy Communion He will enlighten and cheer, and comfort and help you. But there is another thing He will do for you: He will *reprove* you. Why do you look so surprised?

"Because we thought our Lord loved us and liked to be with us, and came to give us graces and things to make us happy."

You were quite right, and you have put it capitally—that is just what He does—just what He comes for—to make us happy. Because He loves us, He gives us His graces, and among His best graces are those words of reproof which seem to you so strange. Let us see if they are so strange after all. I suppose you will own that we all have our faults—the Saints had theirs; the Apostles had theirs; these two disciples had theirs. Now our Lord loved dearly all these servants of His. We know how He loved His Apostles. Did He show that love by passing over their faults, or by pointing them out so that they might be corrected? Look how He reproved the Boanerges, and St. Peter still oftener.

One day our Lord was speaking to the Twelve of His Passion, which was drawing near. He told them that the Son of Man should be mocked and scourged and spit upon. St. Peter's loyal heart was filled with indignant sorrow to think that His Master, Whom he knew to be God, should have to suffer pain and shame like that. So he took Him aside and began to rebuke Him. You see, St. Peter did not think rebuke a sign of unkindness. And our Lord turned upon him and said, "Get thee behind Me, Satan." What tremendous words! How they must have startled poor St. Peter, who only meant to be kind. Notice, too, that this severe reproof was not given for any grievous fault, but for one which we should have thought scarcely a fault at all, perhaps an act of virtue even. But St. Peter ought to have known better, and as he was to be raised very high, our Lord rebuked him for what He might have passed over in another. This looks as if reproof was one of the ways in which love and confidence are shown. And so indeed it is. Reproof is not the unkind thing we take it to be. It does not show that our parents or masters or friends dislike us because they find fault now and then.

If ever there was a loving heart, it was the heart of St. Paul. He loved his friends and his converts so dearly, that he said he could not bear to go to Heaven if they were not to go. Yet how do we find him writing to them at times: "O senseless Galatians, who hath bewitched you?" How should we like a letter from a friend to begin so? St. Paul wanted to bring his friends to their senses; he could do nothing for them till this was done. And our friends can do nothing with us till we can be brought to see what is amiss.

Look at this class of babies. They have got a pencil into their little fat hands and are full of glee, for to-day they are writing quite by themselves. We are called here and there and expected to greatly admire their first efforts. If we suggest that the pot-hooks should be kept inside the lines, and that those O's should be closed, our hints may be taken in different ways. Baby No. 1 listens patiently to what we say, tries to see the faults we see, and to do better. Baby No. 2 turns upon us and says the pot-hooks *are* inside the lines and it can't shut up the O's any better. What do we do? Leave the little stupid, of course, in its self-content and pass to No. 3. The first writer will get on, and after a time its work will really deserve admiration—the second will go on blundering till it can be got to see its faults.

It is the same with us in regard to those faults that belong not to our fingers; but to our minds and our hearts. The moment we begin to notice them, that moment our chances of improvement begin. Why, then, should we be so cross with those who point them out to us? We do not act like this in school matters. We complain that the drawing-master never makes any remark upon *our* work, and he is always touching up So-and-so's. Yet if a friend wants us to touch up this or that in ourselves, that so we may be more like our Model, we take offence, we like to go our own way and not to be interfered with. Clearly there is something to mend here. We must not treat our best Friend in this way. He expects us to be docile to His lessons, and when He finds fault with us, He wants us to own we are in the wrong and try to mend. One of the chief things He will do for us now in His Visits in Holy Communion, will be to show us where He wants to see improvement. Our business must be to listen to Him and to carry out what He tells us.

"But we do not hear Him speak. How can we tell what He wants?"

We can tell quite well, for we do hear Him speak. That low voice in your conscience telling you when you do wrong is His. Do not turn away; do not pretend not to hear; do not try to forget it because it says what is troublesome or uncomfortable. Everything in this life and in the next depends upon the way we listen to that Voice.

If you ask those who have lost their souls, and are now in Hell, why they are there, they will tell you it is because they turned a deaf ear to that Voice, and so its whispers grew fainter and fainter, and their hearts harder and harder, till mortal sin came, and death, and Hell for ever.

And, on the other hand, the bright-faced Saints will tell you that it was by listening to that Voice that their thrones were reached and their crowns won. Let us listen to it then, whether the reproof comes to us through His Voice speaking straight to us through our conscience, or through the lips of those who have a right to speak in His Name, or through those who, without having this right, are still made use of by Him to carry His warning words. You remember how it was through baby-lips that a Catholic father was reproved for breaking the Church's law of abstinence. We, too, at times, hear very plain truths about ourselves from those around us. Instead of firing up and answering back, might we not think to ourselves, "Well, there really is some truth in that—here is our Lord's Voice speaking to me. I must say I do not like it to come in this shape and through this channel—but that cannot be helped. If it *is* His Voice, I will not mind the channel, but take His words to heart in whatever way they come to me, and profit by them."

"But what had these disciples done to deserve reproof?" you say. "They were only discouraged, and there is no harm in that."

Oh, pardon me, but there *is* harm—and very great harm—so much, that if the devil can do nothing more than discourage us, he is perfectly satisfied. Nay, more: he would rather bring us to discouragement than bring us to sin, because after a sin we can rise again quickly, but if we are so cast down that we will not try to get up and return to God, we fall from one sin into another, and get further and further away from Him. Is there no harm, then, in discouragement? Look at it this way. If one of your companions were trying to serve God faithfully, but fell from time to time into the same old faults, and came to you in his trouble for some good advice; and instead of cheering him, you were to tell him it was no use trying and he might as well give it all up, would not you think that wrong? "Very wrong," you say. Then what right have you to do that wrong to yourself by saying, "It is no use my trying—I may as well give it up." There *is* harm, then, in giving way to discouragement, and so our Lord reproved these disciples for it.

They took His reproof well. Oh, was it not well for them that they did! Think what they would have missed had they turned away huffed. They owned they had done wrong, and this was all He wanted. Then He began to comfort them and make them happy. Little by little, the charm of His Presence and the sweetness of his words penetrated into those sad hearts. They had made Him come between them that they might hear Him better, and they listened eagerly to all He said. He showed them things they had never understood before—how God permits suffering for our good—how it was by suffering that the world was to be redeemed and made happy once more—how even Christ was to enter into His glory by the way of suffering, and His followers must go after Him along the same path. So that they must not think all was lost now, though things did look so dark. All this seemed clear as He explained it, and their hearts began to burn with the desire to follow their Master in the way He had gone.

The sun sank lower and lower—that glorious Easter Day was nearly spent. In the society of their Companion, the two travellers had forgotten all about their troubles. Look at them. Are they the same men that left Jerusalem a while ago? They have so enjoyed His conversation; it has so absorbed them, that they have noticed nothing else—neither the passers-by, nor the evening shadows closing round them, nor the little inn they are nearing.

Now they are at the door, and their Fellow-Traveller bids them good-bye. He is passing on. But they cannot part with Him. He has made all the difference in their lives. They must ask, and beg, and if need be *force* Him to go in and stay with them.

And our Lord goes in—He was only *pretending* to leave them, that they might press Him to stay. He goes in with them and they sit down to table.

Look at them—one on each side of Him. How peaceful they are, how contented, how happy! The little room of that little place, how bright He is making it for them. They look at Him with loving, reverent awe. But what is their amazement, when they see Him take bread and lift His Eyes to Heaven—and bless and break, just as they had heard He had done in the Supper-room on Mount Sion. They fall on their knees before Him. He gives them their First Communion, and instantly their eyes are opened—and they know Him—and He vanishes out of their sight.

See the fruit of that Communion—how they discerned the Body of the Lord—how they knew Him at last—their Master, Who had been with them all the afternoon and been treated as a stranger—how they made their acts of adoration, and thanksgiving, and love, and sorrow for having been so slow of heart. Were they not glad that they had invited Him, and constrained Him to go in with them! This is what we too must do, if we want Him to come to us and stay with us.

"If any man shall hear My Voice and open to Me the door, I will come in to him and will sup with him and he with Me."

These are the tender words of Jesus in which He speaks of our First Communion—His Communion and ours. He has stood at the door of our hearts and knocked. And we have heard His Voice and opened to Him, and He has come in and supped with us and we with Him. It has been the Supper-room on Mount Sion over again—only *my* head on His Breast this time instead of John's, *my* love to be His joy and His comfort, instead of the love of His youngest there. *I* to be now the disciple whom Jesus loves. What kind of a welcome have I given Him?

There is something very sweet in those words, "I will sup with him and he with Me." Not dine with him, but "sup." There is a rest and a stillness, a tender familiarity, and an intimacy of intercourse suggested in that word "sup." The hour is late; the door closed; the dark world shut out; no noise without

## The Last Supper

"Jesus took bread: and blessing brake, and gave to them, and said: Take ye, This is My Body."  (Mark 14:22)

breaks the stillness of the little room where the two friends are together; no sound within disturbs their whispered words of confidence and love. They are alone; they may speak freely of their troubles and disappointments; they may tell the secrets that are for each other only. Whatever interests one interests the other; joys and sorrows are shared between them; plans are talked over; difficulties foreseen and provided against. Each feels stronger in the support of the other; help is given freely whenever help is possible, and even when all other help fails, sympathy is unfailing. It is a restful time—there is no need for haste; no duties press; to-morrow's cares are not yet upon them; to-morrow's toil has not yet begun. They may enjoy each other's company; they may rest in each other's love. So must it be in the little room of our hearts when our Lord says, "I will come in and sup with him and he with Me."

Notice the amendment that followed on the First Communion of the two disciples at Emmaus. They had not done right in leaving the company of the Apostles that morning, and they determined to go back without delay. "Rising up the same hour they went back to Jerusalem," says St. Luke. We must see where our Lord expects amendment from us and set to work at once.

This First Communion at Emmaus seems to have been specially intended to show the effects of Holy Communion in enlightening us *to see* and strengthening us *to do* what God wants of us. And this will be the effect, not of First Communion only, but of all the Communions of our lives, provided we go as we ought—frequently and fervently. But how soon after First Communion the fervour of some grows cold! What a difference there is in the second Communion, what a difference after a month's time! Ought this to be? Does our Lord change towards us that we should change so sadly?

Oh, let us ask Him earnestly that we may not grieve His Sacred Heart, either by staying away from Him, or by drawing near with careless and unprepared hearts. His Table is always spread for us. We *must not* stay away. We *cannot afford* to stay away. Our souls *will die* if we stay away. He asks us to come to Him. He wants to give Himself to us now, that He may be able to give Himself to us hereafter. Is He to be all eagerness and are we not to be eager at all? Surely not. "Lord, give us always this Bread."

And what does He *require* of us when we come? One thing only—that we be free from mortal sin. Less than this He could not exact. More we shall surely give Him, but He does not strictly require more.

After the Sacrifice of the Mass, Communion is the holiest, the most sublime, the most glorious action we can offer to God in this life. One good Communion can draw down greater graces than all other acts of religion; by one good Communion we can acquire more merit than by all other holy practices put together. One Communion contains grace enough to make us Saints. If we want to know how it was that the Saints became Saints, the answer is, it was by their Communions. They brought good dispositions, and the Blessed Sacrament did much for them—they brought better and better dispositions, and the Blessed Sacrament did more and more, till our Lord's likeness was perfected in them. No wonder that those who knew by experience what this Divine Food could do for them, hungered after It as they did.

It happens sometimes that the occupant of a carriage, passing swiftly over a long dusty road, comes up with a traveller plodding wearily along, and offers him a lift. He takes from him the different little bundles that are tiring him, makes him sit down beside him, and after beguiling the way with pleasant talk, sets him down refreshed and rested near his journey's end. This is what our Communion-days do for us. They find us trudging along our daily path, which is often monotonous and weary enough, and they take us up and give us a lift. What a lift it often is! What a lift it may *always* be if we choose! How fast and how far it takes us, depends very much on ourselves.

We must come to our Lord then—we must not stay away. And we must come *fervently*. Custom must not lessen our reverence or cool our love. Shall we see how a Saint kept up his fervour from one Communion to another?

Those who lived with St. Aloysius used to say that when he was praying before the Tabernacle, his faced glowed like the face of a seraph. Why was this? You are getting clever in these matters now, and you answer at once, "It must have been his faith." Of course it was. And suppose we go a little further and ask, "How is it that our faith, which is the same as his, does not show the same fruits? How is it that we are so sadly unlike seraphs when we kneel where he knelt? Can you answer that?"

"He must have exercised his faith, and so kept it always fresh and strong."

And we do not? Capital! Why, you are quite theologians! Yes, it was exercise that made the faith of the Saints so different from ours. And their faith made them industrious in finding out ways of strengthening it and keeping it in good practice.

What can we do, then, to keep up fervour in our hearts? As every science has its secrets, so has the science of holiness. But these secrets are for careful students only. Smatterers do not find them out. St. Aloysius was a careful student, and he had a secret for making his Communions always fervent and fruitful. He went to Communion every Sunday, and he turned the whole week into preparation and thanksgiving. The first three days were spent in thanksgiving for his last Communion, and the last three in preparation for the next. This did not interfere in the least with his ordinary duties. On the contrary, it helped them, for it was a motive for doing them all as perfectly as possible. If something hard had to be done on Monday, Tuesday, or Wednesday, he would say, "This is not pleasant, certainly, but I will offer it up to our Lord as a little return for His visit to me last Sunday." The prayers, work, and sufferings of the other three days were offered in preparation—that our Lord might find his heart more ready for His Coming next time. Suppose we were to imitate St. Aloysius in this!

We know what his Communions did for him. It was these visits of our Lord, so fervently expected, so fruitfully employed, that made him a Saint so soon. It is the Sacraments that make all the Saints. Our Lord gave them for this. The two great Sacraments of Penance and the Holy Eucharist work together in the cultivation of the soul as the sun and the Nile work together in producing the rich crops of Egypt. The great river overflows its banks and floods the country all round with its purifying and fertilizing waters. Then the sun comes out in his strength and draws from the moist earth the most luxuriant vegetation. So Penance cleanses and prepares the soul for the Sun of Justice, Who warms and vivifies and covers it with the fruits of holiness.

We see how we may make our Communions fervent as well as regular. But what has this to do with thanksgiving after Communion, which is our point now?

It has everything to do with it. *Thanksgiving shows itself by perseverance.* The only real thanksgiving is perseverance. Whatever helps us to persevere in good, to go on trying in spite of our difficulties and our falls, is in reality helping us to thank our Lord for His unspeakable Gift.

# XXXIII
## "Lord, Give us always this Bread."

> Multiply our graces,
>   Chiefly love and fear,
> And, dear Lord, the chiefest,
>   Grace to persevere.

Yes, *the* grace we have to ask of our Lord now is the grace to *go on* being good—overcoming ourselves, going regularly and carefully to the Sacraments, rising quickly after our falls, and returning to God without discouragement—the grace to do this, not for a month or a year, but always—to the end. "He that shall persevere to the end," says our Lord, "he shall be saved." "Be thou faithful unto death and I will give thee the crown of Life."

Six days before His Passion, our Lord entered Jerusalem in triumph. He came from Bethany over the Mount of Olives, and on reaching the brow of the hill, where the road turns downward into the valley of Kedron, beheld Jerusalem at His Feet. "And seeing the city He wept over it." When the air was resounding with the joyous cries of the multitude and the *hosannas* of the little children, the Sacred Heart was sad. He knew that in a few days all would be changed. There would be this one welcome, and only one. Jerusalem, which was now opening her gates to receive Him as her King, would turn against Him when He came again and cast Him forth, and crucify Him.

Had the little children any share in causing that sadness of the Sacred Heart? Those little voices that sang "*Hosanna* to the Son of David,"—did they join a few days later in the awful cry, "Crucify Him"? Did our Lord look sadly on them—on any one of them—as they sang their welcome to Him? Were any of the tears He shed that day as He looked down upon Jerusalem, shed over them? Or did He think of any other children, who, after receiving Him in joy, would turn away and forget Him, or welcome Him coldly when He came again?

It is not the First Communion only to which He looks. Let us hope He generally gets a warm and loving welcome then. But the second and the third, what of them? What of the Communions weeks after, and months—are they what He has a right to expect?

A friend who has been staying with us soon finds out whether we were really glad to see him. If he is not asked again for a long while; if at his second and third visit he finds he is not put into the best room as before, and that in the room where he is put, little or no preparation has been made for him; if he is left a good deal to himself, and when we see him we have nothing to say, he will not think our thanks for his visit mean much.

Our Lord is our Friend. He watches to see what welcome we give Him when He comes again. He does not look for any very grand preparation. A straw shows which way the wind blows, and very little things tell the secrets of our hearts. Who does not feel that a fresh rose on her table will welcome mother when she has been from home for a week? Can we not find some little acts that will be roses and violets for our Lord when He comes?

All is not over now that our First Communion is over. Quite the contrary. Our Lord has done all He can for us and He will go on doing all He can. But He expects us to correspond with

## Christ Blessing Little Children

"And they brought to Him young children, that He might touch them...
And embracing them, and laying His Hand upon them, He blessed them."
(Mark 10:13, 16)

His graces. We must not be content to go on as we were before First Communion. We must *grow* upon this Divine Food; we must *improve*; we must *persevere*. Our Lord will help us and help us to the end.

Final perseverance is a grace so great that we cannot merit it. God keeps it in His own Hands. But we can certainly obtain it, if we ask for it. "Ask and you shall receive." "Whatsoever you shall ask the Father in My Name, He will give it to you." That is, whatsoever will help us to save our souls. Perseverance is *the* grace on which salvation depends: it puts us in possession of Heaven; therefore we shall certainly obtain it, if we ask as we ought. Ask it every day, and it will be given to you every day. Ask it to the end and it will be given you at the end. Ask it always at the Elevation at Mass. Ask it after your confessions. Ask it above all in your Communions. "Lord, give us always this Bread." Give us the true Manna to feed us right through the desert till we come to the Promised Land. Give us, not the bread of Elias, but the Bread from Heaven, to help us right up to the top of the Mount where we shall see God. Let me never tire of this Bread as the Hebrews tired of the manna, never stay away or make excuses like the guests invited to the marriage.

"He that eateth this Bread shall live for ever." It is a grand promise You have made me, dear Lord, and You will keep it, for You are the "Faithful and True." I have made my little promises to You; help me to show myself faithful and true, by keeping them to the end.

One bitter morning in December, when the cold air outside was making its way even into snug bedrooms, and people who heard the clocks strike were glad it was not yet time to get up, the father of a large family lay awake thinking—thinking of the many little ones fast asleep overhead, whom he had to love and care for.

Suddenly there was a noise in the passage—a sound as of something being laid down at his door—then a fumbling at the handle as if someone were trying to get in. At last the door opened softly, and a small white figure with bare feet crept in on tiptoe, carrying something in its arms. As it came near the gas, which burned low above the fire-place, he made out the fluffy head of little Effie, his youngest child. Yes, it was Effie sure enough, and, as usual, with her beloved Noah's ark. But what business had either of them here at this hour in the dark and the cold?

Arrived at the mantel-piece, she lifted her load on to it, got a chair, mounted it, and proceeded to set out in procession all the inhabitants of the ark—beasts and birds, two and two, beginning with the smallest, Noah, Sem, Cham, and Japhet bringing up the rear. This arranged to her satisfaction, she dismounted, moved her chair to the other end of the mantel-piece, and started there a second procession of china dogs and woolly sheep to meet the first.

What could it all mean—this early visit and display of treasures? Oh, he remembered—it was his birthday, and this must be the beginning of the day's proceedings. Yes, it was father's birthday. He was invited to some grand doings after breakfast; but after breakfast was not soon enough for little Effie. She had gone to bed with her head full of the surprise it had been planning for days past, and here she was carrying it out joyfully, and, as she thought, unperceived.

At last all was ready, and having put the chair back in its place, she was creeping quietly to the door, the empty ark under her arm, when she was startled by hearing her name. How could her father let her go without a kiss and an embrace! He called her to him and told her how he had watched all her loving preparations when she thought he was asleep; how pleased he was, and how proud he would be of his mantel-piece in the morning with all those pretty things upon it. At first Effie was disappointed. Her secret was found out and father would not be surprised after all. But when he said He really had been surprised and that she had made him very happy, she was happy too, and went back to bed full of the thought that hers had been the first kiss and "the soonest present" that day.

What a pity the story does not end here. Perhaps we had better let it end here. But there was an unfortunate promise at the beginning of the book that the stories should all be true. This is a true story, and it has a second part, and as you have been promised I suppose you must have it.

Well, next morning father was lying awake again, when to his great surprise the door opened as before and in came Effie with the empty ark under her arm. What could she want this time? She mounted the chair as before, put her arm round the long procession on the mantel-piece, and with one vigorous stroke swept half of it into the ark. Poor animals, if they could have made a noise, what a roaring and howling there would have been, as with broken legs and tails they fell pell-mell over each other, Noah, Sem, Cham, and Japhet on the top!

Alas! alas! It was but too plain what Effie had come for, and a voice from the blankets cried out:

"Stop thief! Stop thief! Those things are mine—my presents—given to me yesterday by somebody with her arms round my neck—given to me for my very own." Effie turned round unabashed.

"Only for yesterday, father. It was your birthday you know—but it's to-morrow now," and there was another sweep into the ark. Then the chair was moved to the other corner, and in an instant dogs and woolly sheep were falling headlong upon Noah and his sons to complete the havoc. Her work accomplished, Effie gravely descended with her load, replaced the chair and marched out of the room, turning round, however, at the door, to repeat her explanation—"It was only for yesterday, you know."

"*Only for yesterday*." Are we going to say this to our Lord? Are we going to take away the presents we have given Him—to break our promises to Him, saying—"It's to-morrow now"?

But it will cost us something to keep our promises. Of course. Who ever doubted it? When did you buy father or mother something that cost nothing? No, we are not going to be shabby. We are not going to be content with a quarter of an hour's thanksgiving after Communion. We want it to be something that will last, something our Lord will care for—the keeping of those promises we have made Him. Such gifts must cost. *Let them cost.* What has been given to our Lord for His "very own," we are not going to take away again, like little Effie.

We must ask the grace of perseverance, not coldly, not carelessly, but with our whole hearts—"I ask *for what I want*," says St. Ignatius—what *I must have, what I am determined to get* from God. And so I say earnestly:

> Multiply our graces,
> Chiefly love and fear,
> And, dear Lord, the chiefest,
> Grace to persevere.

"Why fear?" you say. "We thought our Lord did not want us to be afraid of Him."

Our Lord does not want us to be afraid to come to Him, but He wants us very much to have that holy fear which is the beginning of wisdom, and one of the great means to perseverance. There are two kinds of fear, one servile—the fear of slaves; the other loving—the fear of children. The first is not a fear of offending God, but of being punished by God. The other is the dread of grieving the Father Whom we love.

"Is the first kind bad then?"

No, it is less perfect than the second, but it is good and sometimes necessary for us. There are times when temptation is so strong, that only the fear of Hell will keep us from falling into sin. At such times, this fear is like a guard before the fire. David knew how necessary it is when he said to God: "Pierce Thou my flesh with Thy fear, for I am afraid of Thy judgments." This holy fear of God has saved many a soul, by keeping it in the love and friendship of God, or by bringing it back when it had gone astray. Listen to the prayer of one of God's greatest Saints: "If ever through my fault Thy love should grow cold in my heart, at least let the fear of Thy punishments keep me from falling into sin."

This fear of God, then, is a grace to be prayed for. There is little of it in the world around us. Yet we all need it. Even the Saints need it. Our Lord Himself tells us so: "And I say *to you, My friends*: Be not afraid of them who kill the body, and after that, have no more that they can do. But I will show you Whom ye shall fear: fear ye Him, Who after He hath killed hath power to cast into Hell. Yes, I say to you, fear Him." The Saints armed themselves with the fear of God as with a shield, and turned quickly in time of temptation to the Four Last Things, the remembrance of which God has promised will keep us in the fear of God and so help us to perseverance.

Death, Judgment, Hell, Heaven—those Four Last Things! The Catechism says they are to be ever remembered. Yet there are people who never remember any one of them. And there are children who suppose these words of the Catechism were never meant for them, but only for grown up people. As for Hell, it is too dreadful to think about, and Death and Judgment are far off yet. It will be time enough to think of them when we get old or sick. Are you so sure of that? Why, we hear on all sides of children dying! Sometimes at home after a few days' illness; sometimes at school, when they were looking forward to the holidays; sometimes in a railway accident; sometimes at their play. If any of us more than others ought to be always ready for death, it is the children. Death is nearer to them than to others, and if it were not for their good Angels, who, we know, are charged to bear them up in their hands, we should be afraid to trust some of them out of our sight. So they, at least, cannot afford to think of death as far off.

If it is not far off—if it may come at any moment—is it not foolish to drive away the thought of it as we do? There are some people who fear the thought of death almost as much as they fear the thought of Hell. When it comes, it must find us ready, and we are not ready for things we never think about. To see the care with which some of us avoid thinking and speaking of death, one would suppose that thinking about it provokes it and brings it nearer. To think about death does not hasten its coming, but it makes all the difference with us when it does come. To those who have made it a familiar thought in life, it comes quietly and sweetly at last: those are frightened of it to whom it comes as a stranger and a dreaded foe. It is not meant to frighten us, but only to make us careful, and if we are wise, we shall accustom ourselves to the thought of it, instead of driving it away when it comes.

Death is the first among those Four Last Things which we are told ever to remember, because it will come first, and because if we are ready for death, we have nothing to fear from the rest. We *shall* be ready for it, if we often remember it, and lay to heart the lessons it teaches us. These lessons are so important and so necessary for us, that it would be very foolish indeed to stop our ears and run away for fear of hearing them. Instead of this, we will draw near, and listen attentively, and try to let one at least of these lessons sink deep, deep down into our hearts.

It is quite certain that I shall die. About other things there is a great deal of uncertainty. Perhaps I shall pass such an examination. Perhaps I shall go home for the holidays. But there is no *perhaps* about death. Everyone dies, the old and the young, the rich and the poor. Our Lord died and His Blessed Mother, and *I too shall die.*

It is certain I shall die, but everything else about my death is uncertain. Will it be by a slow disease, or after a few days' illness? Shall I have a sudden death, by heart complaint, by lightning, a fall, a railway accident? Shall I die in my bed, on the sea, in a place of amusement? After many years, or next year, or to-night? Of all this I know nothing; it is all hidden from me. All I know is that there are many sudden deaths, and that many who are as young and strong as I am, will die before the year is out.

I hear every day of people dying. I see the hearses go by. I feel again and again the same strange fear when there is a death anywhere near me. And yet, for all that, it is so hard to bring it home to myself that *I* shall die—that what happens to everybody will happen *to me*—that the day will come when it will be said of me: "Have you heard that N.N. is dead?"

At death, I shall be alone with God and my past life. All that past life I shall see as in a picture, from the time when I was a little child, beginning to know God, till the hour when He is going to ask me for an account of my life, and whether I have spent it as He meant it to be spent. What kind of a picture will it be? Will it make me afraid, or fill me with joy and confidence? Shall I look back upon a well spent, or upon a useless and wasted life? It will be too late then to wish it had been different. I cannot alter my life then. I cannot call it back to spend it better a second time. Then, surely, I must make it now—now when it *is* in my power—what I shall one day wish it to have been: a life spent for God and the salvation of my soul.

There will be many things along that road of my past life which will be signs of what my life has been. And among these signs, none will be more marked and unmistakable than the Sacraments and the use I have made of them. If those helps God has provided for me have been faithfully used all along, then I may hope my past will be a bright journey to look back upon.

What a traveller likes to see is a road lighted from end to end by lamps placed at regular intervals, for he knows that a well-lit road marks a well-kept, safe, and cheery road, and that robbers and murderers, who lurk in dark places and on neglected paths, will be scared away by the lights. And so with the road of my life. If, on looking back, I find it lit up all the way by those burning and shining lamps—the Sacraments of Penance and the Eucharist—I may be exceedingly glad and thankful. Those bright guardians, watching over my life, will have kept it pure and safe, and the thieves of Hell and the murderers who kill the soul will have been driven far away. The steady light of those lamps will show a careful, well-spent life, filled with good works, for it is not possible to go to the Sacraments regularly and fervently and live in negligence.

Do I want these lamps to cheer me at the last by brightening the road I look back upon? Then I must place them there now. *Now*, after my First Communion, I must make a firm resolve that all through my life I will go regularly and carefully to confession and Holy Communion. A better resolution I could hardly draw out of a meditation on death than this—to make all the Sacraments I shall receive during my life a preparation for those Last Sacraments which will be my immediate preparation for Eternity.

If I am not taken away suddenly, but have an illness by way of preparation, the time will come when the doctor, seeing how this illness is going to end, will warn my friends. And they will tell me gently that they *hope* I shall get better, but that it will be *safer* for me to have the Last Sacraments. This means that it is more than likely I shall not get better.

And so I have to prepare for death—for my last confession and my last Communion. How glad I shall be if I have not driven away the thought of death during life, but used it as God means me to use it—to keep myself from sin, and to make me fervent in His service and in earnest about saving my soul.

My Last Confession! I shall be very weak then—perhaps in great pain—able to do very little. What a happiness it will be for me, if there is little to do, if all has been done already, if there is nothing to trouble my conscience, nothing I have left to say at the last and which I should not like to die without saying—if I have had the custom of leaving the confessional *always*, as if it were for the last time and I should never be absolved any more. Above all, if I have been careful *always* about my contrition. The danger all my life through is not so much of not *remembering* my sins when I go to confession, as of not *being sorry* for them. I will make the resolution of never going to confession without "taking time and care to make a good act of contrition," as the Catechism tells me, both for the sins since my last confession, that I am going to confess, and for a sin of my past life.

And then will come my Last Communion—the last of all those lamps which are to guard and brighten my road to Heaven. Oh, Communions of my life, may you be there, every one, to cheer me as blessed lamps in the darkness of that hour! May I look back upon you from my bed of death, and see you stretching like a path of light, from this First happy one, to the Last, still happier, which is to guide me safely to my Home and to the unveiled Face of Jesus!

If I want this happiness to be mine when I come to die, I must secure it now. There will be no time then to learn the lessons Death was meant to teach me, to set mistakes right, to resolve to spend my life better and avoid sin, which is *the* thing that makes Death terrible. Time, like the sands of a glass, will be nearly run out, and the great Eternity be close at hand. *Now*, then, whilst I have time, I will get ready for Eternity. Like the wise Saints of God, I will make death a familiar thought in life. I will live like one who has to die. When I find myself hesitating whether to do this or that, my thought shall be—not, "what do I like best?" but "what shall I wish to have done when I come to die?" Every day I will ask for the grace of a happy death. I will think of death when I am tempted to sin. And every night before going to sleep, I will make a hearty act of contrition, that so—should I never wake again in this world—I may pass safely into the next.

Why, too, should I not make this compact with our Lady—that whenever I say the Hail Mary, I mean to ask her to pray for me "now," that all my life through I may receive the Sacraments of Holy Church as I shall wish to have done when I come to die—and "at the hour of my death," that they may be to me then the happy ending of time and the entrance to a happy Eternity?

Holy Mary, Mother of God, pray for us sinners, *now*, and *at the hour of our death.* Amen.

"I see quite well," you say, "that the thought of death is very useful. Even if it did nothing more for me than this—to make me careful in my preparation for the Sacraments all my life through, it would help wonderfully towards my salvation. But I cannot help thinking it is a very dreadful thought too and must make people sad and gloomy."

We might very naturally think so. But it is not true at all. The gayest of the Saints were just those into whose hearts the thought of death had sunk deepest, and who were most anxious to bring it home to the hearts of those they loved. Shall we see how the "sweet-faced old man," the Apostle of Rome, brought it home to one, who perhaps had thought as little about it as some of us have done?

No one who knew St. Philip—and was there any one in Rome who did not know him?—would accuse him of being gloomy or sad. It would be hard to find another Saint about whom so many funny stories and sayings are told, or one whose winning ways made him more tenderly beloved by all who came in contact with him. It was the sunshine of his smile quite as much as the fame of his sanctity that attracted to him so many and such different kinds of visitors. Cardinals and soldiers, nobles and poor artisans, English students, for whom the martyrs' crown was waiting, and children with no thought beyond their play—all made their way to St. Girolamo, for Philip's big heart had room for every one and made itself all to all.

Perhaps the children were the favourites. We are told that he often left his prayers to laugh and joke with the boys who came to see him; and that to keep them out of mischief he would set them to play at ball just opposite his room. One day when they were enjoying themselves famously, some people of the house came suddenly upon the scene, and scolded them well for the noise they were making. But Philip would not have their fun stopped.

"Never mind," he said, "what these good people say. Amuse yourselves, and be as merry as you like—all I want of you is not to sin."

Another time, when a gentleman asked in surprise how he could bear such an uproar, the Saint replied, "Provided only they do not offend God, I would willingly let them chop wood on my back."

Dear, kind St. Philip! No wonder the young Romans flocked to him from all parts and besieged his confessional.

Would you like to know the kind of meditations he gave these beginners, many of whom became later great servants of God? He set them to think seriously about *the Four Last Things*. And when he noticed in any of them a reluctance to meditate on such subjects as if they were unnecessary, he told them plainly that those who do not go down into Hell during life, run a great risk of going there after death.

One day a youth goes bounding up the stairs at St. Girolamo. He has made up his mind to win a great name in the world, and is studying hard in the hope of advancing to high honours. And now he has come full of joy to tell the result of a successful examination. His face is flushed with excitement as he enters "the holy Father's" room and kneels down at his feet.

"It has gone well with me, Father, and I have come to tell you, for I know you will be glad."

"Yes, my son, I am glad." And the old man's face beams with pleasure. Then, taking the youth's head tenderly into his hands, he says, "What a lucky fellow you are—you are studying now—by-and-bye you will be made a priest—after that a canon—then perhaps a Bishop." And so he goes on, laying before him all his secret ambitious thoughts, and all the world can give him. "You will become so famous and mount so high, that there is no telling where you will stop. It is quite possible you may become a Cardinal—nay, Francesco—who knows—you may be Pope some day."

Francesco is overjoyed, for he thinks the Saint is in earnest. But at last Philip draws the young student closer to him and whispers in his ear, "O happy you, when you have got all you desire—*And then?*"

Francesco looks up. There is a grave tenderness, such as he has never seen before in the Saint's face as he repeats—*And then?* The words go straight home to his heart. A new light breaks in upon him, and he goes away, saying to himself, "It will all be over some day—*And then?*" Day and night, in the crowded lecture-hall, among his companions, in the midst of his studies and amusements, those words sound in his ear, till at last a change comes over him. His fellow-students notice that Francesco Zazzari has altered. He is as diligent as ever and his work is as well done. But his mind seems set on higher things than formerly, and his life is becoming more holy.

Years pass by: the end comes, and he dies—not a Pope nor Cardinal, but a simple son of St. Philip in the Congregation of the Oratory—thanking God for the words that made him turn all his thoughts and desires to heavenly things, and resolve to seek the greatness and the glory that will last for ever.

And why, my God, should not those words sink into *my* heart too! Like Francesco, I set my heart on this and that, and think that when I have got what I want I shall be happy. But You who made my heart for Yourself know that none of these things will satisfy it—that it will never rest until it gives itself entirely to You. Help me, my God, to do this quickly. You do not want us all to give up everything like Francesco, but we must all care more for You than for anything in this world, and be resolved never to offend You by a wilful sin. Help me to love You like this. Come to me often in Holy Communion to help me to love You like this.

Let St. Philip's words "And then?" come often to my mind, and remind me of the eternity that is coming. Let the Four Last Things warn me while there is time, and keep me safe from sin, so that when the end of my life comes, there may be nothing in Death, or Judgment, or Hell to frighten me. Be with me in Death, and smile upon me and welcome me when I see You for the first time at Judgment. Purgatory I know there must be, but it will not last for ever. The time will come when the last debt will have been paid—the last stain from my wedding garment have gone—and then, O my God, my God—*And then!*

# XXXIV

## "He that Eateth this Bread Shall Live Forever."

> O Paradise, O Paradise,
> I greatly long to see
> The special place, my dearest Lord
> Is furnishing for me,
> Where loyal hearts and true
> Stand ever in the light,
> All rapture through and through
> In God's most holy sight.

How often we long to know what the Home is like to which we are to be taken when this short life is done! We think if we could only get one peep inside, and see its brightness and its glory, we could go away again, and be content to wait outside in the darkness and the cold, till our time should come and our Father send for us,to go away no more.

The Saints had a peep now and then. St. Paul had his, and he tells us that eye hath not seen, nor ear heard, nor the heart of man conceived, what God has prepared for those who love Him. And the Beloved Disciple had his. He tells us of a wonderful invitation he had when he was in banishment in the island of Patmos: "for the testimony of Jesus. I was in the spirit on the Lord's day"—see how he notes lovingly that it was the Lord's day—"and I looked, and behold a door was opened in Heaven and a Voice...said: Come up hither, and I will show thee the things which must be done hereafter."

What did he see? He saw our Mother the Church in all her finished beauty, "not having spot or wrinkle." He saw the glad hosts of the Redeemed, the great multitude which no man could number, of all nations and tribes and peoples and tongues, standing before the Throne and in sight of the Lamb, clothed with white robes and palms in their hands—Apostles and Martyrs and Confessors; Popes and little children; kings like David and our own St. Edward, and beggars like Lazarus; those who have done great things for God like St. Francis Xavier, and oh, such numbers of whom the world knows nothing—the poor and the despised and the sorrowful, who have got to Heaven by the very things that were their troubles in this life. He saw "the hundred and forty-four thousand that follow the Lamb," and "the nine rings of Angels encircling the Throne;" our Lady clothed with the sun and the moon beneath her feet; our Lord with His many diadems—unveiled at last—showing Himself to all as King of Kings and Lord of Lords, yet tender and familiar as of old when He walked through the cornfields or taught by the Lake—the Son of Man, Jesus of Nazareth still. And God upon His Throne—the songs of His rejoicing Saints going up before Him for ever, for He has wiped away all tears from their eyes, and death and mourning and crying and sorrow are not any more.

To think that I shall be there some day in the midst of all that grandeur—quite at home, not shy at all—*fit* for that glorious Companionship; To think that even now our Lord and His glorious Mother and all the Heavenly Court are looking at me lovingly, and saying, "Come up hither"—my good Angel pointing to a throne somewhere in those bright ranks, that is kept *for me*—to a crown laid upon it, unfinished as yet, waiting *for me*. All praying for me, that I may reach that throne and wear that crown, and be safe among them in my Father's House, in my true Home—some day. Am I going to be the only one that does not care much about it? Oh, surely not.

Our Lord loves to say to us: "*Come.*" "*Come* to Me all you that labour and are heavy burdened." "Suffer the little children to *come* unto Me." "*Come* and rest a little." "All that My Father gives Me shall *come* to Me, and him that *comes* to Me I will not cast out." "You will not *come* to Me that you may have life." He seems to be rehearsing for that Great Day, the Day for which He is longing, when He will open His Arms to all His elect and say to us, "*Come!*" "Come, blessed of My Father."

Why should we not rehearse too? The cry of the elect when they see Him coming in the East will be, "*Come Lord Jesus!*" Why should we not practise it now as St. John teaches us to do? "Come, come, Lord Jesus!" "In the hour of my death call me and bid me come to Thee." Why should we not look forward as our Lord does, and refresh ourselves by thinking of the place He is gone to prepare for us?

Whenever we receive Him in Holy Communion, a pledge of future glory is given to us. You know what a pledge is—something given as security that we shall not be cheated out of our rights later on. Our Lord has given to all who eat this Bread from Heaven a right to a blessed eternity: "If any man eat of this Bread he shall live for ever." He looks upon Heaven as our right by reason of our Communions. His Body is risen again in glory; so must ours, not only because they have been so often and so inseparably united with His, but because we are the very members of His Body and must be with our Head. The Head ascends first into Heaven, but the members are soon to follow. And that we may know how true a right we have to ascend with Him to His Father and to our Father, to His God and to our God, and that He is really preparing *our place* in His Heavenly Kingdom, He leaves us a pledge. But what a pledge! Nothing less than Himself.

We read in history of kings who, being taken prisoners on the field of battle, left their sons in the hands of the conquerors as hostages and security for the payment of the ransom exacted. So is the King's Son, the Son of God, left in our hands as our security. We have only to hold Him fast and Heaven is ours. "O Sacred Banquet in which Christ is received and a pledge of future glory is given to us!"

Yes, what we have to do now is to hold Him fast. It is His own advice: "Hold fast that which thou hast." What I have now since my First Communion is Yourself, dear Lord. I hold You and will not let You go—no, not even if You bless me.

"Hold fast," shows that it is not only possible to lose what we have got, but that it needs effort to keep it. "The great multitude which no man could number," had palms in their hands. They were not only clothed in white, but they carried palms; they were not only spotless, they were conquerors.

These palms, like the lamps of the virgins, have to be made ready in this life; there is no getting them afterwards. When we knock at the door of Heaven, we must have our palms in our hands if we want to be let in. Our Lord says so again and again: "*He that shall overcome*, I will make him a pillar in the temple of My God: and he shall go out no more...To him *that shall overcome*, I will give to sit with Me on My Throne..." "Them *that had overcome*," says St. John, "I saw standing on the sea of glass, having the harps of God and singing...the canticle of the Lamb...And He that sat on the Throne said: He *that shall overcome* shall possess these things, and I will be his God and he shall be My son."

The Saints pondered these words and made them the rule of their lives. They set to work to overcome themselves, and they bid us do the like: "Go against yourself." "Conquer yourself," said St. Ignatius. "We must labour in this world," said the Curé d'Ars, "we must suffer and fight, there will be plenty of time to rest during eternity."

"Quite true," we say. "How wise the Saints are to take these things home to themselves as they do, to put their hands to the work and to make everything safe for eternity."

And why should not we be wise too! These things are said for all who mean to get to Heaven, and those amongst us who are not Saints may well take them home to ourselves.

It was the Feast of the Holy Innocents, and the infants of a native orphanage in India were keeping it in festive fashion. The little ones of the East have surely a special right to claim the Holy Innocents as their patrons. So, at least, thought the good Sister who had decorated the school so gaily. At the top, fronting the desks, stood the Crib of the Holy Child, one blaze of light; and all around, the walls were bright with many coloured flags. The desks were bright, too, little heaps of goodies, of all shapes and sizes, red and green, and yellow, marking each child's place. Eager feet pressed in as soon as the door was opened, and black eyes twinkled with delight as they spied the tempting heaps on the desks. But these were not to be attacked till Catechism was over, and Sister Xavier had told them about the Infant Martyrs who had died for the Holy Child.

She told them how the Babe of Bethlehem loved little children and little Indian children; how He had made a beautiful place for them up in the blue sky and had come a long, long way to fetch them. What would they give Him back? All who liked might pick out one of their sweets and bring it to Him after Catechism.

Of course the small, brown faces beamed with delight, and the picking out began immediately in spite of Sister Xavier's remonstrances. In vain did she endeavour to calm the excitement and recall her babies to thoughts wholly spiritual.

The selection of gifts absorbed all minds; her advice was wanted in every direction, and she had to pass backwards and forwards between the rows, suggesting, approving, or deciding.

A tiny fellow of three and a half, baptized the week before, had soon made his choice, and having placed his offering on one side, surveyed it with mingled feelings of gratification and pride.

It happened to be the smallest sugar-plum in the heap, but we will not rashly judge him; no doubt it was the first that came to hand. A neighbour, however, who had noted—not without envy—a large square morsel, bright green, and sparkling with sugar, suggested that "Little Jesus would like the big one best."

Tommy's answer was a howl of indignation, so loud, that the other, alarmed at the result of his interference, scattered back to his place, leaving Tommy in peace. But no—not in peace. Left to himself, his howling indeed subsided, but not his interior trouble. An new idea had made its way into his mind—"Little Jesus would like the big one best," and it was so hard to give it to Him.

There was no more gratified pride for poor Tommy. Sad and thoughtful he sat at his desk, gazing mournfully at the two bits of sugar, whilst the silent tears that trickled down his cheeks showed how hard was the struggle.

At last his mind was made up. When the signal was given, he got out of his place and made his way up to the Crib, carrying his offering with him. There, at the Feet of the Holy Child, he laid, with a heavy sigh, a large square—no—it had somehow become a small round lump of melting sugar, very sticky and messy.

The pitying Sister who had watched the conflict, comforted him, and was praising his generosity, when the sharp-eyed neighbour, who had never lost sight of the green square, exclaimed, "Yes, Sister, but he *bit off the corners* as we were coming up."

The sharp-eyed neighbour was hard. Do you think our Lord was hard? Do you think little Jesus despised that poor baby's offering? Surely not. Then we must not despise it either. Is it fair for us to laugh at Tommy's tears when perhaps we have never made a sacrifice that cost us a single one; or at his want of generosity, when we think of our own shabbiness! At least let us wait till all those resolutions of ours are perfectly kept before we blame him. Meanwhile, perhaps, the best thing we can do is to follow humbly in Tommy's footsteps, imitating him at any rate, in earnest efforts to do what will please our Lord, and hoping the time will come when we shall be brave and generous enough to make Him gifts unspoilt by corners nibbled off for ourselves.

It is not safe for us to do as little as ever we can to get to Heaven. There are not two Heavens, one for heroes and one for cowards. When some one asked our Lord, "Lord, are they few that are saved?" His answer was, "Strive to enter by the narrow gate, for many, I say to you, shall seek to enter and shall not be able." What will He say to those who never think of anything else but of pleasing themselves; whose life is nothing but one round of amusements, parties, theatres, novel-reading; whose one thought every hour of the day and every day of their lives is to kill time by cramming all the enjoyment they can into the twenty-four hours? How can our Lord give an eternal reward to such as these! Let us be wise like the Saints, and resolve to be His true disciples, loving Him not only "in word and in tongue, but in deed and in truth."

"But it would be absurd for *us* to try to be Saints," you say, "for *me* at least."

Why? If all the Saints had said that, the Church's calendar would be empty and Heaven would not be the glorious place it is. What! is *no one*, then, to try for *honours*? Are we all to be contented with a miserable *pass*? Does not God deserve better things at our hands than this? Those who pass well are a credit to their school. Are we going to let our Lord's School turn out such poor specimens as we are at present? Is this to be our return for all we have cost Him—for all His trouble in our training? His Saints had higher and more generous thoughts. Of them, and of us, He said to His Eternal Father at the Last Supper, "For them do I sanctify Myself." And they in return say: For Him do I sanctify myself—for His glory, for His service, to make Him some return, to be of more use to Him in helping others whom He loves.

Why should we not say the same? We all serve the same God. Why are some of us to serve Him well, and some to serve Him badly? Why should we say, "He loved the Saints and delivered Himself for them, and they have made Him a grand return and served Him splendidly: He loved *me* and delivered Himself for *me*, and I am going to be content to serve Him shabbily, to make Him a miserably poor return." Are we going to say that? No, indeed!

It is not to have "St." put before our name, nor to have all the faithful bowing as they pass our statue in the niche, that we want to distinguish ourselves in His service. But it is that our names may be written in the Sacred Heart, graven deeply there as dear and faithful servants—that we may have the higher places in His Kingdom, where He gets *more* praise, *more* glory, *more* love from His Elect.

For His sake, then, if not for our own, we must try to get on, to be a credit to our Master, *to pass with honours* as the Saints did. What excuse can we find for our laziness? If we were obliged to have ecstasies or to work miracles, we might despair, but we have to do nothing of the kind. St. John Baptist and our Lady had no ecstasies and worked no miracles that we know of. When Mary cooked the dinner and washed the dishes in the Holy House, God was more glorified than by any other acts on earth, excepting only the acts of her Divine Son, Who was mending carts and sweeping up the shavings in His shop up the village street.

The materials of holiness are not miracles and ecstasies, but the little daily duties of our lives. If we pray well, study well, play well, do *well* all we do, with a pure intention to please God, we are on the high road to sanctity. Shall we not make the effort? Shall we not try? Our Lord comes to us on purpose to help us to try, as He came to His Saints. It was not by their own strength that they conquered themselves and got on so fast. "I can do all things *in Him* Who strengtheneth me," said St. Paul, and so we will say.

And then think of the reward. A Day is coming when all the trying and the trouble will be over, and our Lord will call us Home, and reward us for every least little thing we have done to please Him. A Day is coming when we shall hear Him say to us, "*Come up hither.*" And we shall be fetched from Purgatory by our good Angel, and presented by our Lady before His Throne. Then we shall be taken back to our own throne, and there, safe at last, we shall look back upon our life on earth.

All the graces strewn along my way—all God's Providence over me along that road of my life—it will all be clear to me then. Why this disappointment happened—and that loss which was such a pain at the time. My sins and infidelities—and God patient, forgiving me over and over again. My struggles—my victories—the strength that came to me from Mass and from the Sacraments, from my Communions in particular, those bright lamps that lit up my road and scared away the enemy—all this I shall see then.

And at last the end came. And I lay on my death-bed, so weak, so trembling, so fearful. Then, just when I seemed able to bear least, the devil came to me "having great wrath, knowing that he had but a short time"—came with temptations

I never suspected. What should I have done then without the strong Sacraments of the Church that bore me up? What without the prayers of the friends I saw around me and of the friends I did not see? There was my last absolution and my last Communion, when our Lord came to carry me Himself over the gulf. And Extreme Unction to comfort and strengthen me in my last passage, and to take away the fear of death. My Angel stood by me, and my holy Patrons protected me. St. Joseph was there to assist me in my last agony, and St. Michael, "the Prince of all the souls to be received." Our Lady prayed for me in that hour of my death. Our Lord was in my heart—and so I persevered to the end.

My eyes closed—closed for ever on the world down there, and on the things of time—and opened in another world—in Eternity. The world where I was living a moment ago—the only world I had ever known—seemed, oh, so far away, with all I had left behind—and I was alone and had come so far. And yet, in that very room where I died—in the presence of my body, the constant companion of my life in all the good and evil I had done—in its presence I was judged. The Throne was set up there. The Judge was there. I saw Him for the first time. I noticed how He looked at me. His Face was beautiful, but stern, for He was Judge now.

He went over my life with me, from the first moment when I came to the use of reason till my last breath—the time up to my First Communion—the preparation for my First Communion, what it was like, whether I was in earnest—the time after my First Communion, whether I went on being good, whether I persevered. Every thought, every word, every act, weighed with perfect justice, the scales in His Hand—all the good in one, all the bad in the other—this act to be rewarded, that one to be punished. I saw it all with Him. I saw how just it was. I said: Yes, Lord, "Thou art just and Thy Judgment is right." It was but for an instant; those around me did not yet know I was dead—and all was over—my Eternity fixed.

I looked up trembling into His Face. There was so little, so very little good for Him to reward; so much that called for His anger and for punishment. I looked up into His Face. It was very gracious, and I saw, I felt He was going to say to me, "*Come.*" In spite of all my carelessness in His service, my little love of Him, He was going to say "*Come.*" Because I did try, and went on trying, and came back to Him after my falls, He would not cast me away from Him nor let me be separated from Him, but in this hour of my death called me and bade me come to Him, that with His Saints I might praise Him for all eternity. He said to me, "*Well done.* Come, blessed of My Father, possess you the Kingdom prepared for you from the foundation of the world."

He held out His Arms to me—oh, how I longed to fling myself into them! But I was held back; I was not ready. The guilt of my sins had fallen from me in my act of love when I first saw His Face, but there was the punishment to be undergone. So much might have been done in life, by good works, by Indulgences, by bearing crosses patiently. And some little *was* done. The rest must be done now. I turned to my good Angel. I asked him to take me away to Purgatory. I longed for those fearful fires which were the only way now to fit me for Christ's Presence. Any pain, however fierce, so that I might come to Him soon again and be clasped in His Embrace. And my good Angel took me to Purgatory, and laid me down amidst the fires, and went back to earth to see if he could get some prayers for me.

The long time of dreary suffering began. Oh, how long it seemed! What pain, what weary waiting, what sad thoughts, what remorse filled the unbroken night! The intense pain—but much more the intense longing for God! The sorrow for all I had done on earth that kept me from Him when my crown was won! The thought of so much wasted time! The many Masses, the many visits to the Blessed Sacrament, in which I might have got pardon for my sins and remission of punishment! The many little crosses badly borne that would have been instead of those tormenting flames!

I noticed the truth of our Lord's words, "With the measure that you mete it shall be measured to you again." Those who had helped others much, who had prayed during life for the Holy Souls, were helped much in their time of need; those who had forgotten the Holy Souls were in their turn forgotten. How I wished that I had thought more of them; that when waiting in church for Mass or Benediction, or when walking about the streets, or in the house, I had said oftener those little Indulgenced prayers which came down in Purgatory like refreshing rain: "Jesus! Mary!" "My Jesus, mercy!" "Jesus my God, I love Thee above all things!" Over and over again I said in my Catechism that "I should do well to say often such little Indulgenced prayers as these," and then I went off and did nothing of the kind. It would have cost me so little and it would have done so much. I saw all around me the holy sufferers I might have helped, and I longed to help them because they deserved help—favourites of Jesus and Mary whom I could have pleased so much by relieving them. I had relieved them a little. Once I got a Mass said for the soul dearest to the Sacred Heart. That soul was delivered, and I had its constant prayers, helping and refreshing me when my turn came to need help. The Sacred Heart, too, was grateful, and when some one on earth had Mass said for His intention, our Lord gave it to me, and I was lifted more out of the flames and my turn of waiting was shortened.

There were no days or nights there—only one long night. On earth we used to think the day began *after* Mass. It seemed to us in Purgatory that the day on earth was over in each place when Mass was over there. The help that came to us from good works—Communion and the Stations, and alms, were like showers of rain falling softly and keeping down the flames. But the Mass—how we looked to that for extinguishing them altogether! What we felt for those who heard Mass or had Mass said for us!

How we looked forward to our Lady's Feasts, when she came down into Purgatory and comforted us, and went away taking so many back with her! How glad we were to see them go, even though our turn had not yet come—for there is no selfishness in that land of bitter pain, but holy charity! How we begged them to remember us in the Presence of God, and sent on sweet messages before us!

And suddenly there was a stir around me! My time had come and I was sent for. My Angel was at my side to fetch me. He lifted me from the flames. He led me through those fiery dungeons. The gates of Purgatory closed behind me. And in front were the gates of my Home—my Father's House with its many Mansions, opening to receive me. And I passed in and was among the Blessed, and I did not feel shy nor strange, but at home at once.

My Angel took me to Mary, that she might take me to Jesus. How strange it seemed—coming from earth and Purgatory—to see and hear the sights and sounds of rejoicing on every side! What welcomes there were all along that road, as we made our way through the throngs of the Blessed up to our Mother's throne! Those whom I had loved on earth were there to meet me, more loving than ever, and oh, so glad that I had come.

The Guardian Angels congratulated my Angel as we passed swiftly by. I kept looking up into his "beautiful bright face," so jubilant, so satisfied. I did not speak; it was enough to be with him. And to think I had been with him all my life—that all through my life I had had a Guardian *like that!*

And I knelt at Mary's feet. And she laid her hand on my head and welcomed me with a smile. I knew she would be glad to see me, but I did not know *how* glad till I saw that smile.

And she took me to Jesus. He stretched out His Arms to me. He welcomed me to my Home. He said to me, "*Come!*" I longed to rush into His embrace, but I had fallen at His Feet. How tenderly He raised me and spoke to me. And then I looked up into His Face. I saw the King in His Beauty—Jesus Who had died for me and washed me from my sins in His Blood—Who had been my Companion all through my life—Who had given Himself to me so often beneath the veils—Who had loved me to the end. I saw Him, and I spoke to Him face to face. I saw how happy He was to have me with Him. I saw—and felt—and was lost in the overflowing love and gladness of the Sacred Heart.

And then I was strengthened for the sight which is *the* joy of Heaven, which makes Heaven what it is—the unveiled Face of God. I saw Him Who had loved me with an everlasting love and created me to His own image and likeness; Who sent me into the world for a little while that I might know Him and love Him and serve Him there, and Who, my trial over, recalled me back to Himself to be my Reward exceeding great. I saw my God *and was satisfied.* "Thou hast made us for Thyself, O God, and our hearts will never be at rest until they rest in Thee."

> Jerusalem, my happy Home,
>   When shall I come to thee,
> When shall my sorrows have an end?
>   Thy joys when shall I see?
>
> Thy Saints are crowned with glory great,
>   They see God face to face,
> They triumph still, they still rejoice,
>   Most happy is their case.

> We that are here in banishment
>   Continually do moan,
> We sigh and sob, we weep and wail,
>   Perpetually we groan.
>
> But there they live in such delight,
>   Such pleasure and such play,
> As that to them a thousand years
>   Doth seem as yesterday.
>
> There David stands with harp in hand
>   As Master of the Choir,
> Ten thousand times that man were blest
>   That might this music hear
>
> Our Lady sings *Magnificat*
>   With tune surpassing sweet,
> And all the virgins bear their parts
>   Sitting about her feet.
>
> Ah, my sweet Home Jerusalem!
>   Would God I were in thee!
> Would God my woes were at an end,
>   Thy joys that I might see.

And now we have come to the end of our journey and must take leave of one another. We have travelled a long way together—from the Garden of Eden to Bethlehem; from Bethlehem to Egypt; on to Nazareth and Jerusalem and the Lake of Galilee, and back again to the Upper-room in Jerusalem, the room of the Last Supper.

Thus we followed our Lord in His preparation for coming to us. And then we thought of our preparation for meeting Him, and tried to make it as worthy, or rather, as little *unworthy* as we could. All has been done very imperfectly, we are quite conscious of that; but we trust all to the Sacred Heart of our dear Master, Who is content with little when that little is done with love. We have received Him; we have made Him welcome; we have laid our resolutions at His Feet, and now we want Him to bless them.

These resolutions will be very different, varying with the

needs of each. But this one we will all make—to invite our Lord into our hearts *often* and to give Him *a loving welcome each time He comes.* If our Communions are frequent and fervent, all will be well with us.

To keep this resolution you must do two things:

First: learn from your confessor how often you are to go to Communion, and keep regularly to the appointed times. If you foresee you will be prevented from going on the usual day, go before rather than after.

Second: always make your preparation and thanksgiving carefully. On the eve, call to mind now and then the happiness you are going to have next day; invite our Lord by aspirations such as you made before your First Communion; and do all your duties more carefully than usual in order to please Him. This will be an excellent remote preparation. As to the immediate, use your prayer-book or make the acts yourself. Do the same in your thanksgiving.

Get to know our Lord better and so to love Him more by visiting Him when you can. He will welcome you always. It must be very lonely in the Tabernacle, and He is grateful to any one who comes to keep Him company, and talk to Him for a little while. Do not be afraid of having nothing to say. News He does not want, but our difficulties, our troubles, our plans, all these things He likes to hear about, and it is well worth our while to take them to Him. Everything about us interests Him, and everything turns out better when it has been talked over with Him. Try, and you will find it so. Think what you would say if you were alone with the one you love best in the world. Say that to our Lord.

*"And now, little children, abide in Him, that when He shall appear, we may have confidence and not be confounded by Him at His coming."* (1 St. John ii. 28.)

# INDEX

Acts before Communion 204, 312, 340
Acts after Communion 356
Aloysius, St. 5, 9, 99, 262, 291, 320, 377
Apostles 136-150

Berengarius 180-181
Bethlehem 70, 92
Body, the care of 73, 242-247
Books 229, 232-236
Bread of Life 174

Carelessness 229, 260, 310
Children, God's love for 53-55
Christ, attractiveness of 152-161, 164-166
Christ, studying of 61-69
Comfort, love of 73-74
Communion, dispositions for 339-344
—preparation for xvii, 227-240
—effects of 324, 329, 375, 398
—acts before 340
—acts after 356
—First 54, 174
—Last 390
—Beads 365
Companions 229-232
Confession 274-302
—preparation for 274, 297, 359
—general 278
—last 390
Conscience, examination of 275-283

Contrition 289
—necessity of 283-286
—motives for 286-289
—how to get 286-289
—acts of 289

Death 386
Desolation 127-128, 136
Discouragement 128, 261-262, 319, 372
Dispositions of the soul for Holy Communion 339
Dispositions of the body 345
Dryness 305-306

Earnestness xvii
Effects of Holy Communion 324, 329, 375, 398
Elias, food of 56-58
End of our creation 2-6
Examination of conscience 275-283

Faith, how increased 307
Fasting 345
Faults, light 323
Faults, rising after 379
Fervour xviii, 229, 260
Food 329-332
Free-will xvii

Greediness 267
Grumbling 74, 91

Heaven 386, 396, 408-410
Hell 244, 287, 386
Hobbies 235
Honours, trying for 402-403
House, the Holy 97-106
Human respect 230-232
Humility 317-320

Idleness 234
Ignatius, St., Prayer of 94
—Teaching of 143, 259, 261, 333, 385, 399
Imitation of Christ, à Kempis 311
Indulgence, Plenary 351, 363, 407

Jerusalem 107
Jewish History, sketch of 31, 39
Joseph, St. 72, 76, 85-87, 90, 115-116, 130
Judgment, the General 253-254
—the Particular 405-406

Lepers 156
Life of Christ, how to use 13, 61, 69, 102-105
Loreto 98-99
Louis, St. 191

Manna 49-53
Malachias 42-45
Mary 37, 64, 72, 76, 82, 87, 90, 116, 120, 134-136, 212-218, 352, 391
Mass 43-48, 221-223
Melchisedech 42
Mortification 244-255

Naim 156
Nazareth 96, 123

Palestine 6, 42, 96

Parents, behaviour towards 124-125
Penance, the Sacrament of,
—Institution of 295
Penance, Sacramental 292
Pet Passions 265-271
Peter St. 140, 144, 162, 170, 201, 369
Petitions 349, 362, 382
Perseverance 379-382, 385
Philip, St. 392
Poor, the 75
Pride 267, 319
Promise of the Messiah 21-30
Prophecies of the Holy Eucharist 39, 174-180
Purgatory 406
Purpose of Amendment 290-291

Reading 235
Real Presence 177-183, 186-189
Resolutions 290-291, 410-411
Reproof 146-150, 369-374
Riches, how to use 75

Sacrifice 41-48
—ends of 216
—of the Mass 43-48, 221-223
Satisfaction, duty of 291
Slothfulness 268
Scandal-giving 232
Soul, the value of 12-20
Species, the 186, 190, 192
Substance 189

Temple, the 108-112
Temptation 228-229, 256-264
Teresa, St. 7-9
Transubstantiation 186, 189-192
Troubles 83
Types of the Eucharist 40

Additional titles available from
# St. Augustine Academy Press
Books for the Traditional Catholic

### Titles by Mother Mary Loyola:

Blessed are they that Mourn
Confession and Communion
Coram Sanctissimo (Before the Most Holy)
First Communion
First Confession
Forgive us our Trespasses
Hail! Full of Grace
Heavenwards
Home for Good
Jesus of Nazareth: The Story of His Life Written for Children
Questions on First Communion
The Child of God: What comes of our Baptism
The Children's Charter
The Little Children's Prayer Book
The Soldier of Christ: Talks before Confirmation
Trust
Welcome! Holy Communion Before and After
With the Church

### Titles by Father Lasance:

The Catholic Girl's Guide
The Young Man's Guide

### Tales of the Saints:

A Child's Book of Saints by William Canton
A Child's Book of Warriors by William Canton
Legends & Stories of Italy by Amy Steedman
Mary, Help of Christians by Rev. Bonaventure Hammer
Page, Esquire and Knight by Marion Florence Lansing
The Book of Saints and Heroes by Leonora Lang
Saint Patrick: Apostle of Ireland
The Story of St. Elizabeth of Hungary by William Canton

Check our Website for more:
# www.staugustineacademypress.com

Complete in 5 Volumes

# Stories of the Saints for Children
by M. F. S.
Originally published between 1874 and 1878

*The stories of over 180 saints, told for children.*

### Volume One: Well-Known and Beloved Saints
St. Francis & Clare—St. Anthony—St. Benedict—St. Dominic
St. Ignatius—St. Cecilia—St. Agnes—St. Teresa

### Volume Two: More Beloved Saints
St. George—St. Patrick—St. Simon Stock—St. Louis
St. Agatha—St. Lucy—St. Dorothy—St. Bernard

### Volume 3: Bishops, Apostles and Evangelists
St. Martin—St. Augustine—St. Boniface—St. Peter—St. Paul
St. Andrew—St. Stephen—St. Mary Magdalene

### Volume 4: Fathers & Doctors of the Church
St. Ambrose—St. Hilary—St. Jerome—St. Leo the Great
St. Gregory the Great—Venerable Bede

### Volume 5: Saints of the Age of Faith
St. Anselm—St. Hildegard—St. Peter Damian—St. Odilo
St. Norbert—St. Bonaventure—St. Thomas Aquinas

*Plus 3 bonus volumes:*

### Stories of Martyr Priests
Edmund Campion—Robert Southwell—Henry Walpole

### Stories of Holy Lives
St. Margaret Mary—Blessed Imelda—St. John Berchmans
Ven. Anna Maria Taigi—Anne Catherine Emmerich—St. John Vianney

### Legends of the Saints (Short tales for Young Children)
Robin Red-Breast—Our Lady of Guadalupe—The Christmas Rose
The Legend of St. Christopher—St. Francis and the Wolf

# The Seat of Wisdom Series

Learn the lesser-known traditional teachings of our Faith
An excellent supplement to any catechesis program!

## By Mother Mary St. Peter

of the Society of the Holy Child Jesus
originally published between 1905 and 1910

### Mary the Queen:
A Life of the Blessed Mother for her Little Ones

### The Lessons of the King:
Parables Made Plain for His Little Ones

### Talks with the Little Ones about the Apostle's Creed

### The Queen's Festivals:
An Explanation of the Feasts of the Blessed Virgin Mary

### The Story of the Friends of Jesus

### The Story of the Miracles of Our Lord

### The Gift of the King:
A Simple Explanation of the Doctrines & Ceremonies
of the Holy Sacrifice of the Mass

### The Laws of the King:
Talks on the Commandments

"The Sisters of the Holy Child in America have made a distinctly valuable contribution to religious literature for children. There are nearly a dozen neatly printed and illustrated volumes...which are, like Mother Loyola's books, a real joy and help to the child."
—The Ecclesiastical Review, July 1910.

"[Mother Mary St. Peter] has a very clear, pleasing style; and she knows youthful hearts thoroughly. Her talks about the Commandments are excellent, not saying too much, and showing a great deal of shrewdness and discretion in her way of putting things. We are sure that the whole series, of which this is the newest volume, must be very useful for those who are responsible for the instruction of the young."
—The Irish Monthly, July 1910.

# Adventure Books for Boys
## by Father Henry S. Spalding, S.J.

Stories that combine the Love of Country
with Love of the Catholic Faith

Cave by the Beech Fork
The Sheriff of the Beech Fork
The Race for Copper Island
The Marks of the Bear Claws
The Old Mill on the Withrose
The Sugar Camp and After
The Camp by Copper River
At the Foot of the Sand Hills
Held in the Everglades
Signals from the Bay Tree
In the Wilds of the Canyon
Stranded on Long Bar

"In *The Cave by the Beech Fork* a new genre is credited in American Catholic Literature...all the fresh air books provided for boys had hitherto been written by non-Catholics, and the lessons taught were the commercially virtuous maxims of Benjamin Franklin, which are so devoid of spiritual life as those of Polonius in his famous counsels to his son Laertes...A dozen more books as true, as interesting, as honestly religious, as manly as that, are, we hope, to be expected from his pen."

—Maurice Francis Egan (1852-1924), American Catholic Writer and Diplomat

www.ingramcontent.com/pod-product-compliance
Lightning Source LLC
Chambersburg PA
CBHW031610160426
43196CB00006B/79